A GRACE PALEY
READER

A GRACE PALEY READER

STORIES, ESSAYS, AND POETRY

GRACE PALEY

Edited by Kevin Bowen and Nora Paley
Introduction by George Saunders

FARRAR, STRAUS AND GIROUX

NEW YORK

Farrar, Straus and Giroux
18 West 18th Street, New York 10011

This selection was chosen and compiled by Nora Paley and Kevin Bowen.

Library of Congress Cataloging-in-Publication Data
Names: Paley, Grace, author.
Title: A Grace Paley reader : stories, essays, and poetry / Grace Paley.
Description: First edition. | New York : Farrar, Straus and Giroux, 2017. |
  Includes bibliographical references.
Identifiers: LCCN 2016041341 | ISBN 9780374165826 (hardback) |
  ISBN 9780374715106 (e-book)
Subjects: BISAC: LANGUAGE ARTS & DISCIPLINES / Readers.
Classification: LCC PS3566.A46 A6 2017 | DDC 818/.5409—dc23
LC record available at https://lccn.loc.gov/2016041341

Designed by Jo Anne Metsch

www.fsgbooks.com
www.twitter.com/fsgbooks • www.facebook.com/fsgbooks

1 3 5 7 9 10 8 6 4 2

Dedicated to the weave of women and some men,
of her generation, with whom my mother
worked and plotted and cooked:

I have not taken their names out of
conversation   gossip   political argument
my telephone book or card index in
whatever alphabetical or contextual
organizer   I can stop any evening of
the lonesome week at Claiborne Bissinger Bercovici
Vernarelli Gandall Deming and rest a moment
on their seriousness as artists   workers
their excitement as political actors in the
streets of our cities or in their workplaces
the vigiling   fasting   praying in or out
of jail   their lightheartedness which floated
above the year's despair
their courageous sometimes hilarious
disobediences before the state's official
servants   their fidelity to the idea that
it is possible with only a little extra anguish
to live in this world   at an absolute minimum
loving brainy sexual energetic redeemed

—from "Sisters"

CONTENTS

III. POEMS

FOREWORD
by Kevin Bowen

The book you hold in your hand has its origins in a series of gatherings held in and around Boston and Cambridge to celebrate the life and work of the late Grace Paley. These December "Birthday Readings" were reunions of sorts for many of us, opportunities to gather as a community to remember Grace and at the same time find renewal as artists, activists, and citizens through public readings of her works. Our readers were an eclectic group that included writers, journal editors, community activists, veterans, students, teachers, even a banker or two. There were many highlights. I remember one performance by former Bread and Puppet Theater members John Bell and Michael Romanyshyn, who set Grace's words to the accompaniment of drum, trombone, and clarinet. These readings, coming around the date of Grace's birthday and toward the end of the year, seemed always to be a powerful affirmation of the greatness and importance of her work and of the enduring ability of great literature to fire the heart and inspire.

Over the years, I began to notice two discussions typically in the air at the end of the evening. One was of the rejuvenating power of Grace's words, and the other the realization that, while many knew Grace Paley through one or another aspect of her work, few knew her through the full range of stories, poems, involvements, and essays. In late February of 2015, I wrote to Nora Paley about the idea of a "Grace Paley Reader." Nora immediately signed on. The poet Yusef Komunyakaa quickly forwarded a query letter to Jonathan Galassi at FSG. I was in Vietnam, standing in front of a poster of a familiar image of Grace hung alongside those of other writers in Hanoi's eleventh-century Temple of Literature as part of the World Poetry Festival, when I received an e-mail from Jonathan Galassi saying FSG was enthusiastic about the idea. A dozen bus-loads of poets from around the world celebrated the news that night. I think Grace would have appreciated that!

In the months that followed, Nora Paley and I worked to-gether in compiling the reader. The task of making selections was never easy. An initial long list was drawn up and circulated among friends and family, Ruth Perry, Geoffrey Gardner, Marilyn Young, Ursula LeGuin, and others, who offered feedback. Emily Bell, who took on the project for FSG, guided us through the editorial pro-cess. We decided to keep the stories in the order they appeared in individual collections; the poems and essays we organized thematically.

In creating this Reader, Nora and I have had several purposes in mind. One has been to provide readers like ourselves a single manageable collection of the stories, poetry, and essays, a book that would be an essential part of a favorite bookcase, a collection ready to be slipped out for bus trip into the city or a flight to Vietnam. We wanted a book that would be a good companion: an occasion of remembrance, serious thought, for meditations on art, life, poli-tics. We wanted a book that would not only be a reminder of the power of a story well told but would also recognize the achievements of a generation of activists who stood up in the causes of civil rights, social justice, nonviolence, and peace, often putting their bodies on the line as acts of witness.

Our second purpose was to create a book that would be useful to teachers and students. Grace Paley's work cuts famously across the disciplines. By offering a sampling of Grace's work in fiction, poetry, and essays in a single volume, we hoped to offer teachers and students in classes on literature, creative writing, women's studies, American studies, and other interdisciplinary areas of study a new resource.

Finally, and perhaps most important, our purpose was to introduce Grace's work to a new generation of readers, writers, teachers, and activists. I think, selfishly perhaps, of my own daughter, who was just four years old when Grace inscribed a copy of the then just published *Collected Stories* to her, "To Lily, I hope we will be friends for a long time." Lily was fortunate to know Grace, to have Grace and her husband Bob visit each year for our two-week Writers Workshop at the Joiner Center in June. Still it was only after Grace's passing that she came of age as a reader and was able to appreciate the richness and complexities of Grace's writings.

There are many to be thanked. All those who joined us in those Birthday Readings first of all. Thanks to the people at FSG who contributed to making this book a reality. Thanks to the interns who had to type back in the original texts of the stories and essays. Thanks to Emily Bell, who walked us through the sometimes agonizing decisions regarding content and kept us on target through many e-mail and phone exchanges, and Maya Binyam, who filled in during Emily's maternity leave; Jonathan Galassi, whose vision and support made this project possible; and George Saunders, for his wonderful introduction. Thanks, finally, to my daughter, Lily, who helped enter the poems and did so much else, and my wife, Leslie, who has been my partner through thick and thin, and who with Lily and my son, Myles, opened our house those summers when Bob and Grace and dozens of other writers would visit. And of course, thanks most to Nora Paley for her patience and good guidance and for all her work in bringing this book into being. It has been a joy working with her and witnessing her devotion to her family, to her children, Zamir and Sienna, and to her mother's work and her many causes.

INTRODUCTION:
"THE SAINT OF SEEING"
by George Saunders

I.

When photography arrived in the world, or so I've heard, painting had to reconsider itself. "What can I do that photography can't?" painting asked itself in its alarmed French accent. "How may I yet be essential?"

The prime quality of literary prose—that is, the thing it does better than any other form (movies, songs, sculpture, tweets, television, you name it)—is *voice*. A great writer mimicking, on the page, the dynamic energy of human thought is as about as close as we can get to modeling pure empathy.

Grace Paley is one of the great writers of voice of the last century. There's an experience one has reading a stylist like her that has to do with how rich in truth the phrase- or sentence-level bursts are and how quickly they follow upon one another. An image or phrase finds you, pleases you with its wit or vividness, shoehorns open your evolving vision of the fictive world, and before that change gets fully processed, here comes another. You find yourself having trouble believing this much wit is washing over you. A world is appearing before you that is richer and stranger than you could possibly have imagined, and that world gains rooms and vistas and complications with every phrase. What you are experiencing is intimate contact with an extraordinary intelligence, which causes the pleasant sensation of one's personality receding and being replaced by the writer's consciousness.

Paley's approach is to make a dazzling verbal surface that doesn't so much linearly represent the world as remind us of its dazzle. Mere straightforward representation is not her game. In fact, she seems to say, the world has no need to be represented: there it is, all around us, all the time. What it needs is to be *loved better*. Or maybe, what *we* need is to be reminded to love it and to be shown how, because sometimes, busy as we get trying to stay alive, loving the world slips our mind.

2.

I'd always thought of Paley as a realist, but immersing myself again in her work I find that she is actually a thrilling postmodernist, in cahoots with her pal Donald Barthelme to remind us that, yes, there certainly is a World, and there is the Word with which to describe it, and normally World and Word seem like two separate things, but with sufficient authorial attention, Word and World can be made to pop back into their proper relation, which is *unity*.

What I mean by this is that, as you read a Paley story, you will find that it is, yes, set in our world (New York City, most often) and that, O.K., it seems concerned with normal enough things (love, divorce, politics, a day at the park) but then you will start to notice that the language is . . . uncommon. Not quite of this world.

Here is a character in "An Interest in Life," speaking (at a normal-enough kitchen table) of his relation to the Church: "You know . . . we iconoclasts . . . we freethinkers . . . we latter-day Masons . . . we idealists . . . we dreamers . . . we are never far from our nervous old mother, the Church. She is never far from us . . . Wherever we are, we can hear, no matter how faint, her hourly bells, tolling the countryside, reverberating in the cities, bringing in our civilized minds the passionate deed of Mary. Every hour on the hour we are startled with remembrance of what was done for us. FOR US."

Not your normal post-breakfast speech.

Well, yes and no.

Like her hero Isaac Babel, the great Russian, Paley understood that just because such language doesn't normally get spoken aloud in the so-called real world that does not make it unreal, or contrived. On the contrary: language like this is the real language going on in the head of man all the time, whether he can articulate it or not. I find a Shakespearean quality in Paley; the people are very real there on the stage, in their faded coats and crooked hair bows and so on, but their talking is coming from a higher realm, and it has been elevated like that in order to parse and contemplate the big questions with maximal efficiency.

But all this is done with a wondrous ear and a love for the vernacular. Have we had another American writer better at celebrating the poetry in which we Americans think, and into which we sometimes erupt? "You see I can crack a little joke because look at this pleasure," for example. Or: "No reason to worry about me, I got a lot of irons in the fire. I get advanced all the time, matter of fact."

Another writer might say, of a group of teachers just pre-Christmas, "They, each of them, were remembering some happy incident from their own childhood holidays and this made them happy." (Very nice.) Paley says: "The teachers became happier and happier. Their heads were ringing like the bells of childhood." (Boom.) Instead of simply *knowing* that the teachers were happy pre-Christmas, we *are*, for that split second, happy teachers, pre-Christmas. (We smell the pine from the crookedly hanging wreath near the bulletin board, which will be brown by the time school resumes in January.) Another writer might have a character tell her mother to keep her opinions about men to herself; Paley has the narrator of "A Woman, Young and Old" advise dear mother to "keep your taste in your own hatch." Which of us, trying to com-municate to our sister that we feel she somewhat underestimates the extent of our worldliness, would think to tell her, as Aunt Rose does in "Goodbye and Good Luck," that our "heart is a regular col-lege of feelings and there is such information between my corset and me that [your] whole married life is a kindergarten." Well, take that, sister.

"You've used me in a bad way. That's not cool. That smells under heaven," says Dennis the cabdriver/lover/songwriter par crapa-mundo in "Enormous Changes at the Last Minute."

Or how about this, from "Ruthy and Edie": "If you said the word 'city' to Edie, or even the cool adjective 'municipal,' specific children usually sitting at the back of the room appeared before her eyes and refused to answer when she called on them."

This is what I mean by the unity of Word and World: some-thing about the arrangement of the words, read in the context of the story, will not (will no longer) let us experience these sentences as mere words on a page. The words sort of recede as you read them, or, maybe, our attention diverts from their wordness to the "image" that appears in our head (although "image" is not quite right; it is something else going on up there) and suddenly—are we reading, or living "there" in that fictive moment?

Yes.

3.

All these agitated manic New York voices explaining themselves! You feel the stress and pace and wild aspirations of the City as it was. And is. The City is the energy coming off a million hustling souls who have both forgotten they will die soon and are very ac-tively feeling that, ah God, they most definitely will. So what do they do? They talk. They protest, explain, beg to differ. In Paley you hear America singing, yes, but also: bellyaching, kvetching, teasing, advocating, disowning, politicizing, explaining the states of their bodies, assessing friends, lovers, and their children with both clinical distance and aching love, sometimes in the same sentence. When I think to myself, "What was the world of American adults like, back before I was one, in the 1960s and 1970s?" my mind turns to Paley's stories. All those desirous, active souls, with one foot in hippiedom/free love (singing crazy songs by bands named The Lepers—formerly The Split Atom, possibly soon Winter Moss), and the other in the Depression, dusty old progressive dreams in their heads (of Guthrie, of the Wobblies), so alive with the tremendous energy that generation expended to make things better ("the vigil-ing   fasting   praying in or out / of jail   their lightheartedness which floated / about the year's despair"). However, as you will see in this book, these firebrands were sometimes depressingly human in their desire to wring the most out of life and one another. And now those people are old, going, or gone. But here, in these pages, they are alive again, to remind us that our present vitality—our sense of being the first humans ever, and permanent—will too someday seem historical, and will have passed. But, as made by Paley, in her particular, larger-than-life way, these people will live forever: par-ticularized receptacles of the eternal.

4.

Any object, any human gesture, contains an infinity of language with which it might be described. But through habituation, or pau-city of talent, or lack of originality, most of us, writing, reach for the most workaday speech-tools, and in this way the world is made dull. Here comes Paley: seemingly incapable of a banal sentence, a loose observation, or a distracted fictive moment.

Paley is, for me, a kind of secular saint. What is a saint? Some-one particularly attentive to things as they are and extraordinarily accepting of them. Paley honors every person and thing she creates by presenting them at their best, or at least their liveliest—which may be the same thing.

This quality of simple, accepting, energetic *seeing* makes Paley's world feel particularly egalitarian. I think of the family, for example, in "A Woman, Young and Old." They seem, well, working class (in the general mayhem of their lives, and the way their collective eye keeps sliding over to questions of livelihood), but because the Paley-narrator does not hang that sign around their necks, the world they live in seems immense and mutable. Who are these people and of what social class? Paley won't say, exactly. That would be rude. Also, not interesting. And reductive and freedom decreasing. Rather, she just shows them acting and talking and choosing happily enough within their limitations. They have autonomy, agency, desire, a right to their own feelings and flavor of understanding. "Everyone, real or invented, deserves the open destiny of life," she wrote, in "A Conversation with My Father." This results in a fresh angle on things like "gender" or "class"—to the point of destabilizing them and giving the people trapped inside these constructs liberty and a voice. In this sense, Paley is a Whitmanesque writer: she loves what she sees, just as it is, and is in favor of it being even more itself. How do we know she loves it? By how precisely she describes it. ("I am right next to the pickle barrel. My pinky is making tiny whirlpools in the brine.") Also, there is an extraordinary quality of freedom in these narratives. Her people do not merely behave like people in stories, but they also do not behave merely like people in the real world—they behave, satisfyingly, like people in a spectacularly mindful artistic purification of the real. An average writer writes toward a familiar vision, be it shocking or comforting; a genius like Paley creates an entirely new world by leaping from stone to stone, these "stones" being distinct, vivid, fictive moments—vivid in language, vivid in import. The route is not, it seems, planned or pre-vetted, but is continuously creating itself by asking the question: "Where is the *life* here?" which she answers with an essential sub-question: "Where does the language come most alive?" The resulting structure has the effect of startling and refreshing us; or, maybe, refreshing us via startling: the freshness of the world mimicked in the freshness of the shape of the story, the reader reminded of her susceptibility to, and yearning for, freshness.

5.

I've written mostly here about her short stories, because short stories are what I understand best. But I think you will find that Paley was a master of all three genres included here: stories, essays, and poems. In each, she operates in a slightly different mode (the essays more direct and political, the poetry at times unbearably moving and emotionally blunt), but all of her work is marked by heart, precision, and concern for others, and surges with real, messy life, and the way life, lived, actually makes us feel: outgunned, befriended, short on time, long on regret, so happy we can't stand it, so in love we become fools. Moments in her stories, often her endings, cause me real sorrow, and, perhaps acclimated to the contemporary tendency toward compensatory lyrical updraft, I feel myself mentally looking over at the author, for, maybe a conciliatory little suggestion that all will be well? But no. She just shrugs. "It's like that sometimes," she says. I love her for this. She's not big on bromides. Her vision of things is complex, by which I mean: she knows that a person can feel irritated and happy at once; despairing and lucky; pleased to be a mother and sick to the core of being a mother. And she is O.K. with all of that.

Her stories, like all great stories, lead us into that uncomfortable holy of holies, ambiguity. How are we to feel, ultimately, about the intermittently racist Iz of "Zagrowsky Tells"? Or the fourteen-year-old who beds a soldier in "A Woman, Young and Old" and the soldier who beds her right back? About all of these callow, absent husbands, who show up late and immediately start advising? Well, we feel *fully* about them, that's for sure. We walk away from her stories feeling, not, "Oh, he got his, or will," but, rather, "Yes, that's how it is in this world." We see them through the lens of her total acceptance of, and fascination with, them. (Reading Paley will, I predict, make you better understand the idea that love is attention and vice versa.)

I love too her extraordinary happy frankness in all things; that is, her courage. She is unafraid, for example, to cry fraud re. that particular flavor of grinding American optimism. We Americans are addicted to the happy lie and to the associated notion that to critique something—to call it what it is—is a form of negativity; a defeatist buzz-kill. Paley (happily, fearlessly) doesn't buy it. A character tells a dying friend, in "Living," that, well, "Life isn't all that great . . . We've had nothing but crummy days and crummy guys and broke all the time and cockroaches and nothing to do on Sunday but take the kids to Central Park and row on that lousy lake"— and we have to agree with her. "I want to see it all," the dying friend replies, and we agree with her too. Paley, like her spiritual predecessor Chekhov, likes to have it both ways.

"Art does not have to solve problems," Chekhov said. "It just has to formulate them correctly."

"I'm artistic," says a character in "A Woman, Young and Old," "and I sometimes hold two views at once."

6.

Grace Paley has been gone for ten years now. As one of her characters might say: this—this I find hard to believe. I only met her once but have always felt her to be a dear friend. How can that be? Well, I have done with her what we do with the greats among us: I have taken credit for her, by finding herself within me. There is a Grace Paley inside each of us, thank God. That inner Paley is funny; sharp; engaged; worldly; kind but no sucker; weary, but then suddenly not, if there's some fun around; and, always: trying, hoping, questing, going off on some adventure. Then, when we read Paley, we get a shock of recognition: Ah, we feel, I know her. I know her as part of myself; how interesting that she has materialized. David Foster Wallace had this same quality; his particular set of virtues (the crazy-precise loquaciousness; the extreme analytical tendency that moved into and then back out of comic neurosis; the manic introspective tendency that we feel to be a form of positive aspiration) seemed to have emanated from inside us, which is to say:

Paley and Wallace were both very special human beings, composed of mostly primary qualities, with very little of what we might call banal/normalized pollution.

What does a writer leave behind? Scale models of a way of seeing and thinking. Those of us still down here are always in need of these models, especially in times of trouble (and all times are times of trouble). We have, most of us, yet to find a way of seeing and thinking that *works*—that allows us to live comfortably and positively in all of this beautiful mess—but our writers, our dear passed writers, have put forth some pretty good models, so that we might suffer less, or at least suffer within some beautiful context. Faith, in the story "Friends," says something about the act of tutoring children that is also true of the conversation between reader and writer: "Though the world cannot be changed by talking to one child at a time," she says, "it may at least be known." A writer as good as Paley helps us (at least) know our world by modeling a certain stance toward it that is so pure and distinctive that it makes us go back into the world and take a harder, fonder look at it.

Paley's model advises us to suffer less by loving more—love the world more, and each other more—and then she gives us a specific way to love more: see better. If you only really see this world, you will think better of it, she seems to say. And *then* she gives us a way to see better: let language sing, sing precisely, and let it off the tether of the mundane, and watch the wonderful truth it knows how to make.

To see better means more joy, less judgment. There is a roof on our language that holds down our love. What has put that roof there? Our natural dullness, exacerbated by that grinding daily need to survive and grunt instructions back and forth in order to do so, helped along of late by the slow, happy spread of all-purpose materialism, and corporations, and pragmatism, and televisions and computer screens all across the land speaking in cahoots with the corporations, which are, in turn, speaking in cahoots with the military (as much a problem in our time as hers), a military that is (still) doing service for materialism, by metallically communicating the notion that goodness can be attained by killing-to-win.

They have all conspired to stupidify our language and make it more businesslike and brutal. A writer like Paley comes along and brightens language up again, takes it aside and gives it a pep talk, sends it back renewed, so it can do its job, which is to wake us up.

How can we dislike ourselves when she loves us so? Why should we be afraid of suffering when she has used her own suffering (and joy, and confusion, and pleasure) to make such a glorious thing as the book you're now holding? You will close this book, I predict, with a revived concern for other people's suffering and in their pleasures. What we might have looked past, she makes us see. That is a beautiful life's work. Grace Paley lives, in the minds of the readers she has moved, and in the minds of those she will yet move. As long as there are human beings wondering who they are, and how they can be better—looking for a more full-hearted way of being in the world—there will be readers for the great, beloved, much-missed Grace Paley.

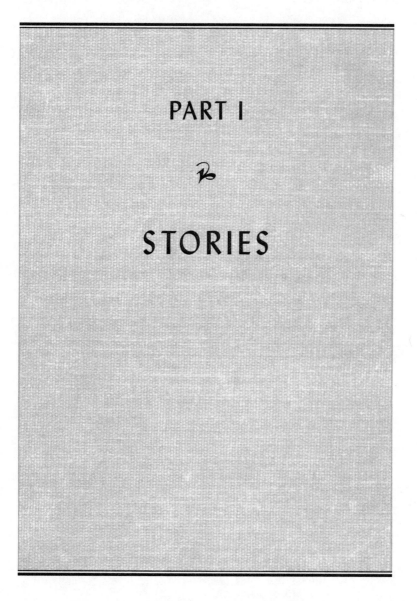

PART I

STORIES

FROM *The Little Disturbances of Man*

Goodbye and Good Luck

I was popular in certain circles, says Aunt Rose. I wasn't no thinner then, only more stationary in the flesh. In time to come, Lillie, don't be surprised—change is a fact of God. From this no one is excused. Only a person like your mama stands on one foot, she don't notice how big her behind is getting and sings in the canary's ear for thirty years. Who's listening? Papa's in the shop. You and Seymour, thinking about yourself. So she waits in a spotless kitchen for a kind word and thinks—poor Rosie . . .

Poor Rosie! If there was more life in my little sister, she would know my heart is a regular college of feelings and there is such information between my corset and me that her whole married life is a kindergarten.

Nowadays you could find me any time in a hotel, uptown or downtown. Who needs an apartment to live like a maid with a dustrag in the hand, sneezing? I'm in very good with the busboys, it's more interesting than home, all kinds of people, everybody with a reason . . .

And my reason, Lillie, is a long time ago I said to the forelady,

"Missus, if I can't sit by the window, I can't sit." "If you can't sit, girlie," she says politely, "go stand on the street corner." And that's how I got unemployed in novelty wear.

For my next job I answered an ad which said: "Refined young lady, medium salary, cultural organization." I went by trolley to the address, the Russian Art Theater of Second Avenue, where they played only the best Yiddish plays. They needed a ticket seller, someone like me, who likes the public but is very sharp on crooks. The man who interviewed me was the manager, a certain type.

Immediately he said: "Rosie Lieber, you surely got a build on you!"

"It takes all kinds, Mr. Krimberg."

"Don't misunderstand me, little girl," he said. "I appreciate, I appreciate. A young lady lacking fore and aft, her blood is so busy warming the toes and the fingertips, it don't have time to circulate where it's most required."

Everybody likes kindness. I said to him: "Only don't be fresh, Mr. Krimberg, and we'll make a good bargain."

We did: Nine dollars a week, a glass of tea every night, a free ticket once a week for Mama, and I could go watch rehearsals any time I want.

My first nine dollars was in the grocer's hands ready to move on already, when Krimberg said to me, "Rosie, here's a great gentleman, a member of this remarkable theater, wants to meet you, impressed no doubt by your big brown eyes."

And who was it, Lillie? Listen to me, before my very eyes was Volodya Vlashkin, called by the people of those days the Valentino of Second Avenue. I took one look, and I said to myself: Where did a Jewish boy grow up so big? "Just outside Kiev," he told me.

How? "My mama nursed me till I was six. I was the only boy in the village to have such health."

"My goodness, Vlashkin, six years old! She must have had shredded wheat there, not breasts, poor woman."

"My mother was beautiful," he said. "She had eyes like stars."

He had such a way of expressing himself, it brought tears.

To Krimberg, Vlashkin said after this introduction: "Who is responsible for hiding this wonderful young person in a cage?"

"That is where the ticket seller sells."

"So, David, go in there and sell tickets for a half hour. I have something in mind in regards to the future of this girl and this company. Go, David, be a good boy. And you, Miss Lieber, please, I suggest Feinberg's for a glass of tea. The rehearsals are long. I enjoy a quiet interlude with a friendly person."

So he took me there, Feinberg's, then around the corner, a place so full of Hungarians, it was deafening. In the back room was a table of honor for him. On the tablecloth embroidered by the lady of the house was *Here Vlashkin Eats*. We finished one glass of tea in quietness, out of thirst, when I finally made up my mind what to say.

"Mr. Vlashkin, I saw you a couple weeks ago, even before I started working here, in *The Sea Gull*. Believe me, if I was that girl, I wouldn't look even for a minute on the young bourgeois fellow. He could fall out of the play altogether. How Chekhov could put him in the same play as you, I can't understand."

"You liked me?" he asked, taking my hand and kindly patting it. "Well, well, young people still like me . . . so, and you like the theater too? Good. And you, Rose, you know you have such a nice hand, so warm to the touch, such a fine skin, tell me, why do you wear a scarf around your neck? You only hide your young, young throat. These are not olden times, my child, to live in shame."

"Who's ashamed?" I said, taking off the kerchief, but my hand right away went to the kerchief's place, because the truth is, it really was olden times, and I was still of a nature to melt with shame.

"Have some more tea, my dear."

"No, thank you, I am a samovar already."

"Dorfmann!" he hollered like a king. "Bring this child a seltzer with fresh ice!"

In weeks to follow I had the privilege to know him better and better as a person—also the opportunity to see him in his profession. The time was autumn; the theater full of coming and going. Rehearsing without end. After *The Sea Gull* flopped, *The Salesman from Istanbul* played, a great success.

Here the ladies went crazy. On the opening night, in the middle of the first scene, one missus—a widow or her husband worked too long hours—began to clap and sing out, "Oi, oi, Vlashkin." Soon there was such a tumult, the actors had to stop acting. Vlashkin stepped forward. Only not Vlashkin to the eyes . . . a younger man with pitch-black hair, lively on restless feet, his mouth clever. A half a century later at the end of the play he came out again, a gray philosopher, a student of life from only reading books, his hands as smooth as silk . . . I cried to think who I was—nothing— and such a man could look at me with interest.

Then I got a small raise, due to he kindly put in a good word for me, and also for fifty cents a night I was given the pleasure together with cousins, in-laws, and plain stage-struck kids to be part of a crowd scene and to see like he saw every single night the hundreds of pale faces waiting for his feelings to make them laugh and bend down their heads in sorrow.

The sad day came, I kissed my mama goodbye. Vlashkin helped me to get a reasonable room near the theater to be more free. Also my outstanding friend would have a place to recline away from the noise of the dressing rooms. She cried and she cried. "This is a different way of living, Mama," I said. "Besides, I am driven by love."

"You! You, a nothing, a rotten hole in a piece of cheese, are you telling me what is life?" she screamed.

Very insulted, I went away from her. But I am good-natured— you know fat people are like that—kind, and I thought to myself, poor Mama . . . it is true she got more of an idea of life than me. She married who she didn't like, a sick man, his spirit already swallowed up by God. He never washed. He had an unhappy smell. His teeth fell out, his hair disappeared, he got smaller, shriveled up little by little, till goodbye and good luck he was gone and only came to Mama's mind when she went to the mailbox under the stairs to get the electric bill. In memory of him and out of respect for mankind, I decided to live for love.

Don't laugh, you ignorant girl.

Do you think it was easy for me? I had to give Mama a little something. Ruthie was saving up together with your papa for linens, a couple knives and forks. In the morning I had to do piecework if I wanted to keep by myself. So I made flowers. Before lunch time everyday a whole garden grew on my table.

This was my independence, Lillie dear, blooming, but it didn't have no roots and its face was paper.

Meanwhile Krimberg went after me too. No doubt observing the success of Vlashkin, he thought, Aha, open sesame . . . Others in the company similar. After me in those years were the following: Krimberg I mentioned. Carl Zimmer, played innocent young fellows with a wig. Charlie Peel, a Christian who fell in the soup by accident, a creator of beautiful sets. "Color is his middle name," says Vlashkin, always to the point.

I put this in to show you your fat old aunt was not crazy out of loneliness. In those noisy years I had friends among interesting people who admired me for reasons of youth and that I was a first-class listener.

The actresses—Raisele, Marya, Esther Leopold—were only interested in tomorrow. After them was the rich men, producers, the whole garment center; their past is a pincushion, future the eye of a needle.

Finally the day came, I no longer could keep my tact in my mouth. I said: "Vlashkin, I hear by carrier pigeon you have a wife, children, the whole combination."

"True, I don't tell stories. I make no pretense."

"That isn't the question. What is this lady like? It hurts me to ask, but tell me, Vlashkin . . . a man's life is something I don't clearly see."

"Little girl, I have told you a hundred times, this small room is the convent of my troubled spirit. Here I come to your innocent shelter to refresh myself in the midst of an agonized life."

"Ach, Vlashkin, serious, serious, who is this lady?"

"Rosie, she is a fine woman of the middle classes, a good mother to my children, three in number, girls all, a good cook, in her youth handsome, now no longer young. You see, could I be more frank? I entrust you, dear, with my soul."

It was some few months later at the New Year's ball of the Russian Artists Club, I met Mrs. Vlashkin, a woman with black hair in a low bun, straight and too proud. She sat at a small table speaking in a deep voice to whoever stopped a moment to converse. Her Yiddish was perfect, each word cut like a special jewel. I looked at her. She noticed me like she noticed everybody, cold like Christmas morning. Then she got tired. Vlashkin called a taxi and I never saw her again. Poor woman, she did not know I was on the same stage as her. The poison I was to her role, she did not know.

Later on that night in front of my door I said to Vlashkin, "No more. This isn't for me. I am sick from it all. I am no home breaker."

"Girlie," he said, "don't be foolish."

"No, no, goodbye, good luck," I said. "I am sincere."

So I went and stayed with Mama for a week's vacation and cleaned up all the closets and scrubbed the walls till the paint came off. She was very grateful, all the same her hard life made her say, "Now we see the end. If you live like a bum, you are finally a lunatic."

After this few days I came back to my life. When we met, me and Vlashkin, we said only hello and goodbye, and then for a few sad years, with the head we nodded as if to say, "Yes, yes, I know who you are."

Meanwhile in the field was a whole new strategy. Your mama and your grandmama brought around—boys. Your own father had a brother, you never even seen him. Ruben. A serious fellow, his idealism was his hat and his coat. "Rosie, I offer you a big new free happy unusual life." How? "With me, we will raise the sands of Palestine to make a nation. That is the land of tomorrow for us Jews."

"Ha-ha, Ruben, I'll go tomorrow then." "Rosie!" says Ruben. "We need strong women like you, mothers and farmers." "You don't fool me, Ruben, what you need is dray horses. But for that you need more money." "I don't like your attitude, Rose." "In that case, go and multiply. Goodbye."

Another fellow: Yonkel Gurstein, a regular sport, dressed to kill, with such an excitable nature. In those days—it looks to me like yesterday—the youngest girls wore undergarments like Battle Creek, Michigan. To him it was a matter of seconds. Where did he practice, a Jewish boy? Nowadays I suppose it is easier, Lillie? My goodness, I ain't asking you nothing—touchy, touchy . . .

Well, by now you must know yourself, honey, whatever you do, life don't stop. It only sits a minute and dreams a dream.

While I was saying to all these silly youngsters "no, no, no," Vlashkin went to Europe and toured a few seasons . . . Moscow, Prague, London, even Berlin—already a pessimistic place. When he came back he wrote a book you could get from the library even today, *The Jewish Actor Abroad*. If someday you're interested enough in my lonesome years, you could read it. You could absorb a flavor of the man from the book. No, no, I am not mentioned. After all, who am I?

When the book came out I stopped him in the street to say congratulations. But I am not a liar, so I pointed out too the egotism of many parts—even the critics said something along such lines.

"Talk is cheap," Vlashkin answered me. "But who are the critics? Tell me, do they create? Not to mention," he continues, "there is a line in Shakespeare in one of the plays from the great history of England. It says, 'Self-loving is not so vile a sin, my liege, as self-neglecting.' This idea also appears in modern times in the moralistic followers of Freud . . . Rosie, are you listening? You asked a question. By the way, you look very well. How come no wedding ring?"

I walked away from this conversation in tears. But this talking in the street opened the happy road up for more discussions. In regard to many things . . . For instance, the management—very narrow-minded—wouldn't give him any more certain young men's parts. Fools. What youngest man knew enough about life to be as young as him?

"Rosie, Rosie," he said to me one day. "I see by the clock on your rosy, rosy face you must be thirty."

"The hands are slow, Vlashkin. On a week before Thursday I was thirty-four."

"Is that so? Rosie, I worry about you. It has been on my mind to talk to you. You are losing your time. Do you understand it? A woman should not lose her time."

"Oi, Vlashkin, if you are my friend, what is time?"

For this he had no answer, only looked at me surprised. We went instead, full of interest but not with our former speed, up to my new place on Ninety-fourth Street. The same pictures on the wall, all of Vlashkin, only now everything painted red and black, which was stylish, and new upholstery.

A few years ago there was a book by another member of that fine company, an actress, the one that learned English very good and went uptown—Marya Kavkaz, in which she says certain things regarding Vlashkin. Such as, he was her lover for eleven years, she's not ashamed to write this down. Without respect for him, his wife and children, or even others who also may have feelings in the matter.

Now, Lillie, don't be surprised. This is called a fact of life. An actor's soul must be like a diamond. The more faces it got the more shining is his name. Honey, you will no doubt love and marry one man and have a couple kids and be happy forever till you die tired. More than that, a person like us don't have to know. But a great artist like Volodya Vlashkin . . . in order to make a job on the stage, he's got to practice. I understand it now, to him life is like a rehearsal.

Myself, when I saw him in *The Father-in-Law*—an older man

in love with a darling young girl, his son's wife, played by Raisele Maisel—I cried. What he said to this girl, how he whispered such sweetness, how all his hot feelings were on his face . . . Lillie, all this experience he had with me. The very words were the same. You can imagine how proud I was.

So the story creeps to an end.

I noticed it first on my mother's face, the rotten handwriting of time, scribbled up and down her cheeks, across her forehead back and forth—a child could read—it said old, old, old. But it troubled my heart most to see these realities scratched on Vlashkin's wonderful expression.

First the company fell apart. The theater ended. Esther Leopold died from being very aged. Krimberg had a heart attack. Marya went to Broadway. Also Raisele changed her name to Roslyn and was a big comical hit in the movies. Vlashkin himself, no place to go, retired. It said in the paper, "An actor without peer, he will write his memoirs and spend his last years in the bosom of his family among his thriving grandchildren, the apple of his wife's doting eye."

This is journalism.

We made for him a great dinner of honor. At this dinner I said to him, for the last time, I thought, "Goodbye, dear friend, topic of my life, now we part." And to myself I said further: Finished. This is your lonesome bed. A lady what they call fat and fifty. You made it personally. From this lonesome bed you will finally fall to a bed not so lonesome, only crowded with a million bones.

And now comes? Lillie, guess.

Last week, washing my underwear in the basin, I get a buzz on the phone. "Excuse me, is this the Rose Lieber formerly connected with the Russian Art Theater?"

"It is."

"Well, well, how do you do, Rose? This is Vlashkin."

"Vlashkin! Volodya Vlashkin?"

"In fact. How are you, Rose?"

"Living, Vlashkin, thank you."

"You are all right? Really, Rose? Your health is good? You are working?"

"My health, considering the weight it must carry, is first-class. I am back for some years now where I started, in novelty wear."

"Very interesting."

"Listen, Vlashkin, tell me the truth, what's on your mind?"

"My mind? Rosie, I am looking up an old friend, an old warm-hearted companion of more joyful days. My circumstances, by the way, are changed. I am retired, as you know. Also I am a free man."

"What? What do you mean?"

"Mrs. Vlashkin is divorcing me."

"What come over her? Did you start drinking or something from melancholy?"

"She is divorcing me for adultery."

"But, Vlashkin, you should excuse me, don't be insulted, but you got maybe seventeen, eighteen years on me, and even me, all this nonsense—this daydreams and nightmares—is mostly for the pleasure of conversation alone."

"I pointed all this out to her. My dear, I said, my time is past, my blood is as dry as my bones. The truth is, Rose, she isn't accustomed to have a man around all day, reading out loud from the papers the interesting events of our time, waiting for breakfast, waiting for lunch. So all day she gets madder and madder. By nighttime a furious old lady gives me my supper. She has information from the last fifty years to pepper my soup. Surely there was a Judas in that theater, saying every day, 'Vlashkin, Vlashkin, Vlashkin . . .' and while my heart was circulating with his smiles he was on the wire passing the dope to my wife."

"Such a foolish end, Volodya, to such a lively story. What is your plans?"

"First, could I ask you for dinner and the theater—uptown, of course? After this . . . we are old friends. I have money to burn. What your heart desires. Others are like grass, the north wind of time has cut out their heart. Of you, Rosie, I re-create only kindness. What a woman should be to a man, you were to me. Do you think, Rosie, a couple of old pals like us could have a few good times among the material things of this world?"

My answer, Lillie, in a minute was altogether. "Yes, yes, come up," I said. "Ask the room by the switchboard, let us talk."

So he came that night and every night in the week, we talked of his long life. Even at the end of time, a fascinating man. And like men are, too, till time's end, trying to get away in one piece.

"Listen, Rosie," he explains the other day. "I was married to my wife, do you realize, nearly half a century. What good was it? Look at the bitterness. The more I think of it, the more I think we would be fools to marry."

"Volodya Vlashkin," I told him straight, "when I was young I warmed your cold back many a night, no questions asked. You admit it, I didn't make no demands. I was softhearted. I didn't want to be called Rosie Lieber, a breaker up of homes. But now, Vlashkin, you are a free man. How could you ask me to go with you on trains to stay in strange hotels, among Americans, not your wife? Be ashamed."

So now, darling Lillie, tell this story to your mama from your young mouth. She don't listen to a word from me. She only screams, "I'll faint, I'll faint." Tell her after all I'll have a husband, which, as everybody knows, a woman should have at least one before the end of the story.

My goodness, I am already late. Give me a kiss. After all, I watched you grow from a plain seed. So give me a couple wishes on my wedding day. A long and happy life. Many years of love. Hug Mama, tell her from Aunt Rose, goodbye and good luck.

A Woman, Young and Old

My mother was born not too very long ago of my grandma, who named lots of others, girls and boys, all starting fresh. It wasn't love so much, my grandma said, but she never could call a spade a spade. She was imagination-minded, read stories all day, and sighed all night, till my grandpa, to get near her at all, had to use that particular medium.

That was the basic trouble. My mother was sad to be so surrounded by brothers and sisters, none of them more good-natured than she. It's all part of the violence in the atmosphere is a theory—wars, deception, broken homes, all the irremediableness of modern life. To meet her problem my mother screams.

She swears she wouldn't scream if she had a man of her own, but all the aunts and uncles, solitary or wed, are noisy. My grandpa is not only noisy, he beats people up, that is to say—members of the family. He whacked my mother every day of her life. If anyone ever touched me, I'd reduce them to fall-out.

Grandma saves all her change for us. My uncle Johnson is in the nuthouse. The others are here and now, but Aunty Liz is seventeen and my mother talks to her as though she were totally grown up. Only the other day she told her she was just dying for a man, a real one, and was sick of raising two girls in a world just bristling with goddamn phallic symbols. Lizzy said yes, she knew how it was, time frittered by, and what you needed was a strong kind hand at the hem of your skirt. That's what the acoustics of this barn have to take.

My father, I have been told several hundred times, was a really stunning Latin. Full of *savoir-faire*, *joie de vivre*, and so forth. They were deeply and irrevocably in love till Joanna and I revoked everything for them. Mother doesn't want me to feel rejected, but she doesn't want to feel rejected herself, so she says *I* was too noisy and cried every single night. And then Joanna was the final blight and wanted titty all day *and* all night. ". . . a wife," he said, "is a beloved mistress until the children come and then . . ." He would just leave it hanging in French, but whenever I'd hear *les enfants*, I'd throw toys at him, guessing his intended slight. He said *les filles* instead, but I caught that petty evasion in no time. We pummeled him with noise and toys, but our affection was his serious burden is Mother's idea, and one day he did not come home for supper.

Mother waited up reading *Le Monde*, but he did not come home at midnight to make love. He missed breakfast and lunch the next day. In fact, where is he now? Killed in the Resistance, says Mother. A postcard two weeks later told her and still tells us all, for that matter, whenever it's passed around: "I have been lonely for France for five years. Now for the rest of my life I must be lonely for you."

"You've been conned, Mother," I said one day while we were preparing dinner.

"Conned?" she muttered. "You speak a different language than me. You don't know a thing yet, you weren't even born. You know perfectly well, misfortune aside, I'd take another Frenchman—Oh, Josephine," she continued, her voice reaching strictly for the edge of the sound barrier, "oh, Josephine, to these loathsomes in this miserable country I'm a joke, a real ha-ha. But over there they'd know me. They would just feel me boiling out to meet them. Lousy grammar and all, in French, I swear I could write Shakespeare."

I turned away in despair. I felt like crying.

"Don't laugh," she said, "someday I'll disappear Air France and surprise you all with a nice curly Frenchman just like your daddy. Oh, how you would have loved your father. A growing-up girl with a man like that in the vicinity constantly. You'd thank me."

"I thank you anyway, Mother dear," I replied, "but keep your taste in your own hatch. When I'm as old as Aunt Lizzy I might like American soldiers. Or a Marine, I think. I already like some soldiers, especially Corporal Brownstar."

"Is *that* your idea of a man?" asked Mother, rowdy with contempt.

Then she reconsidered Corporal Brownstar. "Well, maybe you're right. Those powerful-looking boots . . . Very masculine."

"Oh?"

"I know, I know. I'm artistic and I sometimes hold two views at once. I realize that Lizzy's going around with him and it does something. Look at Lizzy and you see the girl your father saw. Just like me. Wonderful carriage. Marvelous muscle tone. She could have any man she wanted."

"She's already had some she wanted."

At that moment my grandma, the nick-of-time banker, came in, proud to have saved $4.65 for us. "Whew, I'm so warm," she sighed. "Well, here it is. Now a nice dinner, Marvine, I beg of you, a little effort. Josie, run and get an avocado, and Marvine, please don't be small about the butter. And Josie dear, it's awful warm out and your mama won't mind. You're nearly a young lady. Would you like a sip of icy beer?"

Wasn't that respectful? To return the compliment I drank half a glass, though I hate that fizz. We broiled and steamed and sliced and chopped, and it was a wonderful dinner. I did the cooking and Mother did the sauces. We sicked her on with mouth-watering memories of another more gourmet time and, purely flattered, she made one sauce too many and we had it for dessert on saltines, with iced *café au lait*. While I cleared the dishes, Joanna, everybody's piece of fluff, sat on Grandma's lap telling her each single credible detail of her eight hours at summer day camp.

"Women," said Grandma in appreciation, "have been the pleasure and consolation of my entire life. From the beginning I cherished all the little girls with their clean faces and their listening ears . . ."

"Men are different than women," said Joanna, and it's the only thing she says in this entire story.

"That's true," said Grandma, "it's the men that've always troubled me. Men and boys . . . I suppose I don't understand them. But think of it consecutively, all in a row, Johnson, Revere, and Drummond . . . after all, where did they start from but me? But all of them, all all all, each single one of them is gone, far away in heart and body."

"Ah, Grandma," I said, hoping to console, "they were all so grouchy, anyway. I don't miss them a bit."

Grandma gave me a miserable look. "Everyone's sons are like that," she explained. "First grouchy, then gone."

After that she sat in grieving sorrow. Joanna curled herself round the hassock at her feet, hugged it, and slept. Mother got her last week's copy of *Le Monde* out of the piano bench and calmed herself with a story about a farmer in Provence who had raped his niece and killed his mother and lived happily for thirty-eight years into respected old age before the nosy prefect caught up with him. She translated it into our derivative mother tongue while I did the dishes.

Nighttime came and communication was revived at last by our doorbell, which is full of initiative. It was Lizzy and she did bring Corporal Brownstar. We sent Joanna out for beer and soft drinks and the dancing started right away. He cooperatively danced with everyone. I slipped away to my room for a moment and painted a lot of lipstick neatly on my big mouth and hooked a walleyed brassière around my ribs to make him understand that I was older than Joanna.

He said to me, "You're peaches and cream, you're gonna be quite a girl someday, Alice in Wonderland."

"I am a girl already, Corporal."

"Uh *huh*," he said, squeezing my left bottom.

Lizzy passed the punch and handed out Ritz crackers and danced with Mother and Joanna whenever the corporal danced with me. She was delighted to see him so popular, and it just passed her happy head that he was the only man there. At the peak of the evening he said: "You may all call me Browny."

We sang Air Force songs then until 2 a.m., and Grandma said the songs hadn't changed much since her war. "The soldiers are younger though," she said. "Son, you look like your mother is still worried about you."

"No reason to worry about me, I got a lot of irons in the fire. I get advanced all the time, as a matter of fact. Stem to stern," he said, winking at Lizzy, "I'm O.K. . . . By the way," he continued, "could you folks put me up? I wouldn't mind sleeping on the floor."

"The floor?" expostulated Mother. "Are you out of your mind? A soldier of the Republic. My God! We have a cot. You know . . . an Army cot. Set it up and sleep the sleep of the just, Corporal."

"Oh, goodness"—Grandma yawned—"talking about bed—Marvine, your dad must be home by now. I'd better be getting back."

Browny decided in a courteous way to take Lizzy and Grandma home. By the time he returned, Mother and Joanna had wrapped their lonesome arms around each other and gone to sleep.

I sneakily watched him from behind the drapes scrubbing himself down without consideration for his skin. Then, shining and naked, he crawled between the sheets in totality.

I unshod myself and tiptoed into the kitchen. I poured him a cold beer. I came straight to him and sat down by his side. "Here's a nice beer, Browny. I thought you might be hot after such a long walk."

"Why, thanks, Alice Palace Pudding and Pie, I happen to be pretty damn hot. You're a real pal."

He heaved himself up and got that beer into his gut in one gulp. I looked at him down to his belly button. He put the empty glass on the floor and grinned at me. He burped into my face for a joke and then I had to speak the truth. "Oh, Browny," I said, "I just love you so." I threw my arms around his middle and leaned my face into the golden hairs of his chest.

"Hey, pudding, take it easy. I like you too. You're a doll."

Then I kissed him right on the mouth.

"Josephine, who the hell taught you that?"

"I taught myself. I practiced on my wrist. See?"

"Josephine!" he said again. "Josephine, you're a liar. You're one hell of a liar!"

After that his affection increased, and he hugged me too and kissed me right on the mouth.

"Well," I kidded, "who taught you that? Lizzy?"

"Shut up," he said, and the more he loved me the less he allowed of conversation.

I lay down beside him, and I was really surprised the way a man is transformed by his feelings. He loved me all over myself, and to show I understood his meaning I whispered: "Browny, what do you want? Browny, do you want to do it?"

Well! He jumped out of bed then and flapped the sheet around his shoulders and groaned, "Oh, Christ . . . Oh," he said, "I could be arrested. I could be picked up by M.P.'s and spend the rest of my life in jail." He looked at me. "For godsakes button your shirt. Your mother'll wake up in a minute."

"Browny, what's the matter?"

"You're a child and you're too damn smart for your own good. Don't you understand? This could ruin my whole life."

"But, Browny . . ."

"The trouble I could get into! I could be busted. You're a baby. It's a joke. A person could marry a baby like you, but it's criminal to lay a hand on your shoulder. That's funny, ha-ha-ha."

"Oh, Browny, I would love to be married to you."

He sat down at the edge of the cot and drew me to his lap.

"Gee, what a funny kid you are. You really like me so much?"

"I love you. I'd be a first-class wife, Browny—do you realize I take care of this whole house? When Mother isn't working, she spends her whole time mulling over Daddy. I'm the one who does Joanna's hair every day. *I* iron her dresses. I could even have a baby for you, Browny, I know just how to—"

"No! Oh no. Don't let anyone ever talk you into that. Not till you're eighteen. You ought to stay tidy as a doll and not strain your skin at least till you're eighteen."

"Browny, don't you get lonesome in that camp? I mean if Lizzy isn't around and I'm not around . . . Don't you think I have a nice figure?"

"Oh, I guess . . ." He laughed, and put his hand warmly under my shirt. "It's pretty damn nice, considering it ain't even quite done."

I couldn't hold my desire down, and I kissed him again right into his talking mouth and smack against his teeth. "Oh, Browny, I would take care of you."

"O.K., O.K.," he said, pushing me kindly away. "O.K., now listen, go to sleep before we really cook up a stew. Go to sleep. You're a sweet kid. Sleep it off. You ain't even begun to see how wide the world is. It's a surprise even to a man like me."

"But my mind is settled."

"Go to sleep, go sleep," he said, still holding my hand and patting it. "You look almost like Lizzy now."

"Oh, but I'm different. I know exactly what I want."

"Go to sleep, little girl," he said for the last time. I took his hand and kissed each brown fingertip and then ran into my room and took all my clothes off and, as bare as my lonesome soul, I slept.

————

The next day was Saturday and I was glad. Mother is a waitress all weekend at the Paris Coffee House, where she has been learning French from the waiters ever since Daddy disappeared. She's lucky because she really loves her work; she's crazy about the customers, the coffee, the décor, and is only miserable when she gets home.

I gave her breakfast on the front porch at about 10 a.m. and Joanna walked her to the bus. "Cook the corporal some of those frozen sausages," she called out in her middle range.

I hoped he'd wake up so we could start some more love, but instead Lizzy stepped over our sagging threshold. "Came over to fix Browny some breakfast," she said efficiently.

"Oh?" I looked at her childlike in the eye. "I think *I* ought to do it, Aunty Liz, because he and I are probably getting married. Don't you think I ought to in that case?"

"What? Say that slowly, Josephine."

"You heard me, Aunty Liz."

She flopped in a dirndl heap on the stairs. "*I* don't even feel old enough to get married and *I've* been seventeen since Christmas time. Did he really ask you?"

"We've been talking about it," I said, and that was true. "I'm in love with him, Lizzy." Tears prevented my vision.

"Oh, love . . . I've been in love twelve times since I was your age."

"Not me, I've settled on Browny. I'm going to get a job and send him to college after his draft is over . . . He's very smart."

"Oh, smart . . . everybody's smart."

"No, they are not."

When she left I kissed Browny on both eyes, like the Sleeping Beauty, and he stretched and woke up in a conflagration of hunger.

"Breakfast, breakfast, breakfast," he bellowed.

I fed him and he said, "Wow, the guys would really laugh, me thiefin' the cradle this way."

"Don't feel like that. I make a good impression on people, Browny. There've been lots of men more grown than you who've made a fuss over me."

"Ha-ha," he remarked.

I made him quit that kind of laughing and started him on some kisses, and we had a cheerful morning.

"Browny," I said at lunch, "I'm going to tell Mother we're getting married."

"Don't she have enough troubles of her own?"

"No, no," I said. "She's all for love. She's crazy about it."

"Well, think about it a minute, baby face. After all, I might get shipped out to some troubled area and be knocked over by a crazy native. You read about something like that every day. Anyway, wouldn't it be fun to have a real secret engagement for a while? How about it?"

"Not me," I said, remembering everything I'd ever heard from Liz about the opportunism of men, how they will sometimes dedicate with seeming goodwill thirty days and nights, sleeping and waking, of truth and deceit to the achievement of a moment's pleasure. "Secret engagement! Some might agree to a plan like that, but not me."

Then I knew he liked me, because he walked around the table and played with the curls of my home permanent a minute and whispered, "The guys would really laugh, but I get a big bang out of you."

Then I wasn't sure he liked me, because he looked at his watch and asked it: "Where the hell is Lizzy?"

I had to do the shopping and put off some local merchants in a muddle of innocence, which is my main Saturday chore. I ran all the way. It didn't take very long, but as I rattled up the stairs and into the hall, I heard the thumping tail of a conversation. Browny was saying, "It's your fault, Liz."

"I couldn't care less," she said. "I suppose you get something out of playing around with a child."

"Oh no, you don't get it at all . . ."

"I can't say I want it."

"Goddamnit," said Browny, "you don't listen to a person. I think you stink."

"Really?" Turning to go, she smashed the screen door in my face and jammed my instep with the heel of her lavender pump.

"Tell your mother we will," Browny yelled when he saw me. "She stinks, that Liz, goddamnit. Tell your mother tonight."

I did my best during that passing afternoon to make Browny more friendly. I sat on his lap and he drank beer and tickled me. I laughed, and pretty soon I understood the game and how it had to have variety and ran shrieking from him till he could catch me in a comfortable place, the living-room sofa or my own bedroom.

"You're O.K.," he said. "You are. I'm crazy about you, Josephine. You're a lot of fun."

So that night at 9:15 when Mother came home I made her some iced tea and cornered her in the kitchen and locked the door. "I want to tell you something about me and Corporal Brownstar. Don't say a word, Mother. We're going to be married."

"What?" she said. "Married?" she screeched. "Are you crazy? You can't even get a job without working papers yet. You can't even get working papers. You're a baby. Are you kidding me? You're my little fish. You're not fourteen yet."

"Well, I decided we could wait until next month when I will be fourteen. Then, I decided, we can get married."

"You can't, my God! Nobody gets married at fourteen, nobody, nobody. I don't know a soul."

"Oh, Mother, people do, you always see them in the paper. The worst that could happen is it would get in the paper."

"But I didn't realize you had much to do with him. Isn't he Lizzy's? That's not nice—to take him away from her. That's a rotten sneaky trick. You're a sneak. Women should stick together. Didn't you learn anything yet?"

"Well, she doesn't want to get married and I do. And it's essential to Browny to get married. He's a very clean-living boy, and when his furlough's over he doesn't want to go back to those camp followers and other people's wives. You have to appreciate that in him, Mother—it's a quality."

"You're a baby," she droned. "You're my slippery little fish."

Browny rattled the kitchen doorknob ten minutes too early.

"Oh, come in," I said, disgusted.

"How's stuff? Everything settled? What do you say, Marvine?"

"I say shove it, Corporal! What's wrong with Lizzy? You and she were really beautiful together. You looked like twin stars in the summer sky. Now I realize I don't like your looks much. Who's your mother and father? I never even heard much about them. For all I know, you got an uncle in Alcatraz. And your teeth are in terrible shape. I thought the Army takes care of things like that. You just don't look so hot to me."

"No reason to be personal, Marvine."

"But she's a baby. What if she becomes pregnant and bubbles up her entire constitution? This isn't India. Did you ever read what happened to the insides of those Indian child brides?"

"Oh, he's very gentle, Mother."

"What?" she said, construing the worst.

That conference persisted for about two hours. We drank a couple of pitcherfuls of raspberry Kool-Aid we'd been saving for Joanna's twelfth birthday party the next day. No one had a dime, and we couldn't find Grandma.

Later on, decently before midnight, Lizzy showed up. She had a lieutenant (j.g.) with her and she introduced him around as Sid. She didn't introduce him to Browny, because she has stated time and time again that officers and enlisted men ought not to mix socially. As soon as the lieutenant took Mother's hand in greeting, I could see he was astonished. He began to perspire visibly in long welts down his back and in the gabardine armpits of his summer uniform. Mother was in one of those sullen, indolent moods which really put a fire under some men. She was just beady to think of my stubborn decision and how my life contained the roots of excitement.

"France is where I belong," she murmured to him. "Paris, Marseilles, places like that, where men like women and don't chase little girls."

"I have a lot of sympathy with the Gallic temperament and I do like a real woman," he said hopefully.

"Sympathy is not enough." Her voice rose to the requirements of her natural disposition. "Empathy is what I need. The empathy of a true friend is what I have lived without for years."

"Oh yes, I feel all that, empathy too." He fell deeply into his heart, from which he could scarcely be heard . . . "I like a woman who's had some contact with life, cradled little ones, felt the pangs of birth, known the death of loved ones . . ."

". . . and of love," she added sadly. "That's unusual in a young good-looking man."

"Yet that's my particular preference."

Lizzy, Browny, and I borrowed a dollar from him while he sat in idyllic stupor and we wandered out for some ice cream. We took Joanna because we were sorry to have drunk up her whole party. When we returned with a bottle of black-raspberry soda, no one was in sight. "I'm beginning to feel like a procurer," said Lizzy.

That's how come Mother finally said yes. Her moral turpitude took such a lively turn that she gave us money for a Wassermann. She called Dr. Gilmar and told him to be gentle with the needles. "It's my own little girl, Doctor. Little Josie that you pulled right out of me yourself. She's so headstrong. Oh, Doctor, remember me and Charles? She's a rough little customer, just like me."

Due to the results of this test, which is a law, and despite Browny's disbelief, we could not get married. Grandma, always philosophical with the advantage of years, said that young men sowing wild oats were often nipped in the bud, so to speak, and that modern science would soon unite us. Ha-ha-ha, I laugh in recollection.

Mother never even noticed. It passed her by completely, because of large events in her own life. When Browny left for camp drowned in penicillin and damp with chagrin, she gave him a giant jar of Loft's Sour Balls and a can of walnut rum tobacco.

Then she went ahead with her own life. Without any of the disenchantment Browny and I had suffered, the lieutenant and Mother got married. We were content, all of us, though it's common knowledge that she has never been divorced from Daddy. The name next to hers on the marriage license is Sidney LaValle, Jr., Lieut. (j.g.), U.S.N. An earlier, curlier generation of LaValles came to Michigan from Quebec, and Sid has a couple of usable idioms in Mother's favorite tongue.

I have received one card from Browny. It shows an aerial view of Joplin, Mo. It says: "Hi, kid, chin up, love, Browny. P.S. Health improved."

Living as I do on a turnpike of discouragement, I am glad to hear the incessant happy noises in the next room. I enjoyed hugging with Browny's body, though I don't believe I was more to him than a hope for civilian success. Joanna has moved in with me. Though she grinds her teeth well into daylight, I am grateful for her company. Since I have been engaged, she looks up to me. She is a real cuddly girl.

The Loudest Voice

There is a certain place where dumbwaiters boom, doors slam, dishes crash; every window is a mother's mouth bidding the street shut up, go skate somewhere else, come home. My voice is the loudest.

There, my own mother is still as full of breathing as me and the grocer stands up to speak to her. "Mrs. Abramowitz," he says, "people should not be afraid of their children."

"Ah, Mr. Bialik," my mother replies, "if you say to her or her father, 'Ssh,' they say, 'In the grave it will be quiet.'"

"From Coney Island to the cemetery," says my papa. "It's the same subway; it's the same fare."

I am right next to the pickle barrel. My pinky is making tiny whirlpools in the brine. I stop a moment to announce: "Campbell's Tomato Soup. Campbell's Vegetable Beef Soup. Campbell's S-c-otch Broth . . ."

"Be quiet," the grocer says, "the labels are coming off."

"Please, Shirley, be a little quiet," my mother begs me.

In that place the whole street groans: Be quiet! Be quiet! but steals from the happy chorus of my inside self not a tittle or a jot.

There too, but just around the corner, is a red brick building that has been old for many years. Every morning the children stand before it in double lines which must be straight. They are not insulted. They are waiting anyway.

I am usually among them. I am, in fact, the first, since I begin with "A."

One cold morning the monitor tapped me on the shoulder. "Go to Room 409, Shirley Abramowitz," he said. I did as I was told. I went in a hurry up a down staircase to Room 409, which contained sixth-graders. I had to wait at the desk without wiggling until Mr. Hilton, their teacher, had time to speak.

After five minutes he said, "Shirley?"

"What?" I whispered.

He said, "My! My! Shirley Abramowitz! They told me you had a particularly loud, clear voice and read with lots of expression. Could that be true?"

"Oh yes," I whispered.

"In that case, don't be silly; I might very well be your teacher someday. Speak up, speak up."

"Yes," I shouted.

"More like it," he said. "Now, Shirley, can you put a ribbon in your hair or a bobby pin? It's too messy."

"Yes!" I bawled.

"Now, now calm down." He turned to the class. "Children, not a sound. Open at page 39. Read till 52. When you finish, start again." He looked me over once more. "Now, Shirley, you know, I suppose, that Christmas is coming. We are preparing a beautiful play. Most of the parts have been given out. But I still need a child with a strong voice, lots of stamina. Do you know what stamina is? You do? Smart kid. You know, I heard you read 'The Lord is my shepherd' in Assembly yesterday. I was very impressed. Wonderful delivery. Mrs. Jordan, your teacher, speaks highly of you. Now listen to me, Shirley Abramowitz, if you want to take the part and be in the play, repeat after me, 'I swear to work harder than I ever did before.'"

I looked to heaven and said at once, "Oh, I swear." I kissed my pinky and looked at God.

"That is an actor's life, my dear," he explained. "Like a soldier's, never tardy or disobedient to his general, the director. Everything," he said, "absolutely everything will depend on you."

That afternoon, all over the building, children scraped and scrubbed the turkeys and the sheaves of corn off the schoolroom windows. Goodbye Thanksgiving. The next morning a monitor brought red paper and green paper from the office. We made new shapes and hung them on the walls and glued them to the doors.

The teachers became happier and happier. Their heads were ringing like the bells of childhood. My best friend, Evie, was prone to evil, but she did not get a single demerit for whispering. We learned "Holy Night" without an error. "How wonderful!" said Miss Glacé, the student teacher. "To think that some of you don't even speak the language!" We learned "Deck the Halls" and "Hark! The Herald Angels" . . . They weren't ashamed and we weren't embarrassed.

Oh, but when my mother heard about it all, she said to my father: "Misha, you don't know what's going on there. Cramer is the head of the Tickets Committee."

"Who?" asked my father. "Cramer? Oh yes, an active woman."

"Active? Active has to have a reason. Listen," she said sadly. "I'm surprised to see my neighbors making tra-la-la for Christmas."

My father couldn't think of what to say to that. Then he decided: "You're in America! Clara, you wanted to come here. In Palestine the Arabs would be eating you alive. Europe you had pogroms. Argentina is full of Indians. Here you got Christmas . . . Some joke, ha?"

"Very funny, Misha. What is becoming of you? If we came to a new country a long time ago to run away from tyrants, and instead we fall into a creeping pogrom, that our children learn a lot of lies, so what's the joke? Ach, Misha, your idealism is going away."

"So is your sense of humor."

"That I never had, but idealism you had a lot of."

"I'm the same Misha Abramovitch, I didn't change an iota. Ask anyone."

"Only ask me," says my mama, may she rest in peace. "I got the answer."

Meanwhile the neighbors had to think of what to say too.

Marty's father said: "You know, he has a very important part, my boy."

"Mine also," said Mr. Sauerfeld.

"Not my boy!" said Mrs. Klieg. "I said to him no. The answer is no. When I say no! I mean no!"

The rabbi's wife said, "It's disgusting!" But no one listened to her. Under the narrow sky of God's great wisdom she wore a strawberry-blond wig.

Every day was noisy and full of experience. I was Right-hand Man. Mr. Hilton said: "How could I get along without you, Shirley?"

He said: "Your mother and father ought to get down on their knees every night and thank God for giving them a child like you."

He also said: "You're absolutely a pleasure to work with, my dear, dear child."

Sometimes he said: "For godsakes, what did I do with the script? Shirley! Shirley! Find it."

Then I answered quietly: "Here it is, Mr. Hilton."

Once in a while, when he was very tired, he would cry out: "Shirley, I'm just tired of screaming at those kids. Will you tell Ira Pushkov not to come in till Lester points to that star the second time?"

Then I roared: "Ira Pushkov, what's the matter with you? Dope! Mr. Hilton told you five times already, don't come in till Lester points to that star the second time."

"Ach, Clara," my father asked, "what does she do there till six o'clock she can't even put the plates on the table?"

"Christmas," said my mother coldly.

"Ho! Ho!" my father said. 'Christmas. What's the harm? After all, history teaches everyone. We learn from reading this is a holiday from pagan times also, candles, lights, even Hanukkah. So we learn it's not altogether Christian. So if they think it's a private holiday, they're only ignorant, not patriotic. What belongs to history belongs to all men. You want to go back to the Middle Ages? Is it better to shave your head with a second-hand razor? Does it hurt Shirley to learn to speak up? It does not. So maybe someday she won't live between the kitchen and the shop. She's not a fool."

I thank you, Papa, for your kindness. It is true about me to this day. I am foolish but I am not a fool.

That night my father kissed me and said with great interest in my career, "Shirley, tomorrow's your big day. Congrats."

"Save it," my mother said. Then she shut all the windows in order to prevent tonsillitis.

In the morning it snowed. On the street corner a tree had been decorated for us by a kind city administration. In order to miss its chilly shadow our neighbors walked three blocks east to buy a loaf of bread. The butcher pulled down black window shades to keep the colored lights from shining on his chickens. Oh, not me. On the way to school, with both my hands I tossed it a kiss of tolerance. Poor thing, it was a stranger in Egypt.

I walked straight into the auditorium past the staring children. "Go ahead, Shirley!" said the monitors. Four boys, big for their age, had already started work as propmen and stagehands.

Mr. Hilton was very nervous. He was not even happy. Whatever he started to say ended in a sideward look of sadness. He sat slumped in the middle of the first row and asked me to help Miss Glacé. I did this, although she thought my voice too resonant and said, "Show-off!"

Parents began to arrive long before we were ready. They wanted to make a good impression. From among the yards of drapes I peeked out at the audience. I saw my embarrassed mother.

Ira, Lester, and Meyer were pasted to their beards by Miss Glacé. She almost forgot to thread the star on its wire, but I reminded her. I coughed a few times to clear my throat. Miss Glacé looked around and saw that everyone was in costume and on line waiting to play his part. She whispered, "All right . . ." Then:

Jackie Sauerfeld, the prettiest boy in first grade, parted the curtains with his skinny elbow and in a high voice sang out:

> *Parents dear*
> *We are here*
> *To make a Christmas play in time.*
> *It we give*
> *In narrative*
> *And illustrate with pantomime.*

He disappeared.

My voice burst immediately from the wings to the great shock of Ira, Lester, and Meyer, who were waiting for it but were surprised all the same.

"I remember, I remember, the house where I was born . . ."

Miss Glacé yanked the curtain open and there it was, the house—an old hayloft, where Celia Kornbluh lay in the straw with Cindy Lou, her favorite doll. Ira, Lester, and Meyer moved slowly from the wings toward her, sometimes pointing to a moving star and sometimes ahead to Cindy Lou.

It was a long story and it was a sad story. I carefully pronounced all the words about my lonesome childhood, while little Eddie Braunstein wandered upstage and down with his shepherd's stick, looking for sheep. I brought up lonesomeness again, and not being understood at all except by some women everybody hated. Eddie was too small for that and Marty Grof took his place, wearing his father's prayer shawl. I announced twelve friends, and half the boys in the fourth grade gathered round Marty, who stood on an orange crate while my voice harangued. Sorrowful and loud, I declaimed about love and God and man, but because of the terrible deceit of Abie Stock we came suddenly to a famous moment. Marty, whose remembering tongue I was, waited at the foot of the cross. He stared desperately at the audience. I groaned, "My God, my God, why hast thou forsaken me?" The soldiers who were sheiks grabbed poor Marty to pin him up to die, but he wrenched free, turned again to the audience, and spread his arms aloft to show despair and the end. I murmured at the top of my voice, "The rest is silence, but as everyone in this room, in this city—in this world—now knows, I shall have life eternal."

That night Mrs. Kornbluh visited our kitchen for a glass of tea.

"How's the virgin?" asked my father with a look of concern.

"For a man with a daughter, you got a fresh mouth, Abramovitch."

"Here," said my father kindly, "have some lemon, it'll sweeten your disposition."

They debated a little in Yiddish, then fell in a puddle of Russian and Polish. What I understood next was my father, who said, "Still and all, it was certainly a beautiful affair, you have to admit, introducing us to the beliefs of a different culture."

"Well, yes," said Mrs. Kornbluh. "The only thing . . . you know Charlie Turner—that cute boy in Celia's class—a couple others? They got very small parts or no part at all. In very bad taste, it seemed to me. After all, it's their religion."

"Ach," explained my mother, "What could Mr. Hilton do? They got very small voices; after all, why should they holler? The English language they know from the beginning by heart. They're blond like angels. You think it's so important they should get in the play? Christmas . . . the whole piece of goods . . . they own it."

I listened and listened until I couldn't listen anymore. Too sleepy, I climbed out of bed and kneeled. I made a little church of my hands and said, "Hear, O Israel . . ." Then I called out in Yiddish, "Please, good night, good night. Ssh." My father said, "Ssh yourself," and slammed the kitchen door.

I was happy. I fell asleep at once. I had prayed for everybody: my talking family, cousins far away, passersby, and all the lonesome Christians. I expected to be heard. My voice was certainly the loudest.

An Interest in Life

My husband gave me a broom one Christmas. This wasn't right. No one can tell me it was meant kindly.

"I don't want you not to have anything for Christmas while I'm away in the Army," he said. "Virginia, please look at it. It comes with this fancy dustpan. It hangs off a stick. Look at it, will you? Are you blind or cross-eyed?"

"Thanks, chum," I said. I had always wanted a dustpan hooked up that way. It was a good one. My husband doesn't shop in bargain basements or January sales.

Still and all, in spite of the quality, it was a mean present to give a woman you planned on never seeing again, a person you had children with and got onto all the time, drunk or sober, even when everybody had to get up early in the morning.

I asked him if he could wait and join the Army in a half hour, as I had to get the groceries. I don't like to leave kids alone in a three-room apartment full of gas and electricity. Fire may break out from a nasty remark. Or the oldest decides to get even with the youngest.

"Just this once," he said. "But you better figure out how to get along without me."

"You're a handicapped person mentally," I said. "You should've been institutionalized years ago." I slammed the door. I didn't want to see him pack his underwear and ironed shirts.

I never got farther than the front stoop, though, because there was Mrs. Raftery, wringing her hands, tears in her eyes as though she had a monopoly on all the good news.

"Mrs. Raftery!" I said, putting my arm around her. "Don't cry." She leaned on me because I am such a horsey build. "Don't cry, Mrs. Raftery, please!" I said.

"That's like you, Virginia. Always looking at the ugly side of things. 'Take in the wash. It's rainin'!' That's you. You're the first one knows it when the dumbwaiter breaks."

"Oh, come on now, that's not so. It just isn't so," I said. "I'm the exact opposite."

"Did you see Mrs. Cullen yet?" she asked, paying no attention.

"Where?"

"Virginia!" she said, shocked. "She's passed away. The whole house knows it. They've got her in white like a bride and you never saw a beautiful creature like that. She must be eighty. Her husband's proud."

"She was never more than an acquaintance; she didn't have any children," I said.

"Well, I don't care about that. Now, Virginia, you do what I say now, you go downstairs and you say like this— listen to me—say, 'I hear, Mr. Cullen, your wife's passed away. I'm sorry.' Then ask him how he is. Then you ought to go around the corner and see her. She's in Witson & Wayde. Then you ought to go over to the church when they carry her over."

"It's not my church," I said.

"That's no reason, Virginia. You go up like this," she said, parting from me to do a prancy dance. "Up the big front steps, into the church you go. It's beautiful in there. You can't help kneeling only for a minute. Then round to the right. Then up the other stairway. Then you come to a great oak door that's arched above you, then," she said, seizing a deep, deep breath, for all the good it would do her, "and then turn the knob slo-owly and open the door and see for yourself: Our Blessed Mother is in charge. Beautiful. Beautiful. Beautiful."

I sighed in and I groaned out, so as to melt a certain pain around my heart. A steel ring like arthritis, at my age.

"You are a groaner," Mrs. Raftery said, gawking into my mouth.

"I am not," I said. I got a whiff of her, a terrible cheap wine lush.

My husband threw a penny at the door from the inside to take my notice from Mrs. Raftery. He rattled the glass door to make sure I looked at him. He had a fat duffel bag on each shoulder. Where did he acquire so much worldly possession? What was in them? My grandma's goose feathers from across the ocean? Or all the diaper-service diapers? To this day the truth is shrouded in mystery.

"What the hell are you doing, Virginia?" he said, dumping them at my feet. "Standing out here on your hind legs telling everybody your business? The Army gives you a certain time, for godsakes, they're not kidding." Then he said, "I beg your pardon," to Mrs. Raftery. He took hold of me with his two arms as though in love and pressed his body hard against mine so that I could feel him for the last time and suffer my loss. Then he kissed me in a mean way to nearly split my lip. Then he winked and said, "That's all for now," and skipped off into the future, duffel bags full of rags.

He left me in an embarrassing situation, nearly fainting, in front of that old widow, who can't even remember the half of it. "He's a crock," said Mrs. Raftery. "Is he leaving for good or just temporarily, Virginia?"

"Oh, he's probably deserting me," I said, and sat down on the stoop, pulling my big knees up to my chin.

"If that's the case, tell the Welfare right away," she said. "He's a bum, leaving you just before Christmas. Tell the cops," she said. "They'll provide the toys for the little kids gladly. And don't forget to let the grocer in on it. He won't be so hard on you expecting payment."

She saw that sadness was stretched worldwide across my face. Mrs. Raftery isn't the worst person. She said, "Look around for comfort, dear." With a nervous finger she pointed to the truckers eating lunch on their haunches across the street, leaning on the loading platforms. She waved her hand to include in all the men marching up and down in search of a decent luncheonette. She didn't leave out the six longshoremen loafing under the fish-market marquee. "If their lungs and stomachs ain't crushed by overwork, they disappear somewhere in the world. Don't be disappointed, Virginia. I don't know a man living'd last you a lifetime."

Ten days later Girard asked, "Where's Daddy?"

"Ask me no questions, I'll tell you no lies." I didn't want the children to know the facts. Present or past, a child should have a father.

"Where *is* Daddy?" Girard asked the week after that.

"He joined the Army," I said.

"He made my bunk bed," said Philip.

"The truth shall make ye free," I said.

Then I sat down with pencil and pad to get in control of my resources. The facts, when I added and subtracted them, were that my husband had left me with fourteen dollars, and the rent unpaid, in an emergency state. He'd claimed he was sorry to do this, but my opinion is, out of sight, out of mind. "The city won't let you starve," he'd said. "After all, you're half the population. You're keeping up the good work. Without you the race would die out. Who'd pay the taxes? Who'd keep the streets clean? There wouldn't be no Army. A man like me wouldn't have no place to go."

I sent Girard right down to Mrs. Raftery with a request about the whereabouts of Welfare. She responded R.S.V.P. with an extra comment in left-handed script: "Poor Girard . . . he's never the boy my John was!"

Who asked her?

I called on Welfare right after the new year. In no time I discovered that they're rigged up to deal with liars, and if you're truthful it's disappointing to them. They may even refuse to handle your case if you're too truthful.

They asked sensible questions at first. They asked where my husband had enlisted. I didn't know. They put some letter writers and agents after him. "He's not in the United States Army," they said. "Try the Brazilian Army," I suggested.

They have no sense of kidding around. They're not the least bit lighthearted and they tried. "Oh no," they said. "That was incorrect. He is not in the Brazilian Army."

"No?" I said. "How strange! He must be in the Mexican Navy."

By law, they had to hound his brothers. They wrote to his brother who has a first-class card in the Teamsters and owns an apartment house in California. They asked his two brothers in Jersey to help me. They have large families. Rightfully they laughed. Then they wrote to Thomas, the oldest, the smart one (the one they all worked so hard for years to keep him in college until his brains could pay off). He was the one who sent ten dollars immediately, saying, "What a bastard! I'll send something from time to time, Ginny, but whatever you do, don't tell the authorities." Of course I never did. Soon they began to guess they were better people than me, that I was in trouble because I deserved it, and then they liked me better.

But they never fixed my refrigerator. Every time I called I said patiently, "The milk is sour . . ." I said, "Corn beef went bad." Sitting in that beer-stinking phone booth in Felan's for the sixth time (sixty cents) with the baby on my lap and Barbie tapping at the glass door with an American flag, I cried into the secretary's hardhearted ear, "I bought real butter for the holiday, and it's rancid . . ." They said, "You'll have to get a better bid on the repair job."

While I waited indoors for a man to bid, Girard took to swinging back and forth on top of the bathroom door, just to soothe himself, giving me the laugh, dreamy, nibbling calcimine off the ceiling.

On first sight Mrs. Raftery said, "Whack the monkey, he'd be better off on arsenic."

But Girard is my son and I'm the judge. It means a terrible thing for the future, though I don't know what to call it.

It was constantly thinking of my foreknowledge on this and other subjects, it was from observing when I put my lipstick on daily, how my face was just curling up to die, that John Raftery came from Jersey to rescue me.

On Thursdays, anyway, John Raftery took the tubes in to visit his mother. The whole house knew it. She was cheerful even before breakfast. She sang out loud in a girlish brogue that only came to tongue for grand occasions. Hanging out the wash, she blushed to recall what a remarkable boy her John had been. "Ask the sisters around the corner," she said to the open kitchen windows. "They'll never forget John."

That particular night after supper Mrs. Raftery said to her son, "John, how come you don't say hello to your old friend Virginia? She's had hard luck and she's gloomy."

"Is that so, Mother?" he said, and immediately climbed two flights to knock at my door.

"Oh John," I said at the sight of him, hat in hand in a white shirt and blue-striped tie, spick-and-span, a Sunday-school man. "Hello."

"Welcome, John!" I said. "Sit down. Come right in. How are you? You look awfully good. You do. Tell me, how've you been all this time, John?"

"How've I been?" he asked thoughtfully. To answer within reason, he described his life with Margaret, marriage, work, and children up to the present day.

I had nothing good to report. Now that he had put the subject around before my very eyes, every burnt-up day of my life smoked in shame, and I couldn't even get a clear view of the good half hours.

"Of course," he said, "you do have lovely children. Noticeable-looking, Virginia. Good looks is always something to be thankful for."

"Thankful?" I said. "I don't have to thank anything but my own foolishness for four children when I'm twenty-six years old, deserted, and poverty-struck, regardless of looks. A man can't help it, but I could have behaved better."

"Don't be so cruel on yourself, Ginny," he said. "Children come from God."

"You're still great on holy subjects, aren't you? You know damn well where children come from."

He did know. His red face reddened further. John Raftery has had that color coming out on him boy and man from keeping his rages so inward.

Still he made more sense in his conversation after that, and I poured fresh tea to tell him how my husband used to like me because I was a passionate person. That was until he took a look around and saw how in the long run this life only meant more of the same thing. He tried to turn away from me once he came to this understanding, and make me hate him. His face changed. He gave up his brand of cigarettes, which we had in common. He threw out the two pairs of socks I knitted by hand. "If there's anything I hate in this world, it's navy blue," he said. Oh, I could have dyed them. I would have done anything for him, if he were only not too sorry to ask me.

"You were a nice kid in those days," said John, referring to certain Saturday nights. "A wild, nice kid."

"Aaah," I said, disgusted. Whatever I was then was on the way to where I am now. "I was fresh. If I had a kid like me, I'd slap her cross-eyed."

The very next Thursday John gave me a beautiful radio with a record player. "Enjoy yourself," he said. That really made Welfare speechless. We didn't own any records, but the investigator saw my burden was lightened and he scribbled a dozen pages about it in his notebook.

On the third Thursday he brought a walking doll (twenty-four inches) for Linda and Barbie with a card inscribed, "A baby doll for a couple of dolls." He had also had a couple of drinks at his mother's, and this made him want to dance. "La-la-la," he sang, a ramrod swaying in my kitchen chair. "La-la-la, let yourself go . . ."

"You gotta give a little," he sang, "live a little . . ." He said, "Virginia, may I have this dance?"

"Sssh, we finally got them asleep. Please, turn the radio down. Quiet. Deathly silence, John Raftery."

"Let me do your dishes, Virginia."

"Don't be silly, you're a guest in my house," I said. "I still regard you as a guest."

"I want to do something for you, Virginia."

"Tell me I'm the most gorgeous thing," I said, dipping my arm to the funny bone in dish soup.

He didn't answer. "I'm having a lot of trouble at work" was all he said. Then I heard him push the chair back. He came up behind me, put his arm around my waistline, and kissed my cheek. He whirled me around and took my hands. He said, "An old friend is better than rubies." He looked me in the eye. He held my attention by trying to be honest. And he kissed me a short sweet kiss on my mouth.

"Please sit down, Virginia," he said. He kneeled before me and put his head in my lap. I was stirred by so much activity. Then he looked up at me and, as though proposing marriage for life, he offered—because he was drunk—to place his immortal soul in peril to comfort me.

First I said, "Thank you." Then I said, "No."

I was sorry for him, but he's devout, a leader of the Fathers' Club at his church, active in all the lay groups for charities, orphans, etc. I knew that if he stayed late to love with me, he would not do it lightly but would in the end pay terrible penance and ruin his long life. The responsibility would be on me.

So I said no.

And Barbie is such a light sleeper. All she has to do, I thought, is wake up and wander in and see her mother and her new friend John with his pants around his knees, wrestling on the kitchen table. A vision like that could affect a kid for life.

I said no.

Everyone in this building is so goddamn nosy. That evening I had to say no.

But John came to visit, anyway, on the fourth Thursday. This time he brought the discarded dresses of Margaret's daughters, organdy party dresses and glazed cotton for every day. He gently admired Barbara and Linda, his blue eyes rolling to back up a couple of dozen oohs and ahs.

Even Philip, who thinks God gave him just a certain number of hellos and he better save them for the final judgment, Philip leaned on John and said, "Why don't you bring your boy to play with me? I don't have nobody who to play with." (Philip's a liar. There must be at least seventy-one children in this house, pale pink to medium brown, English-talking and gibbering in Spanish, rough-and-tough boys, the Lone Ranger's bloody pals, or the exact picture of Supermouse. If a boy wanted a friend, he could pick the very one out of his neighbors.)

Also, Girard is a cold fish. He was in a lonesome despair. Sometimes he looked in the mirror and said, "How come I have such an ugly face? My nose is funny. Mostly people don't like me." He was a liar too. Girard had a face like his father's. His eyes are the color of those little blue plums in August. He looks like an advertisement in a magazine. He could be a child model and make a lot of money. He is my first child, and if he thinks he is ugly, I think I am ugly.

John said, "I can't stand to see a boy mope like that . . . What do the Sisters say in school?"

"He doesn't pay attention is all they say. You can't get much out of them."

"My middle boy was like that," said John. "Couldn't take an interest. Aaah, I wish I didn't have all that headache on the job. I'd grab Girard by the collar and make him take notice of the world. I wish I could ask him out to Jersey to play in all that space."

"Why not?" I said.

"Why, Virginia, I'm surprised you don't know why not. You know I can't take your children out to meet my children."

I felt a lot of strong arthritis in my ribs.

"My mother's the funny one, Virginia." He felt he had to continue with the subject matter. "I don't know. I guess she likes the idea of bugging Margaret. She says, 'You goin' up, John?' 'Yes, Mother,' I say. 'Behave yourself, John,' she says. 'That husband might come home and hacksaw you into hell. You're a Catholic man, John,' she says. But I figured it out. She likes to know I'm in the building. I swear, Virginia, she wishes me the best of luck."

"I do too, John," I said. We drank a last glass of beer to make sure of a peaceful sleep. "Good night, Virginia," he said, looping his muffler neatly under his chin. "Don't worry. I'll be thinking of what to do about Girard."

I got into the big bed that I share with the girls in the little room. For once I had no trouble falling asleep. I only had to worry about Linda and Barbara and Philip. It was a great relief to me that John had taken over the thinking about Girard.

John was sincere. That's true. He paid a lot of attention to Girard, smoking out all his sneaky sorrows. He registered him into a wild pack of Cub Scouts that went up to the Bronx once a week to let off steam. He gave him a Junior Erector Set. And sometimes when his family wasn't listening he prayed at great length for him.

One Sunday, Sister Veronica said in her sweet voice from another life, "He's not worse. He might even be a little better. How are *you*, Virginia?" putting her hand on mine. Everybody around here acts like they know everything.

"Just fine," I said.

"We ought to start on Philip," John said, "if it's true Girard's improving."

"You should've been a social worker, John."

"A lot of people have noticed that about me," said John.

"Your mother was always acting so crazy about you, how come

she didn't knock herself out a little to see you in college? Like we did for Thomas?"

"Now, Virginia, be fair. She's a poor old woman. My father was a weak earner. She had to have my wages, and I'll tell you, Virginia, I'm not sorry. Look at Thomas. He's still in school. Drop him in this jungle and he'd be devoured. He hasn't had a touch of real life. And here I am with a good chunk of a family, a home of my own, a name in the building trades. One thing I have to tell you, the poor old woman is sorry. I said one day (oh, in passing—years ago) that I might marry you. She stuck a knife in herself. It's a fact. Not more than an eighth of an inch. You never saw such a gory Sunday. One thing—you would have been a better daughter-in-law to her than Margaret."

"Marry me?" I said.

"Well, yes . . . Aaah—I always liked you, then . . . Why do you think I'd sit in the shade of this kitchen every Thursday night? For godsakes, the only warm thing around here is this teacup. Yes sir, I did want to marry you, Virginia."

"No kidding, John? Really?" It was nice to know. Better late than never, to learn you were desired in youth.

I didn't tell John, but the truth is, I would never have married him. Once I met my husband with his winking looks, he was my only interest. Wild as I had been with John and others, I turned all my wildness over to him and then there was no question in my mind.

Still, face facts, if my husband didn't budge on in life, it was my fault. On me, as they say, be it. I greeted the morn with a song. I had a hello for everyone but the landlord. Ask the people on the block, come or go—even the Spanish ones, with their sad dark faces—they have to smile when they see me.

But for his own comfort, he should have done better lifewise and moneywise. I was happy, but I am now in possession of knowledge that this is wrong. Happiness isn't so bad for a woman. She gets fatter, she gets older, she could lie down, nuzzling a regiment of men and little kids, she could just die of the pleasure. But men are different, they have to own money, or they have to be famous, or everybody on the block has to look up to them from the cellar stairs.

A woman counts her children and acts snotty, like she invented life, but men *must* do well in the world. I know that men are not fooled by being happy.

"A funny guy," said John, guessing where my thoughts had gone. "What stopped him up? He was nobody's fool. He had a funny thing about him, Virginia, if you don't mind my saying so. He wasn't much distance up, but he was all set and ready to be looking down on us all."

"He was very smart, John. You don't realize that. His hobby was crossword puzzles, and I said to him real often, as did others around here, that he ought to go out on the '$64 Question.' Why not? But he laughed. You know what he said? He said, 'That proves how dumb you are if you think I'm smart.'"

"A funny guy," said John. "Get it all off your chest," he said. "Talk it out, Virginia; it's the only way to kill the pain."

By and large, I was happy to oblige. Still I could not carry through about certain cruel remarks. It was like trying to move back into the dry mouth of a nightmare to remember that the last day I was happy was the middle of a week in March, when I told my husband I was going to have Linda. Barbara was five months old to the hour. The boys were three and four. I had to tell him. It was the last day with anything happy about it.

Later on he said, "Oh, you make me so sick, you're so goddamn big and fat, you look like a goddamn brownstone, the way you're squared off in front."

"Well, where are you going tonight?" I asked.

"How should I know?" he said. "Your big ass takes up the whole goddamn bed," he said. "There's no room for me." He bought a sleeping bag and slept on the floor.

I couldn't believe it. I would start every morning fresh. I couldn't believe that he would turn against me so, while I was still young and even his friends still liked me.

But he did, he turned absolutely against me and became no friend of mine. "All you ever think about is making babies. This place stinks like the men's room in the BMT. It's a fucking *pissoir.*" He was strong on truth all through the year. "That kid eats more than the five of us put together," he said. "Stop stuffing your face, you fat dumbbell," he said to Philip.

Then he worked on the neighbors. "Get that nosy old bag out of here," he said. "If she comes on once more with 'my son in the building trades' I'll squash her for the cat."

Then he turned on Spielvogel, the checker, his oldest friend, who only visited on holidays and never spoke to me (shy, the way some bachelors are). "That sonofabitch, don't hand me that friendship crap, all he's after is your ass. That's what I need—a little shitmaker of his using up the air in this flat."

And then there was no one else to dispose of. We were left alone fair and square, facing each other.

"Now, Virginia," he said. "I come to the end of my rope. I see a black wall ahead of me. What the hell am I supposed to do? I only got one life. Should I lie down and die? I don't know what to do anymore. I'll give it to you straight, Virginia, if I stick around, you can't help it, you'll hate me . . ."

"I hate you right now," I said. "So do whatever you like."

"This place drives me nuts," he mumbled. "I don't know what to do around here. I want to get you a present. Something."

"I told you, do whatever you like. Buy me a rat trap for rats."

That's when he went down to the House Appliance Store, and he brought back a new broom and a classy dustpan.

"A new broom sweeps clean," he said. "I got to get out of here," he said. "I'm going nuts." Then he began to stuff the duffel bags, and I went to the grocery store but was stopped by Mrs. Raftery, who had to tell me what she considered so beautiful—death—then he kissed and went to join some army somewhere.

I didn't tell John any of this, because I think it makes a woman look too bad to tell on how another man has treated her. He begins to see her through the other man's eyes, a sitting duck, a skinful of flaws. After all, I had come to depend on John. All my husband's friends were strangers now, though I had always said to them, "Feel welcome."

And the family men in the building looked too cunning, as though they had all personally deserted me. If they met me on the stairs, they carried the heaviest groceries up and helped bring Linda's stroller down, but they never asked me a question worth answering at all.

Besides that, Girard and Philip taught the girls the days of the week: Monday, Tuesday, Wednesday, Johnday, Friday. They waited for him once a week, under the hallway lamp, half asleep like bugs in the sun, sitting in their little chairs with their names on in gold, a birth present from my mother-in-law. At fifteen after eight he punctually came, to read a story, pass out some kisses, and tuck them into bed.

But one night, after a long Johnday of them squealing my eardrum split, after a rainy afternoon with brother constantly raising up his hand against brother, with the girls near ready to go to court over the proper ownership of Melinda Lee, the twenty-four-inch walking doll, the doorbell rang three times. Not any of those times did John's face greet me.

I was too ashamed to call down to Mrs. Raftery, and she was too mean to knock on my door and explain.

He didn't come the following Thursday either. Girard said sadly, "He must've run away, John."

I had to give him up after two weeks' absence and no word. I didn't know how to tell the children: something about right and wrong, goodness and meanness, men and women. I had it all at my fingertips, ready to hand over. But I didn't think I ought to take mistakes and truth away from them. Who knows? They might make a truer friend in this world somewhere than I have ever made. So I just put them to bed and sat in the kitchen and cried.

In the middle of my third beer, searching in my mind for the next step, I found the decision to go on *Strike It Rich*. I scrounged some paper and pencil from the toy box and I listed all my troubles, which must be done in order to qualify. The list when complete could have brought tears to the eye of God if He had a minute. At the sight of it my bitterness began to improve. All that is really necessary for survival of the fittest, it seems, is an interest in life, good, bad, or peculiar.

As always happens in these cases where you have begun to help yourself with plans, news comes from an opposite direction. The doorbell rang, two short and two long—meaning John.

My first thought was to wake the children and make them happy. "No! No!" he said. "Please don't put yourself to that trouble. Virginia, I'm dog-tired," he said. "Dog-tired. My job is a damn headache. It's too much. It's all day and it scuttles my mind at night, and in the end who does the credit go to?"

"Virginia," he said, "I don't know if I can come anymore. I've been wanting to tell you. I just don't know. What's it all about? Could you answer me if I asked you? I can't figure this whole thing out at all."

I started the tea steeping because his fingers when I touched them were cold. I didn't speak. I tried looking at it from his man point of view, and I thought he had to take a bus, the tubes, and a subway to see me; and then the subway, the tubes, and a bus to go back home at 1 a.m. It wouldn't be any trouble at all for him to part with us forever. I thought about my life, and I gave strongest consideration to my children. If given the choice, I decided to choose not to live without him.

"What's that?" he asked, pointing out my careful list of troubles. "Writing a letter?"

"Oh no," I said, "it's for *Strike It Rich*. I hope to go on the program."

"Virginia, for goodness' sakes," he said, giving it a glance, "you don't have a ghost. They'd laugh you out of the studio. Those people really suffer."

"Are you sure, John?" I asked.

"No question in my mind at all," said John. "Have you ever seen that program? I mean, in addition to all of this—the little disturbances of man"—he waved a scornful hand at my list—"they *suffer*. They live in the forefront of tornadoes, their lives are washed off by floods—catastrophes of God. Oh, Virginia."

"Are you sure, John?"

"For goodness' sake . . ."

Sadly I put my list away. Still, if things got worse, I could always make use of it.

Once that was settled, I acted on an earlier decision. I pushed his cup of scalding tea aside. I wedged myself onto his lap between his hard belt buckle and the table. I put my arms around his neck and said, "How come you're so cold, John?" He has a kind face and he knew how to look astonished. He said, "Why, Virginia, I'm getting warmer." We laughed.

John became a lover to me that night.

Mrs. Raftery is sometimes silly and sick from her private source of cheap wine. She expects John often. "Honor your mother, what's the matter with you, John?" she complains. "Honor. Honor."

"Virginia dear," she says. "You never would've taken John away to Jersey like Margaret. I wish he'd've married you."

"You didn't like me much in those days."

"That's a lie," she says. I know she's a hypocrite, but no more than the rest of the world.

What is remarkable to me is that it doesn't seem to conscience John as I thought it might. It is still hard to believe that a man who sends out the Ten Commandments every year for a Christmas card can be so easy buttoning and unbuttoning.

Of course we must be very careful not to wake the children or disturb the neighbors, who will enjoy another person's excitement just so far, and then the pleasure enrages them. We must be very careful for ourselves too, for when my husband comes back, realizing the babies are in school and everything easier, he won't forgive me if I've started it all up again—noisy signs of life that are so much trouble to a man.

We haven't seen him in two and a half years. Although people have suggested it, I do not want the police or Intelligence or a private eye or anyone to go after him to bring him back. I know that if he expected to stay away forever he would have written and said so. As it is, I just don't know what evening, any time, he may appear. Sometimes, stumbling over a blockbuster of a dream at midnight, I wake up to vision his soft arrival.

He comes in the door with his old key. He gives me a strict look and says, "Well, you look older, Virginia." "So do you," I say, although he hasn't changed a bit.

He settles in the kitchen because the children are asleep all over the rest of the house. I unknot his tie and offer him a cold sandwich. He raps my backside, paying attention to the bounce. I walk around him as though he were a Maypole, kissing as I go.

"I didn't like the Army much," he says. "Next time I think I might go join the Merchant Marine."

"What Army?" I say.

"It's pretty much the same everywhere," he says.

"I wouldn't be a bit surprised," I say.

"I lost my cuff link, goddamnit," he says, and drops to the floor to look for it. I go down too on my knees, but I know he never had a cuff link in his life. Still I would do a lot for him.

"Got you off your feet that time," he says, laughing. "Oh yes, I did." And before I can even make myself half comfortable on that polka-dotted linoleum, he got onto me right where we were, and the truth is, we were so happy, we forgot the precautions.

Two Short Sad Stories
from a Long and Happy Life

I. THE USED-BOY RAISERS

There were two husbands disappointed by eggs.

I don't like them that way either, I said. Make your own eggs. They sighed in unison. One man was livid; one was pallid.

There isn't a drink around here, is there? asked Livid.

Never find one here, said Pallid. Don't look; driest damn house. Pallid pushed the eggs away, pain and disgust his escutcheon.

Livid said, Now really, isn't there a drink? Beer? he hoped.

Nothing, said Pallid, who'd been through the pantries, closets, and refrigerators looking for a white shirt.

You're damn right, I said. I buttoned the high button of my powder-blue duster. I reached under the kitchen table for a brown paper bag full of an embroidery which asked God to Bless Our Home.

I was completing this motto for the protection of my sons, who were also Livids. It is true that some months earlier, from a far place—the British plains in Africa—he had written hospitably to Pallid: I do think they're fine boys, you understand. I love them too, but Faith is their mother and now Faith is your wife. I'm so much away. If you want to think of them as yours, old man, go ahead.

Why, thank you, Pallid had replied, airmail, overwhelmed.

Then he implored the boys, when not in use, to play in their own room. He made all efforts to be kind.

Now as we talked of time past and upon us, I pierced the ranch house that nestles in the shade of a cloud and a Norway maple, just under the golden script.

Ha-ha, said Livid, dripping coffee on his pajama pants, you'll never guess whom I met up with, Faith.

Who? I asked.

Saw your old boyfriend Clifford at the Green Coq. He looks well. One thing must be said—he addressed Pallid—she takes good care of her men.

True, said Pallid.

How is he? I asked coolly. What's he doing? I haven't seen him in two years.

Oh, you'll never guess. He's marrying. A darling girl. She was with him. Little tootsies, little round bottom, little tummy—she must be twenty-two, but she looks seventeen. One long yellow braid down her back. A darling girl. Stubby nose, fat little underlip. Her eyes put on in pencil. Shoulders down like a dancer . . . slender neck. Oh, darling, darling.

You certainly observed her, said Pallid.

I have a functioning retina, said Livid. Then he went on. Better watch out, Faith. You'd be surprised, the dear little chicks are hatching out all over the place. All the sunny schoolgirls rolling their big black eyes. I hope you're really settled this time. To me, whatever is under the dam is in another county; however, in my life you remain an important person historically, he said. And that's why I feel justified in warning you. I must warn you. Watch out, sweetheart! he said, leaning forward to whisper harshly and give me a terrible bellyache.

What's all this about? asked Pallid innocently. In the first place, she's settled . . . and then she's still an attractive woman. Look at her.

Oh yes, said Livid, looking. An attractive woman. Magnificent, sometimes.

We were silent for several seconds in honor of that generous remark.

Then Livid said, Yes, magnificent, but I just wanted to warn you, Faith.

He pushed his eggs aside finally and remembered Clifford. A mystery wrapped in an enigma . . . I wonder why he wants to marry.

I don't know, it just ties a man down, I said.

And yet, said Pallid seriously, what would I be without marriage? In luminous recollection—a gay dog, he replied.

At this moment, the boys entered: Richard the horse thief and Tonto the crack shot.

Daddy! they shouted. They touched Livid, tickled him, unbuttoned his pajama top, whistled at several gray hairs coloring his chest. They tweaked his ear and rubbed his beard the wrong way.

Well, well, he cautioned. How are you boys, have you been well? You look fine. Sturdy. How are your grades? he inquired. He dreamed that they were just up from Eton for the holidays.

I don't go to school, said Tonto. I go to the park.

I'd like to hear the child read, said Livid.

Me. I can read, Daddy, said Richard. I have a book with a hundred pages.

Well, well, said Livid. Get it.

I kindled a fresh pot of coffee. I scrubbed cups and harassed Pallid into opening a sticky jar of damson-plum jam. Very shortly, what could be read had been, and Livid, knotting the tie strings of his pants vigorously, approached me at the stove. Faith, he admonished, that boy can't read a tinker's damn. Seven years old.

Eight years old, I said.

Yes, said Pallid, who had just remembered the soap cabinet and was rummaging in it for a pint. If they were my sons in actuality as they are in everyday life, I would send them to one of the good parochial schools in the neighborhood where reading is taught. Reading. St. Bartholomew's, St. Bernard's, St. Joseph's.

Livid became deep purple and gasped. Over my dead body. *Merde*, he said in deference to the children. I've said, yes, you may think of the boys as your own, but if I ever hear they've come within an inch of that church, I'll run you through, you bastard. I was fourteen years old when in my own good sense I walked out of that grotto of deception, head up. You sonofabitch, I don't give a damn how *au courant* it is these days, how gracious to be seen under a dome on Sunday . . . Shit! Hypocrisy. Corruption. Cave dwellers. Idiots. Morons.

Recalling childhood and home, poor Livid writhed in his seat. Pallid listened, head to one side, his brows gathering the onsets of grief.

You know, he said slowly, we iconoclasts . . . we freethinkers . . . we latter-day Masons . . . we idealists . . . we dreamers . . . we are never far from our nervous old mother, the Church. She is never far from us.

Wherever we are, we can hear, no matter how faint, her hourly bells, tolling the countryside, reverberating in the cities, bringing to our civilized minds the passionate deed of Mary. Every hour on the hour we are startled with remembrance of what was done for us. FOR US.

Livid muttered in great pain. Those bastards, oh oh oh, those contemptible, goddamnable bastards. Do we have to do the nineteenth century all over again? All right, he bellowed, facing us all, I'm ready. That Newman! He turned to me for approval.

You know, I said, this subject has never especially interested me. It's your little dish of lava.

Pallid spoke softly, staring past the arched purple windows of his soul. I myself, although I lost God a long time ago, have never lost faith.

What the hell are you talking about, you moron? roared Livid.

I have never lost my love for the wisdom of the Church of the World. When I go to sleep at night, I inadvertently pray. I also do so when I rise. It is not to God, it is to that unifying memory out of childhood. The first words I ever wrote were: What are the sacraments? Faith, can you ever forget your old grandfather intoning Kaddish? It will sound in your ears forever.

Are you kidding? I was furious to be drawn into their conflict. Kaddish? What do I know about Kaddish. Who's dead? You know my opinions perfectly well. I believe in the Diaspora, not only as a fact but a tenet. I'm against Israel on technical grounds. I'm very disappointed that they decided to become a nation in my lifetime. I believe in the Diaspora. After all, they *are* the chosen people. Don't laugh. They really are. But once they're huddled in one little corner of a desert, they're like anyone else: Frenchies, Italians, temporal nationalities. Jews have one hope only—to remain a remnant in the basement of world affairs—no, I mean something else—a splinter in the toe of civilizations, a victim to aggravate the conscience.

Livid and Pallid were astonished at my outburst, since I rarely express my opinion on any serious matter but only live out my destiny, which is to be, until my expiration date, laughingly the servant of man.

I continued. I hear they don't even look like Jews anymore. A bunch of dirt farmers with no time to read.

They're your own people, Pallid accused, dilating in the nostril, clenching his jaw. And they're under the severest attack. This is not the time to revile them.

I had resumed my embroidery. I sighed. My needle was now deep in the clouds, which were pearl gray and late afternoon. I am only trying to say that they aren't meant for geographies but for history. They are not supposed to take up space but to continue in time.

They looked at me with such grief that I decided to consider all sides of the matter. I said, Christ probably had all that trouble—

now that you mention it—because he knew he was going to gain the whole world but he forgot Jerusalem.

When you married us, said Pallid, and accused me, didn't you forget Jerusalem?

I never forget a thing, I said. Anyway, guess what. I just read somewhere that England is bankrupt. The country is wadded with installment paper.

Livid's hand trembled as he offered Pallid a light. Nonsense, he said. That's not true. Nonsense. The great British Island is the tight little fist of the punching arm of the Commonwealth.

What's true is true, I said, smiling.

Well, I said, since no one stirred, do you think you'll ever get to work today? Either of you?

Oh my dear, I haven't even seen you and the boys in over a year. It's quite pleasant and cozy here this morning, said Livid.

Yes, isn't it? said Pallid, the surprised host. Besides, it's Saturday.

How do you find the boys? I asked Livid, the progenitor.

American, American, rowdy, uncontrolled. But you look well, Faith. Plumper, but womanly and well.

Very well, said Pallid, pleased.

But the boys, Faith. Shouldn't they be started on something? Just lining up little plastic cowboys. It's silly, really.

They're so young, apologized Pallid, the used-boy raiser.

You'd both better go to work, I suggested, knotting the pearl-gray late-afternoon thread. Please put the dishes in the sink first. Please, I'm sorry about the eggs.

Livid yawned, stretched, peeked at the clock, sighed. Saturday or no, alas, my time is not my own. I've got an appointment downtown in about forty-five minutes, he said.

I do too, said Pallid. I'll join you on the subway.

I'm taking a cab, said Livid.

I'll split it with you, said Pallid.

They left for the bathroom, where they shared things nicely—shaving equipment, washstand, shower, and so forth.

I made the beds and put the aluminum cot away. Livid would find a hotel room by nightfall. I did the dishes and organized the greedy day: dinosaurs in the morning, park in the afternoon, peanut butter in between, and at the end of it all, to reward us for a week of beans endured, a noble rib roast with little onions, dumplings, and pink applesauce.

Faith, I'm going now, Livid called from the hall. I put my shopping list aside and went to collect the boys, who were wandering among the rooms looking for Robin Hood. Go say goodbye to your father, I whispered.

Which one? they asked.

The real father, I said. Richard ran to Livid. They shook hands manfully. Pallid embraced Tonto and was kissed eleven times for his affection.

Goodbye now, Faith, said Livid. Call me if you want anything at all. Anything at all, my dear. Warmly with sweet propriety he kissed my cheek. Ascendant, Pallid kissed me with considerable business behind the ear.

Goodbye, I said to them.

I must admit that they were at last clean and neat, rather attractive, shiny men in their thirties, with the grand affairs of the day ahead of them. Dark night, the search for pleasure and oblivion were well ahead. Goodbye, I said, have a nice day. Goodbye, they said once more, and set off in pride on paths which are not my concern.

2. A SUBJECT OF CHILDHOOD

At home one Saturday and every Saturday, Richard drew eight-by-eleven portraits of stick men waving their arms. Tonto held a plastic horse in his hand and named it Tonto because its eyes were painted blue as his had been. I revised the hem of last year's dress in order to be up to the minute, chic, and *au courant* in the midst of spring. Strangers would murmur, "Look at her, isn't she wonderful? Who's her couturier?"

Clifford scrubbed under the shower, singing a Russian folk song. He rose in a treble of cold water to high C, followed by the scourging of the flesh. At last after four hots and three colds, he was strong and happy and he entered the living room, a steaming emanation. His face was round and rosy. He was noticeably hairless on the head. What prevented rain and shower water from running foolishly down his face? Heavy dark down-sloping brows. Beneath these his eyes were round and dark, amazed. This Clifford, my close friend, was guileless. He would not hurt a fly and he was a vegetarian.

As always, he was glad to see us. He had wrapped a large sun-bathing towel around his damp body. "Behold the man!" he shouted, and let the towel fall. He stood for a moment, gleaming and pleasant. Richard and Tonto glanced at him. "Cover yourself for godsakes, Clifford," I said.

"Take it easy, Faith," he called to the ear of reason, "the world is changing." Actually propriety did not embarrass him. It did not serve him. He peeked from behind the rubber plant where his pants, under and over, were heaped. When he reappeared, snapped and buttoned, he said, "Wake up, wake up. What's everyone slouching around for?" He poked Richard in the tummy. "A little muscle tone there, boy. Wake up."

Richard said, "I want to draw, Clifford."

"You can draw any time. I'm not always here. Draw tomorrow, Rich. Come on—fight me, boy. Fight. Come on . . . let's go, get me. You better get started, Richy, 'cause I'm gonna really punch you one. Here I come, ready or not!"

"Here *I* come," said Tonto, dropping his horse, and he whacked Clifford hard across the kidneys.

"Who did that?" asked Clifford. "What boy did that?"

"Me, me," said Tonto, jumping up and down. "Did I hurt you bad?"

"Killed me, yes sir, yes you did, and now I'm going to get *you*." He whirled. "I'm going to tickle you, that's what." He raised Tonto high above his head, a disposable item, then pitched him into the air-foam belly of the couch.

Richard tiptoed with the teddy bear to a gentle rise, the sofa cushion, from which he crowned Clifford three times.

"Oh, I'm getting killed," cried Clifford. "They're all after me. They're very rough." Richard kicked him in the shin. "That's it," said Clifford. "Get it out! Get it all out! Boys! Out! Out!"

Tonto spit right into his eye. He wiped his cheek. He feinted and dodged the teddy bear that was coming down again on his bowed head. Tonto leaped onto his back and got hold of his ears. "Ouch," said Clifford.

Richard found a tube of rubber cement in the bookcase and squirted it at Clifford's hairy chest.

"I'm wild," said Richard. "I am, I'm wild."

"So am I," said Tonto. "I'm the wildest boy in the whole park." He tugged at Clifford's ears. "I'll ride you away. I'm an elephant boy."

"He's a lazy camel," screamed Richard. "Bubbles, I want you to work."

"Pretend I'm the djinn," said Tonto in a high wail. "Giddap, Clifford."

"Me, me, me," said Richard, sinking to the floor. "It's me. I'm a poison snake," he said, slithering to Clifford's foot. "I'm a poison snake," he said, resting his chin on Clifford's instep. "I'm a terrible poison snake," he swore. Then he raised his head like the adder he is, and after a prolonged hiss, with all his new front teeth, he bit poor

Clifford above the bone, in his Achilles' heel, which is his weak left ankle.

"Oh no, oh no . . ." Clifford moaned, then folded neatly at all joints.

"Mommy, Mommy, Mommy," cried Richard, for Clifford fell, twelve stone, on him.

"Oh, it's me," screamed Tonto, an elephant boy thrown by his horse, headlong into a trap of table legs.

And he was the one I reached first. I hugged him to my lap. "Mommy," he sobbed, "my head hurts me. I wish I could get inside you." Richard lay, a crushed snake in the middle of the floor, without breath, without tears, angry.

Well, what of Clifford? He had hoisted his sorrowful self into an armchair and lay there lisping on a bloody tongue which he himself had bitten, "Faith, Faith, the accumulator, the accumulator!"

Bruised and tear-stricken, the children agreed to go to bed. They forgot to say it was too early to nap. They forget to ask for their bears. They lay side by side and clutched each other's thumb. Here was the love that myth or legend has imposed on brothers.

I re-entered the living room, where Clifford sat, a cone like an astrologer's hat on his skin-punctured place. Just exactly there, universal energies converged. The stationary sun, the breathless air in which the planets swing were empowered now to make him well, to act, in their remarkable art, like aspirin.

"We've got to have a serious talk," he said. "I really can't take those kids. I mean, Faith, you know yourself I've tried and tried. But you've done something to them, corrupted their instincts in some way or other. Here we were, having an absolutely marvelous time, rolling around making all kinds of free noise, and look what happened—like every other time, someone got hurt. I mean I'm really hurt. We should have all been relaxed. Easy. It should have been all easy. Our bodies should have been so easy. No one should've been hurt, Faith."

"Do you mean it's my fault, you all got hurt?"

"No doubt about it, Faith, you've done a rotten job."

"Rotten job?" I said.

"Lousy," he said.

I gave him one more chance. "Lousy?" I asked.

"Oh my God! Stinking!" he said.

Therefore, the following—a compendium of motivations and griefs, life to date:

Truthfully, Mondays through Fridays—because of success at work—my ego is hot; I am a star; whoever can be warmed by me, I may oblige. The flat scale stones of abuse that fly into that speedy atmosphere are utterly consumed. Untouched, I glow my little thermodynamic way.

On Saturday mornings in my own home, however, I face the sociological law called the Obtrusion of Incontrovertibles. For I have raised these kids, with one hand typing behind my back to earn a living. I have raised them all alone without a father to identify themselves with in the bathroom like all the other little boys in the playground. Laugh. I was forced by inclement management into a yellow-dog contract with Bohemia, such as it survives. I have stuck by it despite the encroachments of kind relatives who offer ski pants, piano lessons, tickets to the rodeo. Meanwhile I have serviced Richard and Tonto, taught them to keep clean and hold an open heart on the subjects of childhood. We have in fact risen mightily from toilets in the hall and scavenging in great cardboard boxes at the Salvation Army for underwear and socks. It has been my perversity to do this alone, except for one year their father was living in Chicago with Claudia Lowenstill and she was horrified that he only sent bicycles on the fifth birthday. A whole year of gas and electricity, rent and phone payments followed. One day she caught him in the swiveling light of truth, a grand figure who took a strong stand on a barrel of soapsuds and went down clean. He is now on the gold coast of another continent, enchanted by the survival of clandestine civilizations. Courts of kitchen drama cannot touch him.

All the same, I gave Clifford one more opportunity to renege and be my friend. I said, "Stinking? I raised them lousy?"

This time he didn't bother to answer because he had become busy gathering his clothes from different parts of the room.

Air was filtering out of my two collapsing lungs. Water rose, bubbling to enter, and I would have died of instantaneous pneumonia—something I never have heard of—if my hand had not got hold of a glass ashtray and, entirely apart from my personal decision, flung it.

Clifford was on his hands and knees looking for the socks he'd left under the armchair on Friday. His back was to me; his head convenient to the trajectory. And he would have passed away a blithering idiot had I not been blind with tears and only torn off what is anyways a vestigial earlobe.

Still, Clifford is a gentle person, a consortment of sweet dispositions. The sight of all the blood paralyzed him. He hulked, shuddering; he waited on his knees to be signaled once more by Death, the Sheriff from the Styx.

"You don't say things like that to a woman," I whispered. "You damn stupid jackass. You just don't say anything like that to a woman. Wash yourself, moron, you're bleeding to death."

I left him alone to tie a tourniquet around his windpipe or doctor himself according to present-day plans for administering first aid in the Great Globular and Coming War.

I tiptoed into the bedroom to look at the children. They were asleep. I covered them and kissed Tonto, my baby, and "Richard, what a big boy you are," I said. I kissed him too. I sat on the floor, rubbing my cheek on Richard's rubbly fleece blanket until their sweet breathing in deep sleep quieted me.

A couple of hours later Richard and Tonto woke up picking their noses, sneezing, grumpy, then glad. They admired the ticktacktoes of Band-Aid I had created to honor their wounds. Richard ate soup and Tonto ate ham. They didn't inquire about Clifford, since he had a key which had always opened the door in or out.

That key lay at rest in the earth of my rubber plant. I felt discontinued. There was no one I wanted to offer it to.

"Still hungry, boys?" I asked. "No, sir," said Tonto. "I'm full up to here," leveling at the eyes.

"I'll tell you what." I came through with a stunning notion. "Go on down and play."

"Don't shove, miss," said Richard.

I looked out the front window. Four flights below, armed to the teeth, Lester Stukopf waited for the enemy. Carelessly I gave Richard this classified information. "Is he all alone?" asked Richard.

"He is," I said.

"O.K., O.K." Richard gazed sadly at me. "Only, Faith, remember, I'm going down because I feel like it. Not because you told me."

"Well, naturally," I said.

"Not me," said Tonto.

"Oh, don't be silly, you go too, Tonto. It's so nice and sunny. Take your new guns that Daddy sent you. Go on, Tonto."

"No, sir, I hate Richard and I hate Lester. I hate those guns. They're baby guns. He thinks I'm a baby. You better send him a picture."

"Oh, Tonto—"

"He thinks I suck my thumb. He thinks I wet my bed. That's why he sends me baby guns."

"No, no, honey. You're no baby. Everybody knows you're a big boy."

"He is not," said Richard. "And he does suck his thumb and he does so wet his bed."

"Richard," I said, "Richard, if you don't have anything good to say, shut your rotten mouth. That doesn't help Tonto, to keep reminding him."

"Goodbye," said Richard, refusing to discuss, but very high and first-born. Sometimes he is nasty, but he is never lazy. He returned in forty-five seconds from the first floor to shout, "As long as he doesn't wet my bed, what do I care?"

Tonto did not hear him. He was brushing his teeth, which he sometimes does vigorously seven times a day, hoping they will loosen. I think they are loosening.

I served myself hot coffee in the living room. I organized comfort in the armchair, poured the coffee black into a white mug that said MAMA, tapped cigarette ash into a ceramic hand-hollowed by Richard. I looked into the square bright window of daylight to ask myself the sapping question: What is man that woman lies down to adore him?

At the very question mark Tonto came softly, sneaky in socks, to say, "I have to holler something to Richard, Mother."

"Don't lean out that window, Tonto. Please, it makes me nervous."

"I have to tell him something."

"No."

"Oh yes," he said. "It's awful important, Faith. I really *have* to."

How could I permit it? If he should fall, everyone would think I had neglected them, drinking beer in the kitchen or putting eye cream on at the vanity table behind closed doors. Besides, I would be bereaved forever. My grandmother mourned all her days for some kid who'd died of earache at the age of five. All the other children, in their own municipal-pension and federal-welfare years, gathered to complain at her deathside when she was ninety-one and heard her murmur, "Oh, oh, Anita, breathe a little, try to breathe, my little baby."

With tears in my eyes I said, "O.K., Tonto. I'll hold on to you. You can tell Richard anything you have to."

He leaned out onto the air. I held fast to one thick little knee. "Richie," he howled. "Richie, hey, Richie!" Richard looked up, probably shielding his eyes, searching for the voice. "Richie, hey, listen, I'm playing with your new birthday-present Army fort and all them men."

Then he banged the window shut as though he knew nothing about the nature of glass and tore into the bathroom to brush his teeth once more in triumphant ritual. Singing through toothpaste and gargle, "I bet he's mad," and in lower key, "He deserves it, he stinks."

"So do you," I shouted furiously. While I sighed for my grandmother's loss, he had raised up his big mouth against his brother. "You really stink!"

"Now listen to me. I want you to get out of here. Go on down and play. I need ten minutes all alone. Anthony, I might kill you if you stay up here."

He reappeared, smelling like peppermint sticks at Christmas. He stood on one foot, looked up into my high eyes, and said, "O.K., Faith. Kill me."

I had to sit immediately then, so he could believe I was his size and stop picking on me.

"Please," I said gently, "go out with your bother. I have to think, Tonto."

"I don't wanna. I don't have to go anyplace I don't wanna," he said. "I want to stay right here with you."

"Oh, please, Tonto, I have to clean the house. You won't be able to do a thing or start a good game or anything."

"I don't care," he said. "I want to stay here with you. I want to stay right next to you."

"O.K., Tonto. O.K. I'll tell you what, go to your room for a couple of minutes, honey, go ahead."

"No," he said, climbing onto my lap. "I want to be a baby and stay right next to you every minute."

"Oh, Tonto," I said, "please, Tonto." I tried to pry him loose, but he put his arm around my neck and curled up right there in my lap, thumb in mouth, to be my baby.

"Oh, Tonto," I said, despairing of one solitary minute. "Why can't you go play with Richard? You'll have fun."

"No," he said, "I don't care if Richard goes away, or Clifford.

They can go do whatever they wanna do. I don't even care. I'm never gonna go away. I'm gonna stay right next to you forever, Faith."

"Oh, Tonto," I said. He took his thumb out of his mouth and placed his open hand, its fingers stretching wide, across my breast. "I love you, Mama," he said.

"Love," I said. "Oh love, Anthony, I know."

I held him so and rocked him. I cradled him. I closed my eyes and leaned on his dark head. But the sun in its course emerged from among the water towers of the downtown office buildings and suddenly shone white and bright on me. Then through the short fat fingers of my son, interred forever, like a black-and-white-barred king in Alcatraz, my heart lit up in stripes.

FROM *Enormous Changes at
the Last Minute*

Living

Two weeks before Christmas, Ellen called me and said, "Faith, I'm dying." That week I was dying too.

After we talked, I felt worse. I left the kids alone and ran down to the corner for a quick sip among living creatures. But Julie's and all the other bars were full of men and women gulping a hot whiskey before hustling off to make love.

People require strengthening before the acts of life.

I drank a little California Mountain Red at home and thought— why not—wherever you turn someone is shouting give me liberty or I give you death. Perfectly sensible, thing-owning, Church-fearing neighbors flop their hands over their ears at the sound of a siren to keep fallout from taking hold of their internal organs. You have to be cockeyed to love, and blind in order to look out the window at your own ice-cold street.

I really was dying. I was bleeding. The doctor said, "You can't bleed forever. Either you run out of blood or you stop. No one bleeds forever."

It seemed *I* was going to bleed forever. When Ellen called to say she was dying, I said this clear sentence: "Please! I'm dying too, Ellen."

Then she said, "Oh, oh, Faithy. I didn't know." She said, "Faith, what'll we do? About the kids. Who'll take care of them? I'm too scared to think."

I was frightened too, but I only wanted the kids to stay out of the bathroom. I didn't worry about them. I worried about me. They were noisy. They came home from school too early. They made a racket.

"I may have another couple of months," Ellen said. "The doctor said he never saw anyone with so little will to live. I don't want to live, he thinks. But Faithy, I do, I do. It's just I'm scared."

I could hardly take my mind off this blood. Its hurry to leave me was draining the red out from under my eyelids and the sunburn off my cheeks. It was all rising from my cold toes to find the quickest way out.

"Life isn't that great Ellen," I said. "We've had nothing but crummy days and crummy guys and no money and broke all the time and cockroaches and nothing to do on Sunday but take the kids to Central Park and row on that lousy lake. What's so great, Ellen? What's the big loss? Live a couple more years. See the kids and the whole cruddy thing, every cheese hole in the world go up in heat blast firewaves . . ."

"I want to see it all," Ellen said.

I felt a great gob making its dizzy exit.

"Can't talk," I said. "I think I'm fainting."

Around the holly season, I began to dry up. My sister took the kids for a while so I could stay home quietly making hemoglobin, red corpuscles, etc., with no interruption. I was in such first-class shape by New Year's, I nearly got knocked up again. My little boys came home. They were tall and handsome.

Three weeks after Christmas, Ellen died. At her funeral at that very neat church on the Bowery, her son took a minute out of crying to tell me, "Don't worry Faith, my mother made sure of everything. She took care of me from her job. That man came and said so."

"Oh. Shall I adopt you anyway?" I asked, wondering, if he said yes, where the money, the room, another ten minutes of good nights, where they would all come from. He was a little older than my kids. He would soon need a good encyclopedia, a chemistry set. "Listen Billy, tell me the truth. Shall I adopt you?"

He stopped all his tears. "Why thanks. Oh no. I have an uncle in Springfield. I'm going to him. I'll have it O.K. It's in the country. I have cousins there."

"Well," I said, relieved. "I just love you Billy. You're the most wonderful boy. Ellen must be so proud of you."

He stepped away and said, "She's not anything of anything, Faith." Then he went to Springfield. I don't think I'll see him again.

But I often long to talk to Ellen, with whom, after all, I have done a million things in these scary, private years. We drove the kids up every damn rock in Central Park. On Easter Sunday, we pasted white doves on blue posters and prayed on Eighth Street for peace. Then we were tired and screamed at the kids. The boys were babies. For a joke we stapled their snowsuits to our skirts and in a rage of slavery every Saturday for weeks we marched across the bridges that connect Manhattan to the world. We shared apartments, jobs, and stuck-up studs. And then, two weeks before last Christmas, we were dying.

Come On, Ye Sons of Art

The way Zandakis comes on smiling! says Jerry Cook, biggest archbishopric in New Jersey in the palm of his hand; shy saints, relics all kinds; painted monks blessed by the dumbest ladies, bawling madonnas.

Everywhere in America, he says, giving Kitty a morning hour, New Jersey and Long Island man is looking at God and about Him, says Jerry Cook, I dream.

Oh, he says further, turning over to stare, as far as money is concerned, I love the masters. Baby, admit it, the masters are scientists. They add and they multiply. After that they water and they weigh. They're artists. They lay low. They are smiling in a hot bath and the whole damn East Coast leather-goods industry grows up out of the crap in their teeth. They are bulldozers. Two Jew experts in any regular recession can mash twenty-five miserable Syrians. One old Greek, he's half asleep, he puts his marble shoulder on fifty Jews. Right away a hundred thousand plastic briefcases get dumped into bargain bins of Woolworth, New York. Don't mention the Japanese.

Why not? asked Kitty.

Never, said Jerry Cook, no matter to whom, I never mention the Japanese.

Who Cook worked for was Gladstein. There were billings up and down 46, 1, 22 for maybe 285,000 all in secular goods. If you see a cheap wallet in Orange County, Jerry Cook put it there.

But what is Gladstein compared to Zandakis? Zandakis, so help me, he is touched by the pinky of the Holy Spirit and the palm of Eastern Orthodox. You can see Gladstein from here, put-putting behind that greasy genius, giving out 20-by-60 Flushing building lots at swamp-bottom prices to his wife's nephews. Dumbhead Gladstein is not even afraid of Taiwan. He is on the high seas, but he thinks it's Central Park Lake. He holds a dance for the showoff of it all once a month out on deck, which is a twentieth-floor penthouse over Broadway and Seventh Avenue, the black tidewaters. In the war he turned old maid's sweater buttons into golden captain's buttons and internal security exploded in him—to his fingertips—like a dumdum, and now he includes the switchboard girls in his party, the key-punch girls, the Dictaphone girls, the groovy bookkeepers, he even includes Jerry Cook, very democratic.

Only Karl Marx, the fly in the ointment, knows how come Zandakis turned on Gladstein just when his in-laws loved him the most and ground him into drygoods. In a minute 325,000 little zippered real-leather ladies' change purses were rammed into the digestion of starving Mrs. Lonesome, the Jersey Consumer.

Envy of Zandakis and pain about Gladstein made Jerry Cook bitter.

Business! he said. You think I'm in business. You think Gladstein is business—with his Fulton Street molds and his Florentine bookmarks. You think tobacco pouches is business! He bit his nails.

No! But diamonds! Kitty, say it to me, say diamonds, he said.

O.K. Diamonds, she said.

Well, that's better. That's business. I call that business. I should go right to diamonds. Kitty, it's a fact, old bags, you slip them the salami nice, they buy anything. That's what I hear everywhere.

Don't go into diamonds, said Kitty.

Oh yes, he said, giving the pillow a rabbit punch. I know you Kitty. You're one of that crowd. You're the kind thinks the world is round. Not like my sister, he said. Not Anna Marie. She knows the real shape. She lived, Anna Marie. What did she have, when she was a kid, what'd my father give her, a little factory to begin with, embroidery, junk, but she's shrewd and crooked and she understands. My two brothers are crooked. Crooked, crooked. They have crooked wives. The only one is not crooked, the one who is straight and dumb like you Kitty—Kitty, Kitty—he said, dragging her to him for a minute's kiss—is her husband, Anna Marie's. He was always dumb and straight, but they have got him now, all knotted up, you wouldn't unravel him if you started in August.

Kitty, with your personality, you should be in some business. Only for a year, to buy and sell, it's a gimmick.

But they are thieves. Baby. My brothers. Oh listen they worked for famous builders one time. They're known. Planit Brothers. Millions of dollars. You don't know reality. Kitty, you're not in contact, if you don't realize what a million dollars is. (It is one and six zeroes running after.) That was the Planit Corner Cottages, Every Cottage a Corner Plot. How they did it was short blocks. Every penny they stole from the government. So? What's the government for? The people? Kitty, you're right. And Planit Brothers is people, a very large family.

Four brothers and three sisters, they wouldn't touch birth control with a basement beam. Orthodox. Constructive fucking. Builders, baby.

Meanwhile my brother Skippy mentions $40,000. Come on! What is $40,000. Ask the bank. Go to the bank. They tear up $40,000. They jump up and down on it. They spit on it. They laugh. You want to sink in one stick of a foundation, the cost is maybe $12,000. It disappears into the ground. Into the ground and farewell.

But listen Kitty. Anna Marie is shrewd. She has a head, hollered Jerry Cook, leaping out of bed and rapping his own with his pointing forefinger. Anna Marie, she tells my brothers, while you're working for Planit, take something, for godsakes. Take a little at a time. Don't be greedy. Don't be dumb. The world is an egg, jackasses, suck it. It's pure protein, you won't get fat on your heart. You might get psychosomatic, but you won't get fat.

Jerry Cook sighed. He fell back into bed, exhausted, and talked softly against Kitty's soft breast. Take something, Anna Marie said, sinks, boilers, stoves, washing machines, lay it up, lay it up. Slowly. Where, my brothers ask, should we lay up? Where? they asked. It was my brothers. I wasn't there. I'm not in on it. Kitty, I don't know why, he said sadly. I'm crooked too.

Sure you are, said Kitty.

You guys make me puke, said Anna Marie. I took care of all that already. She had really done that. Taken care of where to stack it away. She had gone and bought a warehouse. In an auction. Where else do you get one?

Tie! Tie bid! the auctioneer hollers. A quarter of a million, screams one sharpie. At the same simultaneous minute, a quarter of a million, screams the other sharpie. Ha! The auctioneer bangs the gavel. Bang! Tie bid!

I never heard of that, said Kitty.

You sheltered yourself, said Jerry Cook. My sister says to him, Marv. You look like a pig half the time. You look like a punk, you don't look like an auctioneer. What do you look like? Name it. Schlep, he says. Laughs. Right-o. Schlep. Listen, Marv, give me this warehouse for 70,000. I'll slip you back 7 and an Olds. Beautiful car, like a horse, she says. I know your wife's a creep, she don't put out. I'll fix you up nice. You don't deserve to look such a bum. Right away he's grateful. Hahahah, breathes hard. He thinks he's getting laid. What? My sister? Anna Marie. Not her. No. She wouldn't do that. Never. Still, that's what he thinks.

My brothers say, Sure, introduce him. A nice brunette, a blonde, redhead, something from Brooklyn. You know? Not Anna Marie. Too smart. I ain't in the roast-beef business, Skippy, she says to my brother Skippy . . .

Because she's not! Anna Marie could be in any business she chose. She learned from my mother and father. They knew. But what did she do when her time came to do? She looked up at the sky. It was empty. Where else could she put her name and fame? Oh Anna Marie. High-risers! she said. Oh, she could choose to be in anything. She could sell tushies in Paris. She could move blondes in Sweden. Crooked, he said, his heart jumping like a fool in his throat. He sat up straight. High-risers!

On the East Side, on the North Side. Democratic. She put one up in Harlem. She named it. She digs spades. Not what you think, Kitty. Digs them. She sees it coming, Anna Marie. She sees who she's dealing with in ten years, twenty years. Life is before her. You have to watch *The New York Times*. The editorial section, who they're for. *Then* do business.

Harriet Tubman Towers, that's what I name you, twenty-seven stories. Looks out over Central Park, Madison Avenue, the Guggenheim Museum. If you happen to live in the back, the Harlem River, bridges, the South Bronx, and a million slaves.

A colonial power I planted here, she says. She missed the boat though, naming it that way. She's putting up another one more west, she already got the name for it, black, like onyx halls, a sphinx fountain, a small Cleopatra's needle in the playground, you know, for the kids to climb on. *Egypt*, she calls it. They like that. She doesn't build, Anna Marie, till she got the name. In the Village, what do you see, for instance: Cézanne, Van Gogh, St. Germain . . . Jerks, transient tenancy, concessions, vacancies in the second year . . . She reads the papers there, *The Villager*, the *Voice*. She sniffs. Anna Marie is shrewd. Quiet, she looks the contractor in the face. *Franz Kline*. And she is oversubscribed the day after they paste the plans up.

You ought to go into business, Kitty. You're not shrewd. But you're loving and you got tolerance. There's a place for that. You wouldn't be a millionaire, but you'd get out of this neighborhood. What have your kids got here, everywhere they go, shvartzes, spics, and spades. Not that I got a thing against them, but who needs the advance guard.

Kitty put her finger over his lips. Ssh, she said. I am tolerant and loving.

Come on, Kitty. Did you like the mockies right out of steerage? They stunk. Those Yids, you could smell them a precinct away. Beards like a garlic farm. What can you do . . . Europe in those days . . . Europe was backwards. Today you could go into a gym with the very same people. People forget today about the backwardness of Europe.

But listen, Kitty, once my sister decided about high-risers . . .

Who? said Kitty. Decided what?

My sister decided. High-risers. That's where her future was. Way up. She called up Skippy. She called up the bank. They each of them got into their own car and they head for the warehouse. Collateral for a life of investments. The warehouse is laying out there in Jersey, in the sun, beautiful, grass all around, a swamp in the back, barbed wire, electrified in case of trouble, a watchman, the windows clean. The bank takes one look, the warehouse is so stuffed, stovepipes are sticking out the window, cable is rolling off the gutters, the bank doesn't have to look twice. It signs right away on the dotted line.

Oh Anna Marie! Out of her head all that came. Jerry, she asks me, what do you use your head for, headaches? Headaches. How come I'm not one of them, Kitty? I asked Skippy for a house once. He said, Sure, I'll five a $35,000 house for maybe 22. Is that good, Kitty? Should he have given it to me straight, Kitty? Oh, if I could lay my hand on some of that jack, if you figure me out a way.

I wish I could help you be more crooked, said Kitty.

He put his hand on Kitty's high belly. Kitty, I would personally put that kid in Harvard if I could figure the right angle.

Well, what happened to Zandakis?

What'd you bring him up for? He's no businessman, he's a murderer and a creep.

Where's Gladstein?

Him too? He doesn't exist. They hung him up by his thumbs in his five-and-ten on 125th Street with mercerized cotton no. 9.

God?

Kitty, you're laughing at me. Don't laugh.

O.K., said Kitty and leaned back into the deep pillows. She thought life on Sunday was worth two weeks of waiting.

Now me, said Jerry. What I am really: I am the Sunday-breakfast chef. I will make thirty pancakes, six per person, eggs, bacon, fresh ham, and a gallon of juice. I will wake up those lazy kids of yours, and I will feed them and feed them until I see some brains wiggling in their dumb heads. I hate a dumb kid. I always think it's me.

Oh, Jerry, said Kitty, what would I do without you?

Well, you wouldn't be knocked up is one thing, he said.

Is that so? said Kitty.

It wasn't cold, but she snuggled down deep under the blanket. It was her friend Faith's grandmother's patchwork quilt that kept her so warm in the warm room. The old windowshades made the morning dusk. She listened to the song of Jerry's brother Skippy's orange radio which was:

"Come, come, ye sons of art . . ."

The bacon curled fearfully on the hot griddle, the waffles popped out of the toaster, and a countertenor called:

> Strike the viol
> Touch
>   oh touch the lute . . .

Well, it was on account of the queen's birthday, the radio commentator said, that such a lot of joy had been transacted in England the busy country, one day when Purcell lived.

Faith in a Tree

Just when I most needed important conversation, a sniff of the man-wide world, that is, at least one brainy companion who could translate my friendly language into his tongue of undying carnal love, I was forced to lounge in our neighborhood park, surrounded by children.

All the children were there. Among the trees, in the arms of statues, toes in the grass, they hopped in and out of dog shit and dug tunnels into mole holes. Wherever the children ran, their mothers stopped to talk.

What a place in democratic time! One God, who was King of the Jews, who unravels the stars to this day with little hydrogen explosions, He can look down from His Holy Headquarters and see us all: heads of girl, ponytails riding the springtime luck, short black bobs, and an occasional eminence of golden wedding rings. He sees south into Brooklyn how Prospect Park lies in its sand-rooted trees among Japanese gardens and police, and beyond us north to dangerous Central Park. Far north, the deer-eyed eland and kudu survive, grazing the open pits of the Bronx Zoo.

But me, the creation of His soft second thought, I am sitting on the twelve-foot-high, strong, long arm of a sycamore, my feet swinging, and I can only see Kitty, a co-worker in the mother trade—a topnotch craftsman. She is below, leaning on my tree, rumpled in a black cotton skirt made of shroud remnants at about fourteen cents a yard. Another colleague, Anne Kraat, is close by on a hard park bench, gloomy, beautiful, waiting for her luck to change.

Although I can't see them, I know that on the other side of the dry pool, the thick snout of the fountain spout, hurrying along the circumference of the parched sun-struck circle (in which, when Henry James could see, he saw lilies floating), Mrs. Hyme Caraway pokes her terrible seedlings, Gowan, Michael, and Christopher, astride an English bike, a French tricycle, and a Danish tractor. Beside her, talking all the time in fear of no response, Mrs. Steamy Lewis, mother of Matthew, Mark, and Lucy, tells of happy happy life in a thatched hotel on a Greek island where total historical recall is indigenous. Lucy limps along at her skirt in muddy cashmere. Mrs. Steamy Lewis really swings within the seconds of her latitude and swears she will have six, but Mr. Steamy Lewis is not expected to live.

I can easily see Mrs. Junius Finn, my up-the-block neighbor and evening stoop companion, a broad barge, like a lady, moving slow—a couple of redheaded cabooses dragged by clothesline at her stern; on her fat upper deck, Wiltwyck,* a pale three-year-old roaring captain with smoky eyes, shoves his wet thumb into the wind. "Hurry! Hurry!" he howls. Mrs. Finn goes puff puffing toward the opinionated playground, that sandy harbor.

Along the same channel, but near enough now to spatter with spite, tilting delicately like a boy's sailboat, Lynn Ballard floats past my unconcern to drop light anchor, a large mauve handbag, over the green bench slats. She sighs and looks up to see what (if any-

---

* Wiltwyck is named for the school of his brother Junior, where Junior, who was bad and getting worse, is still bad, but is getting better (as man is perfectible).

thing) the heavens are telling. In this way, once a week, toes in, head high and in three-quarter turn, arms at her side, graceful as a seal's flippers, she rests, quiet and expensive. She never grabs another mother's kid when he falls and cries. Her particular Michael on his little red bike rides round and round the sandbox, while she dreams of private midnight.

"Like a model," hollers Mrs. Junius Finn over Lynn Ballard's head.

I'm too close to the subject to remark. I sniff, however, and accidentally take sweetness into my lungs. Because it's the month of May.

Kitty and I are nothing like Lynn Ballard. You will see Kitty's darling face, as I tell her, slowly, but me—quick—what am I? Not bad if you're a basement shopper. On my face are a dozen messages, easy to read, strictly for friends, Bargains Galore! I admit it now.

However, the most ordinary life is illuminated by a great event like fame. Once I was famous. From the meaning of that flow, the most hardhearted me is descended.

Once, all the New York papers that had the machinery to do so carried a rotogravure picture of me in a stewardess's arms. I was, it is now thought, the third commercial air-flight baby passenger in the entire world. This picture is at the Home now, mounted on laundry cardboard. My mother fixed it with glass to assail eternity. The caption says: One of Our Youngest. Little Faith Decided to Visit Gramma. Here She Is, Gently Cuddled in the Arms of Stewardess Jeannie Carter.

Why would anyone send a little baby anywhere alone? What was my mother trying to prove? That I was independent? That she wasn't the sort to hang on? That in the sensible, socialist, Zionist world of the future, she wouldn't cry at my wedding? "You're an American child. Free. Independent." Now what does that mean? I have always required a man to be dependent on, even when it appeared that I had one already. I own two small boys whose dependence on me takes up my lumpen time and my bourgeois feelings.

I'm not the least bit ashamed to say that I tie their shoes and I have wiped their backsides well beyond the recommendations of my friends, Ellen and George Hellesbraun, who are psychiatric social workers and appalled. I kiss those kids forty times a day. I punch them just like a father should. When I have a date and come home late at night, I wake them with a couple of good hard shakes to complain about the miserable entertainment. When I'm not furiously exhausted from my low-level job and that bedraggled soot-slimy house, I praise God for them. One Sunday morning, my neighbor, Mrs. Raftery, called the cops because it was 3 a.m. and I was vengefully singing a praising song.

Since I have already mentioned singing, I have to tell you: it is not Sunday. For that reason, all the blue-eyed, boy-faced policemen in the park are worried. They can see that lots of our vitamin-enlarged high-school kids are planning to lug their guitar cases around all day long. They're scared that one of them may strum and sing a mountain melody or that several, a gang, will gather to raise their voices in medieval counterpoint.

Question: Does the world know, does the average freedman realize that, except for a few hours on Sunday afternoon, the playing of fretted instruments is banned by municipal decree? Absolutely forbidden is the song of the flute and oboe.

Answer (explanation): This *is* a great ballswinger of a city on the constant cement-mixing remake, battering and shattering, and a high note out of a wild clarinet could be the decibel to break a citizen's eardrum. But what if you were a city-loving planner leaning on your drawing board? Tears would drop to the delicate drafting sheets.

Well, you won't be pulled in for whistling and here come the whistlers—the young Saturday fathers, open-shirted and ambitious. By and large they are trying to get somewhere and have to go to a lot of parties. They are sleepy but pretend to great energy for the sake of their two-year-old sons (little boys need a recollection of Energy as a male resource). They carry miniature footballs though the season's changing. Then the older fathers trot in, just a few minutes slower, their faces scraped to a clean smile, every one of them wearing a fine gray head and eager eyes, his breath caught, his hand held by the baby daughter of a third intelligent marriage.

One of them, passing my tree, stubs his toe on Kitty's sandal. He shades his eyes to look up at me against my sun. That is Alex O. Steele, who was a man organizing tenant strikes on Ocean Parkway when I was a Coney Island Girl Scout against my mother's socialist will. He says, "Hey, Faith, how's the world? Heard anything from Ricardo?"

I answer him in lecture form:

Alex Steele. Sasha. Yes. I have heard from Ricardo. Ricardo even at the present moment when I am trying to talk with you in a civilized way, Ricardo has rolled his dove-gray brain into a glob of spit in order to fly secretly into my ear right off the poop deck of Foamline's World Tour Cruiseship *Eastern Sunset*. He is stretched out in my head, exhausted before dawn from falling in love with an *Eastern Sunset* lady passenger on the first leg of her many-masted journey round the nighttimes of the world. He is *this minute* saying to me,

"Arcturus Rise, Orion Fall . . ."

"Cock-proud son of a bitch," I mutter.

"Ugh," he says, blinking.

"How are the boys?" I make him say.

"Well, he really wants to know how the boys are," I reply.

"No, I don't," he says. "Please don't answer. Just make sure they don't get killed crossing the street. That's your job."

"What?" says Alex Steele. "Speak clearly, Faith, you're garbling like you used to."

"I'm joking. Forget it. But I did hear from him the other day." Out of the pocket of my stretch denims I drag a mashed letter with the exotic stamp of a new underdeveloped nation. It is a large stamp with two smiling lions on a field of barbed wire. The letter says: "I am not well. I hope I never see another rain forest. I am sick. Are you working? Have you seen Ed Snead? He owes me $180. Don't badger him about it if he looks broke. Otherwise send me some to Guerra Verde c/o Dotty Wasserman. Am living here with her. She's on a Children's Mission. Wonderful girl. Reminds me of you ten years ago. She acts on her principles. I *need* the money."

"That is Ricardo. Isn't it, Alex? I mean, there's no signature."

"Dotty Wasserman!" Alex says. "So, that's where she is . . . a funny plain girl. Faith, let's have lunch some time. I work up in the East Fifties. How're your folks? I hear they put themselves into a Home. They're young for that. Listen, I'm the executive director of Incurables, Inc., a fund-raising organization. We do wonderful things, Faith. The speed of life-extending developments . . . By the way, what do you think of this little curly Sharon of mine?"

"Oh, Alex, how old is she? She's darling, she's a little golden baby, I love her. She's a peach."

"Of course! *She's* a peach, you like anyone better'n you like us," says my son Richard, who is jealous—because he came first and was deprived at two and one-half by his baby brother of my single-hearted love, my friend Ellie Hellesbraun says. Of course, that's a convenient professional lie, a cheap hindsight, as Richard, my older son, is brilliant, and I knew it from the beginning. When he was a baby all alone with me, and Ricardo, his daddy, was off exploring some deep creepy jungle, we often took the ferry to Staten Island. Then we sometimes took the ferry to Hoboken. We walked bridges, just he and I, I said to him, Richie, see the choo-choos on the barges, Richie, see the strong fast tugboat, see the merchant ships with their tall cranes, see the *United States* sail away for a week and a day, see the Hudson River with its white current. Oh, it isn't really the Hudson River, I told him, it's the North River; it isn't really a river, it's an estuary, part of the sea, I told him, though he was only two. I could tell him scientific things like that, because I considered him absolutely brilliant. See how beautiful the ice is on the river, see the stony palisades, I said, I hugged him, my pussycat, I said, see the interesting world.

So he really has no kicks coming, he's just peevish.

"We're really a problem to you, Faith, we keep you not free," Richard says. "Anyway, it's true you're crazy about anyone but us."

It's true I do like the other kids. I am not too cool to say Alex's Sharon really is a peach. But you, you stupid kid, Richard! Who could match me for pride or you for brilliance? Which one of the smart third-grade kids in a class of learned Jews, Presbyterians, and bohemians? You are one of the two smartest and the other one is Chinese—Arnold Lee, who does make Richard look a little simple, I admit it. But did you ever hear of a child who, when asked to write a sentence for the word "who" (they were up to the hard wh's), wrote and then magnificently, with Oriental lisp, read the following: "Friend, tell me who among the Shanghai merchants does the largest trade?"*

"That's typical yak yak out of you, Faith," says Richard.

"Now Richard, listen to me, Arnold's an interesting boy; you wouldn't meet a kid like him anywhere but here or Hong Kong. So use some of these advantages I've given you. I could be living in the country, which I love, but I know how hard that is on children—I stay here in this creepy slum. I dwell in soot and slime just so you can meet kids like Arnold Lee and live on this wonderful block with all the Irish and Puerto Ricans, although God knows why there aren't any Negro children for you to play with . . ."

"Who needs it?" he says, just to tease me. "All those guys got knives anyway. But you don't care if I get killed much, do you?"

How can you answer that boy?

"You don't," says Mrs. Junius Finn, glad to say a few words.

---

* The teacher, Marilyn Gewirtz, the only real person in this story, a child admirer, told me this.

"You don't have to answer them. God didn't give out tongues for that. You answer too much, Faith Asbury, and it shows. Nobody fresher than Richard."

"Mrs. Finn," I scream in order to be heard, for she's some distance away and doesn't pay attention the way I do, "what's so terrible about fresh. EVIL is bad. WICKED is bad. ROBBING, MURDER, and PUTTING HEROIN IN YOUR BLOOD is bad."

"Blah, blah," she says, deaf to passion. "Blah to you."

Despite no education, Mrs. Finn always is more in charge of word meanings than I am. She is especially in charge of Good and Bad. My language limitations here are real. My vocabulary is adequate for writing notes and keeping journals but absolutely useless for an active moral life. If I really knew this language, there would surely be in my head, as there is in Webster's or the *Dictionary of American Slang*, that unreducible verb designed to tell a person like me what to do next.

Mrs. Finn knows my problems because I do not keep them to myself. And I am reminded of them particularly at this moment, for I see her roughly the size of life, held up at the playground by Wyllie, who has rolled off the high ruddy deck of her chest to admire all the English bikes filed in the park bike stand. Of course that is what Junior is upstate for: love that forced possession. At first his father laced him on his behind, cutting the exquisite design known to generations of daddies who labored at home before the rise of industrialism and group therapy. Then Mr. Finn remembered his childhood, that it was Adam's Fall not Junior that was responsible. Now the Finns never see a ten-speed Italian racer without family sighs for Junior, who is still not home as there were about 176 bikes he loved.

Something is wrong with the following tenants: Mrs. Finn, Mrs. Raftery, Ginnie, and me. Everyone else in our building is on the way up through the affluent society, putting five to ten years into low rent before moving to Jersey or Bridgeport. But our four

family units, as people are now called, are doomed to stand cultur-
ally still as this society moves on its caterpillar treads from ordinary affluent to absolute empire. All this in mind, I name names
and dates. "Mrs. Finn, darling, look at my Richard, the time Junior
took his Schwinn and how Richard hid in the coal in the basement
thinking of a way to commit suicide," but she coolly answers, "Faith,
you're not a bit fair, for Junior give it right back when he found out
it was Richard's."

O.K.

Kitty says, "Faith, you'll fall out of the tree, calm yourself." She
looks up, rolling her eyes to show direction, and I see a handsome
man in narrow pants whom we remember from other Saturdays.
He has gone to sit beside Lynn Ballard. He speaks softly to her left
ear while she maintains her profile. He has never spoken to her
Michael. He is a famous actor trying to persuade her to play opposite him in a new production of *She*. That's what Kitty, my kind
friend, says.

I am above that kindness. I often see through the appearance of
things right to the apparition itself. It's obvious that he's a weekend
queer, talking her into the possibilities of a neighborhood three-
some. When her nose quivers and she agrees, he will easily get his
really true love, the magnificent manager of the supermarket, who
has been longing for her at the check-out counter. What they will
do then, I haven't the vaguest idea. I am the child of puritans and
I'm only halfway here.

"Don't even think like that," says Kitty. No. She can see a contract in his pocket.

There is no one like Kitty Skazka. Unlike other people who have
similar flaws that doom, she is tolerant and loving. I wish Kitty
could live forever, bearing daughters and sons to open the heart
of man. Meanwhile, mortal, pregnant, she has three green-eyed
daughters and they aren't that great. Of course, Kitty thinks they
are. And they are no worse than the average gifted, sensitive child
of a wholehearted mother and half a dozen transient fathers.

Her youngest girl is Antonia, who has no respect for grown-ups. Kitty has always liked her to have no respect; so in this, she is quite satisfactory to Kitty.

At some right moment on this Saturday afternoon, Antonia decided to talk to Tonto, my second son. He lay on his belly in the grass, his bare heels exposed to the eye of flitting angels, and he worked at a game that included certain ants and other bugs as players.

"Tonto," she asked, "what are you playing, can I?"

"No, it's my game, no girls," Tonto said.

"Are you the boss of the world?" Antonia asked politely.

"Yes," said Tonto.

He thinks, he really believes, he is. To which I must say, Righto! you are the boss of the world, Anthony, you are prince of the day-care center for the deprived children of working mothers, you are the Lord of the West Side loading zone whenever it rains on Sundays. I have seen you, creepy chief of the dark forest of four gingko trees. The Boss! If you would only look up, Anthony, and boss me what to do, I would immediately slide down this scabby bark, ripping my new stretch slacks, and do it.

"Give me a nickel, Faith," he ordered at once.

"Give him a nickel, Kitty," I said.

"Nickels, nickels, nickels, whatever happened to pennies?" Anna Kraat asked.

"Anna, you're rich. You're against us," I whispered, but loud enough to be heard by Mrs. Junius Finn, still stopped at the mouth of the playground.

"Don't blame the rich for everything," she warned. She herself, despite the personal facts of her economic position, is disgusted with the neurotic rise of the working class.

Lynn Ballard bent her proud and shameless head.

Kitty sighed, shifted her yardage, and began to shorten the hem of the enormous skirt which she was wearing. "Here's a nickel, love," she said.

"Oh boy! Love!" said Anna Kraat.

Antonia walked in a wide circle around the sycamore tree and put her arm on Kitty, who sewed, the sun just barely over her left shoulder—a perfect light. At that very moment, a representational artist passed. I think it was Edward Roster. He stopped and kneeled, peering at the scene. He squared them off with a filmmaker's viewfinder and said, "Ah, what a picture!" then left.

"Number one!" I announced to Kitty, which he was, the very first of the squint-eyed speculators who come by to size up the stock. Pretty soon, depending on age and intention, they would move in groups along the paths or separately take notes in the shadows of the statues.

"The trick," said Anna, downgrading the world, "is to know the speculators from the investors . . ."

"I will never live like that. Not I," Kitty said softly.

"Balls!" I shouted, as the two men strolled past us, leaning toward one another. They weren't lovers, they were Jack Resnick and Tom Weed, music lovers inclining toward their transistor, which was playing the "Chromatic Fantasy." They paid no attention to us because of their relation to this great music. However, Anna heard them say, "Jack, do you hear what I hear?" "Damnit yes, the overromanticizing and the under-Baching, I can't believe it."

Well, I must say when darkness covers the earth and great darkness the people, I will think of you: two men with smart ears. I don't believe civilization can do a lot more than educate a person's senses. It's truth and honor you want to refine, I think the Jews have some insight. Make no images, imitate no God. After all, in His field, the graphic arts, he is pre-eminent. Then let that One who made the tan deserts and the blue Van Allen belt and the green mountains of New England be in charge of Beauty, which He obviously understands, and let man, who was full of forgiveness at Jerusalem, and full of survival at Troy, let man be in charge of Good.

"Faith, you will quit with your all-the-time philosophies," says Richard, my first- and disapproving-born. Into our midst, he'd galloped, riding an all-day rage. Brand-new ball bearings, roller skates, heavy enough for his big feet, hung round his neck.

I decided not to give in to Richard by responding. I digressed and was free: A cross-eyed man with a red beard became president of the Parent-Teachers Association. He appointed a committee of fun-loving ladies who met in the lunchroom and touched up the coffee with little gurgles of brandy.

He had many clever notions about how to deal with the money shortage in the public schools. One of his great plots was to promote the idea of the integrated school in such a way that private-school people would think their kids were missing the real thing. And at 5 a.m., the envious hour, the very pit of the morning of middle age, they would think of all the public-school children deeply involved in the urban tragedy, something their children might never know. He suggested that one month of public-school attendance might become part of the private-school curriculum, as natural and progressive an experience as a visit to the boiler room in first grade. Funds could be split 50-50 or 30-70 or 40-60 with the Board of Education. If the plan failed still the projected effort would certainly enhance the prestige of the public school.

Actually something did stir. Delegations of private progressive-school parents attacked the Board of Ed. for what became known as the Shut-out, and finally even the parents-and-teachers associations of the classical schools (whose peculiar concern always had been educating the child's head) began to consider the value of exposing children who had read about the horror at Ilium to ordinary street fights, so they could understand the Iliad better. Public School (in Manhattan) would become a minor like typing, required but secondary.

Mr. Terry Koln, full of initiative, energy, and lightheartedness, was re-elected by unanimous vote and sent on to the United Parents and Federated Teachers Organization as special council member, where in a tiny office all his own he grew marijuana on the windowsills, swearing it was deflowered marigolds.

He was the joy of our P.T.A. But it was soon discovered that he had no children, and Kitty and I have to meet him now surreptitiously in bars.

"Oh," said Richard, his meanness undeflected by this jolly digression:

> *"The ladies of the P.T.A.*
> *wear baggies in their blouses*
> *they talk on telephones all day*
> *and never clean their houses."*

He really wrote that, my Richard. I thought it was awfully good, rhyme and meter and all, and I brought it to his teacher. I took the afternoon off to bring it to her. "Are you joking, Mrs. Asbury?" she asked.

Looking into her kind teaching eyes, I remembered schools and what it might be like certain afternoons and I replied, "May I have my Richard, please, he has a dental appointment. His teeth are just like his father's. Rotten."

"Do take care of them, Mrs. Asbury."

"God, yes, it's the least," I said, taking his hand.

"Faith," said Richard, who had not gone away. "Why did you take me to the dentist that afternoon?"

"I thought you wanted to get out of there."

"Why? Why? Why?" asked Richard, stamping his feet and shouting. I didn't answer. I closed my eyes to make him disappear.

"Why not?" asked Philip Mazzano, who was standing there looking up at me when I opened my eyes.

"Where's Richard?" I asked.

"This is Philip," Kitty called up to me. "You know Philip, that I told you about?"

"Yes?"

"Philip," she said.

"Oh," I said and left the arm of the sycamore with as delicate a jump as can be made by a person afraid of falling, twisting an ankle, and being out of work for a week.

"I don't mind school," said Richard, shouting from behind the tree. "It's better than listening to her whine."

He really talks like that.

Philip looked puzzled. "How old are you, sonny?"

"Nine."

"Do nine-year-olds talk like that? I think I have a boy who's nine."

"Yes," said Kitty. "Your Johnny's nine, David's eleven, and Mike's fourteen."

"Ah," said Philip, sighing; he looked up into the tree I'd flopped from—and there was Judy, Anna's kid, using my nice warm branch. "God," said Philip, "more!"

Silence followed and embarrassment, because we outnumbered him, though clearly, we tenderly liked him.

"How is everything, Kitty?" he said, kneeling to tousle her hair. "How's everything, my old honey girl? Another one?" He tapped Kitty's tummy lightly with an index finger. "God!" he said, standing up. "Say, Kitty, I saw Jerry in Newark day before yesterday. Just like that. He was standing in a square scratching his head."

"Jerry?" Kitty asked in a high loving squeak. "Oh, I know. Newark all week . . . Why were you there?"

"Me? I had to see someone, a guy named Vincent Hall, a man in my field."

"What's your field?" I asked.

"Daisies," he said. "I happen to be in the field of daisies."

What an answer! How often does one meet, in this black place, a man, woman, or child who can think up a pastoral reply like that?

For that reason I looked at him. He had dark offended eyes deep in shadow, with a narrow rim of whiteness under the eyes, the result, I invented, of lots of late carousing nights, followed by eye-wrinkling examinations of mortalness. All this had marked him lightly with sobriety, the first enhancing manifest of ravage.

Even Richard is stunned by this uncynical openhearted nota-
tion of feeling. Forty bare seconds then, while Jack Resnick puts
his transistor into the hollow of an English elm, takes a tattered
score of *The Messiah* out of his rucksack, and writes a short Elizabe-
than melody in among the long chorus holds to go with the last
singing sentence of my ode to Philip.

"Nice day," said Anna.

"Please, Faith," said Richard. "Please. You see that guy over
there?" He pointed to a fat boy seated among adults on a park
bench not far from listening Lynn Ballard. "He has a skate key and
he won't lend it to me. He stinks. It's your fault you lost the skate
key, Faith. You know you did. You never put anything away."

"Ask him again, Richard."

"You ask him, Faith. You're a grownup."

"I will not. You want the skate key, you ask him. You have to
go after your own things in this life. I'm not going to be around
forever."

Richard gave me a gloomy, lip-curling look. No. It was worse
than that. It was a baleful, foreboding look; a look which as far as
our far-in-the-future relations were concerned could be named
ill-auguring.

"You never do me a favor, do you?" he said.

"*I'll* go with you, Richard." Philip grabbed his hand. "We'll
talk to that kid. He probably hasn't got a friend in the world. I'm
not kidding you, boy, it's hard to be a fat kid." He rapped his belly,
where, I imagine, certain memories were stored.

Then he took Richard's hand and they went off, man and boy,
to tangle.

"Kitty! Richard just hands him his skate, his hand, and just
goes off with him . . . That's not like my Richard."

"Children sense how good he is," said Kitty.

"He's good?"

"He's really not *so* good. Oh, he's good. He's considerate. You
know what kind he is, Faith. But if you don't really want him to be

good, he will be. And he's very strong. Physically. Someday I'll tell you about him. Not now. He has a special meaning to me."

Actually everyone has a special meaning to Kitty, even me, a dictionary of particular generalities, even Anna and all our children.

Kitty sewed as she spoke. She looked like a delegate to a Conference of Youth from the People's Republic of Ubmonsk from Lower Tartaria. A single dark braid hung down her back. She wore a round-necked white blouse with capped sleeves made of softened muslin, woven for aged bridesbeds. I have always listened carefully to my friend Kitty's recommendations, for she has made one mistake after another. Her experience is invaluable.

Kitty's kids have kept an eye on her from their dear tiniest times. They listened to her reasons, but the two eldest, without meaning any disrespect, had made different plans for their lives. Children are all for John Dewey. Lisa and Nina have never believed that Kitty's life really worked. They slapped Antonia for scratching the enameled kitchen table. When Kitty caught them, she said, "Antonia's a baby. Come on now girls, what's a table?"

"What's a *table*?" said Lisa. "What a nut! She wants to know what a table is."

"Well, Faith," said Richard, "*he* got the key for me."

Richard and Philip were holding hands, which made Richard look like a little boy with a daddy. I could cry when I think that I always treat Richard as though he's about forty-seven.

Philip felt remarkable to have extracted that key. "He's quite a kid, Faith, your boy. I wish that my Johnny in Chicago was as great as Richard here. Is Johnny really nine, Kitty?"

"You bet," she said.

He kept his puzzled face for some anticipated eventuality and folded down to cross-legged comfort, leaning familiarly on Nina's and Lisa's backs. "How are you two fairy queens?" he asked and tugged at their long hair gently. He peeked over their shoulders. They were reading Classic Comics, *Ivanhoe* and *Robin Hood*.

"I hate to read," said Antonia.

"Me too," hollered Tonto.

"Antonia, I wish *you'd* read more," said Philip. "Antonia, little beauty. These two little ones. Forest babies. Little sunny brown creatures. I think you would say, Kitty, that they understand their bodies?"

"Oh, yes, I would," said Kitty, who believed all that.

Although I'm very shy, I tend to persevere, so I said, "You're pretty sunny and brown yourself. How do you make out? What are you? An actor or a French teacher, or something?"

"French . . ." Kitty smiled. "He could teach Sanskrit if he wanted to. Or Filipino or Cambodian."

"Cambodge . . ." Philip said. He said this softly as though the wars in Indochina might be the next subject for discussion.

"French teacher?" asked Anna Kraat, who had been silent, grieved by spring, for one hour and forty minutes. "Judy," she yelled into the crossed branches of the sycamore. "Judy . . . French . . ."

"So?" said Judy. "What's so great? Je m'appelle Judy Solomon. Ma père s'appelle Pierre Solomon. How's that folks?"

"Mon père," said Anna. "I told you that before."

"Who cares?" said Judy, who didn't care.

"She's lost two fathers," said Anna, "within three years."

Tonto stood up to scratch his belly and back, which were itchy with wet grass. "Mostly nobody has fathers, Anna," he said.

"Is it true, little boy?" asked Philip.

"Oh yes," Tonto said. "My father is in the Equator. They never even had fathers," pointing to Kitty's daughters. "Judy has two fathers, Peter and Dr. Kraat. Dr. Kraat takes care of you if you're crazy."

"Maybe I'll be your father."

Tonto looked at me. I was too rosy. "Oh no," he said. "Not right now. My father's name is Ricardo. He's a famous explorer. Like an explorer, I mean. He went in the Equator to make contacts. I have two books by him."

"Do you like him?"

"He's all right."

"Do you miss him?"

"He's very fresh when he's home."

"That's enough of that!" I said. It's stupid to let a kid talk badly about his father in front of another man. Men really have too much on their minds without that.

"He's quite a boy," said Philip. "You and your brother are real boys." He turned to me. "What do I do? Well, I make a living. Here. Chicago. Wherever I am. I'm not in financial trouble. I figured it all out ten years ago. But what I really am, really . . ." he said, driven to lying confidence because he thought he ought to try that life anyway. "What I truly am is a comedian."

"That's a joke, that's the first joke you've said."

"But that's what I want to be . . . a comedian."

"But you're not funny."

"But I am. You don't know me yet. I want to be one. I've been a teacher and I've worked for the State Department. And now what I want to be's a comedian. People have changed professions before."

"You can't be a comedian," said Anna, "unless you're funny."

He took a good look at Anna. Anna's character is terrible, but she's beautiful. It took her husbands about two years apiece to see how bad she was, but it takes the average passer, answerer, or asker about thirty seconds to see how beautiful she is. You can't warn men. As for Kitty and me, we love her because she's beautiful.

"Anna's all right," said Richard.

"Be quiet," said Philip. "Say, Anna, are you interested in the French tongue, the French people, French history, or French civilization?"

"No," said Anna.

"Oh," he said, disappointed.

"I'm not interested in anything," said Anna.

"Say!" said Philip, getting absolutely red with excitement, blushing from his earlobes down into his shirt, making me think as I watched the blood descend from his brains that I would like to be the one who was holding his balls very gently, to be exactly present so to speak when all the thumping got there.

Since it was clearly Anna, not I, who would be in that affectionate position, I thought I'd better climb the tree again just for the oxygen or I'd surely suffer the same sudden descent of blood. That's the way nature does things, swishing those quarts and quarts to wherever they're needed for power and action.

Luckily, a banging of pots and pans came out of the playground and a short parade appeared—four or five grownups, a few years behind me in the mommy-and-daddy business, pushing little go-carts with babies in them, a couple of three-year-olds hanging on. They were the main bangers and clangers. The grownups carried three posters. The first showed a prime-living, prime-earning, well-dressed man about thirty-five years old next to a small girl. A question was asked: would you burn a child? In the next poster he placed a burning cigarette on the child's arm. The cool answer was given: WHEN NECESSARY. The third poster carried no words, only a napalmed Vietnamese baby, seared, scarred, with twisted hands.

We were very quiet. Kitty put her head down into the dark skirt of her lap. I trembled. I said, "Oh!" Anna said to Philip, "They'll only turn people against them," and turned against them herself at once.

"You people will have to go," said Douglas, our neighborhood cop. He had actually arrived a few minutes earlier to tell Kitty to beg Jerry not to sell grass at this end of the park. But he was ready. "You just have to go," he said. "No parades in the park."

Kitty lifted her head and with sweet bossiness said, "Hey Doug, leave them alone. They're O.K."

Tonto said, "I know that girl, she goes to Greenwich House. You're in the big fours," he told her.

Doug said, "Listen Tonto, there's a war on. You'll be a soldier too someday. I know you're no sissy like some kids around here. You'll fight for your country."

"Ha ha," said Mrs. Junius Finn, "that'll be the day. Oh, say, can you see?"

The paraders made a little meeting just outside our discussion. They had to decide what next. The four grownups held the tongues of the children's bells until that decision could be made. They were a group of that kind of person.

"What they're doing is treason," said Douglas. He had decided to explain and educate. "Signs on sticks aren't allowed. In case of riot. It's for their own protection too. They might turn against each other." He was afraid that no one would find the real perpetrator if that should happen.

"But Officer, I know these people. They're decent citizens of this community," said Philip, though he didn't live in the borough, city, or state, let alone vote in it.

Doug looked at him thoroughly. "Mister, I could take you in for interference." He pulled his cop voice out of his healthy diaphragm.

"Come on . . ." said Kitty.

"You too," he said fiercely. "Disperse," he said, "disperse, disperse."

Behind his back, the meeting had been neatly dispersed for about three minutes. He ran after them, but they continued on the park's circumference, their posters on the carriage handles, very solemn, making friends and enemies.

"They look pretty legal to me," I hollered after Doug's blue back.

Tonto fastened himself to my leg and stuck his thumb in his mouth.

Richard shouted, "Ha! Ha!" and punched me. He also began to grind his teeth, which would lead, I knew, to great expense.

"Oh, that's funny, Faith," he said. He cried, he stamped his feet dangerously, in skates. "I hate you. I hate your stupid friends. Why didn't they just stand up to that stupid cop and say fuck you. They should have just stood up and hit him." He ripped his skates off, twisting his bad ankle. "Gimme that chalk box, Lisa, just give it to me."

In a fury of tears and disgust, he wrote on the near blacktop in pink flamingo chalk—in letters fifteen feet high, so the entire Saturday walking world could see—WOULD YOU BURN A CHILD? and under it, a little taller, the red reply, WHEN NECESSARY.

And I think that is exactly when events turned me around, changing my hairdo, my job uptown, my style of living and telling. Then I met women and men in different lines of work, whose minds were made up and directed out of that sexy playground by my children's heartfelt brains, I thought more and more and every day about the world.

Enormous Changes at the Last Minute

A young man said he wanted to go to bed with Alexandra because she had an interesting mind. He was a cabdriver and she *had* admired the curly back of his head. Still, she was surprised. He said he would pick her up again in about an hour and a half. Because she was fair and a responsible person, she placed between them a barrier of truthful information. She said, I suppose you don't know many middle-aged women.

You don't look so middle-aged to me. I mean, everyone likes what they like. That is, I'm interested in your point of view, your way of life. Anyway, he said, peering into the mirror, your face is nice and your eyebrows are out of sight.

Make it two hours, she said. I'm visiting my father whom I happen to love.

I love mine too, he said. He just doesn't love me. Too too bad.

O.K. That's enough, she said. Because they had already *had* the following factual and introductory conversation.

How old are your kids?

I have none.

Sorry. Then what do you do for a living?

Children. Early teenage. Adoption, foster homes. Probations. Troubles—well . . .

Where'd you go to school?

City colleges. What about you?

Oh, me. Lots of places. Antioch. Wisconsin. California. I might go back someday. Someplace else though. Maybe Harvard. Why not?

He leaned on his horn to move a sixteen-wheel trailer truck delivering Kleenex to the A&P.

I wish you'd stop that, she said. I hate that kind of driving.

Why? Oh! You're an idealist! He looked through his rearview mirror straight into her eyes. But were you married? Ever?

Once. For years.

Who to?

It's hard to describe. A revolutionist.

Really? Could I know him? What's his name? We say revolutionary nowadays.

Oh?

By the way, my name's Dennis. I probably like you, he said.

You do, do you? Well, why should you? And let me ask you something. What do you mean by nowadays?

By the birdseed of St. Francis, he said, taking a tiny brogue to the tip of his tongue. I meant no harm.

Nowadays! she said. What does that mean? I guess you think you're kind of brand-new. You're not so brand-new. The telephone was brand-new. The airplane was brand-new. You've been seen on earth before.

Wow! he said. He stopped the cab just short of the hospital entrance. He turned to look at her and make decisions. But you're right, he said sweetly. You know the mind *is* an astonishing, long-living, erotic thing.

Is it? she asked. Then she wondered: What is the life expectancy of the mind?

Eighty years, said her father, glad to be useful. Once he had explained electrical storms before you could find the Book of Knowledge. Now in the cave of old age, he continued to amass wonderful information. But he was sick with oldness. His arteries had a hopeless future, and conversation about all that obsolescent tubing often displaced very interesting subjects.

One day he said, Alexandra! Don't show me the sunset again. I'm not interested anymore. You know that. She had just pointed to a simple sunset happening outside his hospital window. It was a red ball—all alone, without its evening streaking clouds—a red ball falling hopelessly west, just missing the Hudson River, Jersey City, Chicago, the Great Plains, the Golden Gate—falling, falling.

Then in Russian he sighed some Pushkin. Not for me, the spring. *Nye dyla menya . . .* He slept. She read the large-print edition of *The Guns of August*. A half hour later, he opened his eyes and told her how, in that morning's *Times*, the Phoenicians had sailed to Brazil in about 500 B.C. A remarkable people. The Vikings too were remarkable. He spoke well of the Chinese, the Jews, the Greeks, the Indians—all the old commercial people. Actually he had never knocked an entire nation. International generosity had been started in him during the late nineteenth century by his young mother and father, candleholders inside the dark tyranny of the tsars. It was childhood training. Thoughtfully, he passed it on.

In the hospital bed next to him, a sufferer named John feared the imminent rise of the blacks of South Africa, the desperate blacks of Chicago, the yellow Chinese, and the Ottoman Turks. He had more reason than Alexandra's father to dread the future because his heart was strong. He would probably live to see it all. He believed the Turks when they came would bring New York City diseases like cholera, virulent scarlet fever, and particularly leprosy.

Leprosy! for godsakes! said Alexandra. John! Upset yourself with reality for once! She read aloud from the *Times* about the bombed, burned lepers' colonies in North Vietnam. Her father said, Please

Alexandra, today, no propaganda. Why do you constantly pick on the United States? He remembered the first time he'd seen the American flag on wild Ellis Island. Under its protection and working like a horse, he'd read Dickens, gone to medical school, and shot like a surface-to-air missile right into the middle class.

Then he said, But they shouldn't put a flag in the middle of the chocolate pudding. It's ridiculous.

It's Memorial Day, said the nurse's aide, removing his tray.

In the early evening Dennis stood at the door of each room of Alexandra's apartment. He looked this way and that. Underuse in a time of population stress, he muttered. He entered the kitchen and sniffed the kitchen air. It doesn't matter, he said aloud. He took a fingerful of gravy out of the pot on the stove. Beef stew, he whispered. Then he opened the door to the freezer compartment and said, Sweet Jesus! because there were eleven batches of the same, neatly stacked and frozen. They were for Alexandra's junkies, whose methadone required lots of protein and carbohydrates.

I wouldn't have them in my house. It's a wonder you got a cup and saucer left. Creeps, said Dennis. However, yes, indeed, I will eat this stuff. Why? Does it make me think of home or something else? he asked. I think, a movie I once saw.

Apple turnovers! You know I have to admit it, our commune isn't working too well. Probably because it's in Brooklyn and the food co-op isn't together. But it's cool, they've accepted the criticism.

You have lots of junk in here, he pointed out after dinner. He had decided to give the place some respectful attention. He meant armchairs, lamps, desk sets, her grandmother's wedding portrait, and an umbrella stand with two of her father's canes.

Um, said Alexandra, it's rent-controlled.

You know what I like to do, Alexandra? I like to sit with a girl and look at a late movie, he said. It's an experience common to Americans at this hour. It's important to be like others, to dig the average dude, you have to be him. Be HIM. It's groovier than a lot of phony gab. You'd be surprised how friendly you get.

I'm not against friendliness, she said, I'm not even against Americans.

They watched half of *A Day at the Races*. This is very relaxing, he said. It's kind of long though, isn't it? Then he began to undress. He held out his arms. He said, Alexandra, I really can't wait anymore. I'm a sunrise person. I like to go to bed early. Can I stay a few days?

He gave reasons: 1. It was a Memorial Day weekend, and the house in Brooklyn was full of tripping visitors. 2. He was disgusted with them anyway because they'd given up the most beautiful batik work for fashionable tie-dying. 3. He and Alexandra could take some good walks in the morning because all the parks to walk in were the lightest green. He had noticed that the tree on the corner though dying of buses was green at the beginning of many twigs. 4. He could talk to her about the kids, help her to understand their hangups, their incredible virtues. He had missed being one of them by about seven useless years.

So many reasons are not essential, Alexandra said. She offered him a brandy. Holy toads! he said furiously. You *know* I'm not into that. Touched by gloom, he began to remove the heavy shoes he wore for mountain walking. He dropped his pants and stamped on them a couple of times to make sure he and they were disengaged.

Alexandra, in the first summer dress of spring, stood still and watched. She breathed deeply because of having been alone for a year or two. She put her two hands over her ribs to hold her heart in place and also out of modesty to quiet its immodest thud. Then they went to bed in the bedroom and made love until that noisy disturbance ended. She couldn't hear one interior sound. Therefore they slept.

In the morning she became interested in reality again, which she had always liked. She wanted to talk about it. She began with a description of John, her father's neighbor in the hospital.

Turks? Far out! Well he's right. And another thing. Leprosy *is* coming. It's coming to the Forest Hills County Fair, the Rikers Island Jamboree, the Fillmore East, and the Ecolocountry Gardens in Westchester. In August.

Reality? A lesson in reality? Am I a cabdriver? No. I drive a cab but I am not a cabdriver. I'm a song hawk. A songmaker. I'm a poet, in other words. Do you know that every black man walking down the street today is a poet? But only one white honky devil in ten. One in ten.

Nowadays I write for the Lepers all the time. Fuck poetry. The Lepers dig me. I dig them.

The Lepers? Alexandra said.

Cool! You know them? No? Well, you may have known them under their old name. They used to be called The Split Atom. But they became too popular and their thing is anonymity. That's what they're known for. They'll probably change their name after the summer festivals. They might move to the country and call themselves Winter Moss.

Do you really make a living now?

Oh yes. I do. I do. Among technicians like myself I do.

Now: I financially carry one-third of a twelve-person, three-children commune. I only drive a cab to keep on top of the world of illusion, you know, Alexandra, to rap with the bourgeoisies, the fancy whores, the straight ladies visiting their daddies. Oh, excuse me, he said.

Now, Alexandra, imagine this: two bass guitars, a country violin, one piccolo, and drums. The Lepers' theme song! He sat up in bed. The sun shone on his chest. He had begun to think of breakfast, but he sang so that Alexandra could know him better and dig his substantialness.

> ooooh
> *first my finger goes   goes   goes*
> *then my nose*
>   *then baby   my toes*

if you love me this way   anyway   any day
I'll go your way
        my Little Neck rose

Well? he asked. He looked at Alexandra. Was she going to cry? I thought you were such a reality freak, Alexandra. That's the way it is in the real world. Anyway! He then said a small prose essay to explain and buttress the poem:

> The kids! the kids! Though terrible troubles hang over them, such as the absolute end of the known world quickly by detonation or slowly through the easygoing destruction of natural resources, they are still, even now, optimistic, humorous, and brave. In fact, they intend enormous changes at the last minute.

Come on, said Alexandra, hardhearted, an enemy of generalization, there are all kinds. My boys aren't like that.

Yes, they are, he said, angry. You bring them around. I'll prove it. Anyway, I love them. He tried for about twenty minutes, forgetting breakfast, to show Alexandra how to look at things in this powerful last-half-of-the-century way. She tried. She had always had a progressive if sometimes reformist disposition, but at that moment, listening to him talk, she could see straight ahead over the thick hot rod of love to solitary age and lonesome death.

But there's nothing to fear my dear girl, her father said. When you get there you will not want to live a hell of a lot. Nothing to fear at all. You will be used up. You are like a coal burning, smoldering. Then there's nothing left to burn. Finished. Believe me, he said, although he hadn't been there yet himself, at that moment you won't mind. Alexandra's face was a bit rumpled, listening.

Don't look at me like that! he said. He was too sensitive to her appearance. He hated her to begin to look older the way she'd had to in the last twenty years. He said, Now *I* have seen people die. A large number. Not one or two. Many. They are good and ready. Pain. Despair. Unconsciousness, nightmares. Perfectly good comas, wrecked by nightmares. They are ready. You will be too, Sashka. Don't worry so much.

Ho ho ho, said John in the next bed listening through the curtains. Doc, I'm not ready. I feel terrible, I got lousy nightmares. I don't sleep a wink. But I'm not ready. I can't piss without this tube. Lonesomeness! Boy! Did you ever see one of my kids visiting? No! Still I am not ready. NOT READY. He spelled it out, looking at the ceiling or through it, to the roof garden for incurables, and from there to God.

The next morning Dennis said, I would rather die than go to the hospital.

For godsakes, why?

Why? Because I hate to be in the hands of strangers. They don't let you take the pills you got that you know work, then if you need one of their pills, even if you buzz, they don't come. The nurse and three interns are making out in the information booth. I've seen it. It's a high counter, she's answering questions, and they're taking turns banging her from behind.

Dennis! You're too dumb. You sound like some superstitious old lady with rape dreams.

That's cool, he said. I *am* an old lady about my health. I mean I like it. I want my teeth to go right on. Right on sister. He began to sing, then stopped. Listen! Your destiny's in their hands. It's up to them. Do you live? Or are you a hippie crawling creep from their point of view? Then die!

Really. Nobody ever decides to let you die. In fact, that's what's wrong. They decide to keep people alive for years after death has set in.

You mean like your father?

Alexandra leaped out of bed stark naked. My father! Why he's got twenty times your zip.

Cool it! he said. Come back. I was just starting to fuck you and you get so freaked.

And another thing. Don't use that word. I hate it. When you're with a woman you have to use the language that's right for her.

What do you want me to say?

I want you to say, I was just starting to make love to you, etc.

Well, that's true, said Dennis, I was. When she returned to him, he only touched the tips of her fingers, though all of her was present. He kissed each finger and said right after each kiss, I want to make love to you. He did this sweetly, not sarcastically.

Dennis, Alexandra said in an embarrassment of recognition, you look like one of my placements, in fact you look like a kid, Billy Platoon. His real name is Platon but he calls himself Platoon so he can go to Vietnam and get killed like his stepbrother. He's a dreamy boy.

Alexandra, you talk a lot, now hush, no politics.

Alexandra continued for a sentence or two. He carries a stick with a ball full of nails attached, like some medieval weapon, in case an enemy from Suffolk Street CIA's him. That's what they call it.

Never heard that before. Besides I'm jealous. And also I'm the enemy from Suffolk Street.

No, no, said Alexandra. Then she noticed in her mother's bedroom bureau mirror across the room a small piece of her naked self. She said, Ugh!

There, there! said Dennis lovingly, caressing what he thought she'd looked at, a couple of rippled inches between her breast and belly. It's natural, Alexandra. Men don't change as much as women. Among all the animals, human females are the only ones to lose estrogen as they get older.

Is that it? she said.

Then there was nothing to talk about for half an hour.

But how come you knew that? she asked. The things you know, Dennis. What for?

Why—for my art, he said. And despite his youth he rested from love the way artists often do in order to sing. He sang:

Camp out
out in the forest daisy
under the gallows tree
with the
ace of pentacles
and me
daisy flower

What of the
earth's ecology
you're drivin too fast
Daisy you're drivin alone

Hey Daisy cut the ignition
let the oil
back in the stone.

Oh I like that one. I admire it! Alexandra said. But in fact, *is* ecology a good word for a song? It's technical . . .

Any word is good, it's the big word today anyway, said Dennis. It's what you do with the word. The language and the idea, they work it out together.

Really? Where do you get most of your ideas?

I don't know if I want to eat or sleep, he said. I think I just want to nuzzle your titty. Talk talk talk. Most? Well, I would say the majority are from a magazine, the *Scientific American*.

During breakfast, language remained on his mind. Because of this, he was silent. After the pancakes, he said, Actually Alexandra, I can use any words I want. And I have. I proved it last week in a conversation just like this one. I asked these blue-eyed cats to give me a dictionary. I just flipped the pages and jabbed and the word I hit was *ophidious*. But I did it, because the word does the dreaming for you. The word.

　　To a tune that was probably "On Top of Old Smoky" he sang:

> *The ophidious garden*
> *was invented by Freud*
>
> 　*where three ladies murdered*
> 　*oh three ladies murdered*
>
> *the pricks of the birds*
>
> *the cobra is buried*
> *the rattlesnake writhes*
>
> 　*in the black snaky garden*
> 　*in the blue snaky garden*
>
> *in the hairs of my wives.*

More coffee, please, he said with pride and modesty.

　　It's better than most of your songs, Alexandra said. It's a poem, isn't it? It *is* better.

　　What? What? It is *not* better, it is not, goddamn. It is not . . . It just isn't . . . oh, excuse me for losing my cool like that.

　　Forget it, sonny, Alexandra said respectfully. I only meant I liked it, but I know, I'm too frank from living alone so much I think. Anyway, how come you always think about wives? Wives, mothers?

　　Because that's me, said peaceful Dennis. Haven't you noticed it yet? That's my bag. I'm a motherfucker.

　　Oh, she said, I see. But I'm not a mother, Dennis.

　　Yes, you are, Alexandra. I've figured out a lot about you. I know. I act like the weekend stud sometimes. But I wrote you a song. Just last night in the cab. I think about you. The Lepers'll never dig it.

They don't know too much about life. They're still baby bees trying to make it to the next flower, but some old-timer'll tape it, some sore dude who's been out of it for a couple of years who wants to grow. He'll smell the shit in it.

> *Oh*
> *I know something about you baby*
> *that's sad*
> *don't be mad*
> *baby*
> *That you will never have children at*
> *rest*
> *at that beautiful breast*
> *my love*

> *But see*
> *everywhere you go, children follow you*
> *for more*
> *many more*
> *are the children of your life*
> *than the children of the married wife.*

That one is out of the Bible, he said.

Pa, Alexandra said, don't you think a woman in this life ought to have at least one child?

No doubt about it, he said. You should have when you were married to Granofsky, the Communist. We disagreed. He had no sense of humor. He's probably boring the Cubans to death this minute. But he was an intelligent person otherwise. I would have brilliant grandchildren. They would not necessarily have the same politics.

Then he looked at her, her age and possibilities. He softened. You don't look so bad. You could still marry, dear girl. Then he softened further, thinking of hopeless statistics he had just read about the ratio of women to men. Actually! So what! It's not important, Alexandra. According to the Torah, only the man is commanded to multiply. You are not commanded. You have a child, you don't have, God doesn't care. You don't have one, you call in the maid. You say to your husband, Sweetie, get my maid with child. O.K. Well, your husband has anyway been fooling around with the maid for a couple of years, but now it's a respectable business. Good. You don't have to go through the whole thing, nine months, complications, maybe a caesarean, no no pronto, a child for the Lord, Hosanna.

Pa, she said, several weeks later, but what if I did have a baby?

Don't be a fool, he said. Then he gave her a terrible long medical look, which included her entire body. He said, Why do you ask this question? He became red in the face, which had never happened. He took hold of his chest with his right hand, the hospital buzzer with the left. First, he said, I want the nurse! Now! Then he ordered Alexandra: Marry!

Dennis said, I don't know how I got into this shit. It's not right, but because your habits and culture are different, I will compromise. What I suggest is this, Alexandra. The three children in our commune belong to us all. No one knows who the father is. It's far out. I swear—by the cock of our hard-up gods, I swear it's beautiful. One of them might be mine. But she doesn't have any distinguishing marks. Why don't you come and live with us and we'll all raise that kid up to be a decent human and humane being in this world. We need a slightly older person, we really do, with a historic sense. We lack that.

Thank you, Alexandra replied. No.

Her father said, Explain it to me, please. For what purpose did you act out this nonsense? For love? At your age. Money? Some conniver flattered you. You probably made him supper. Some starving ne'er-do-well probably wanted a few meals and said, Why not?

This middle-aged fool is an easy mark. She'll give me pot roast at night, bacon and eggs in the morning.

No Pa, no, Alexandra said. Please, you'll get sicker.

John in the next bed dying with a strong heart wrote a little note to him. Doc, you're crazy. Don't leave enemies. That girl is loyal! She hasn't missed a Tues., Thurs., or Sat. Did you ever see one of my kids visit? Something else. I feel worse and worse. But I'm still *not ready*.

I want to tell you one more thing, her father said. You are going to embitter my last days and ruin my life.

After that, Alexandra hoped every day for her father's death, so that she could have a child without ruining his interesting life at the very end of it when ruin is absolutely retroactive.

Finally, Dennis said, Then let me at least share the pad with you. It'll be to *your* advantage.

No, Alexandra said. Please, Dennis. I've got to go to work early. I'm sleepy.

I dig. I've been a joke to you. You've used me in a bad way. That's not cool. That smells under heaven.

No, Alexandra said. Please, shut up. Anyway, how do you know you're the father?

Come on, he said, who else would be?

Alexandra smiled, bit her lip to the edge of blood to show pain politely. She was thinking about the continuity of her work, how to be proud and not lose a productive minute. She thought about the members of her caseload one by one.

She said, Dennis, I know exactly what I'm going to do.

In that case, this is it, I'm splitting.

This is what Alexandra did in order to make good use of the events of her life. She invited three pregnant clients who were fifteen and sixteen years old to live with her. She visited each one and explained to them that she was pregnant too, and that her apartment was very large. Although they had disliked her because she'd always worried more about the boys, they moved out of the homes of their bad-tempered parents within a week. At the very first evening meal they began to give Alexandra good advice about men, which she did appreciate years later. She ensured their health and her own and she took notes as well. She established a precedent in social work which would not be followed or even mentioned in state journals for about five years.

Alexandra's father's life was not ruined, nor did he have to die. Shortly before the baby's birth, he fell hard on the bathroom tiles, cracked his skull, dipped the wires of his brain into his heart's blood. Short circuit! He lost twenty, thirty years in the flood, the faces of nephews, in-laws, the names of two Presidents, and a war. His eyes were rounder, he was often awestruck, but he was smart as ever, and able to begin again with fewer scruples to notice and appreciate.

The baby was born and named Dennis for his father. Of course his last name was Granofsky because of Alexandra's husband, Granofsky, the Communist.

The Lepers, who had changed their name to the Edible Amanita, taped the following song in his tiny honor. It was called "Who? I."

The lyrics are simple. They are:

> *Who is the father?*
> *Who is the father*
> *Who is the father*

> *I! I! I! I!*

> *I am the father*
> *I am the father*
> *I am the father.*

Dennis himself sang the solo which was I! I! I! I! in a hoarse enraged prophetic voice. He had been brave to acknowledge the lyrics. After a thirty-eight-hour marathon encounter at his commune, he was asked to leave. The next afternoon he moved to a better brown-stone about four blocks away where occasional fatherhood was expected.

On the baby's third birthday, Dennis and the Fair Fields of Corn produced a folk-rock album because that was the new sound and exciting. It was called *For Our Son*. Tuned-in listeners could hear how taps played by the piccolo about forty times a verse flitted in and out of the long dark drumrolls, the ordinary banjo chords, and the fiddle tune which was something but not exactly like "Lullaby and Good Night."

Will you come to see me Jack
    When I'm old and very shaky?
Yes I will for you're my dad
    And you've lost your last old lady
    Though you traveled very far
To the highlands and the badlands
    And ripped off the family car
Still, old dad, I won't forsake you.

Will you come to see me Jack?
    Though I'm really not alone.
Still I'd like to see my boy
    For we're lonesome for our own.
    Yes I will for you're my dad
Though you dumped me and my brothers
    And you sizzled down the road
Loving other fellows' mothers.

Will you come to see me Jack?
    Though I look like time boiled over.
Growing old is not a lark.
    Yes I will for you're my dad
    Though we never saw a nickel

As we struggled up life's ladder
     I will call you and together
We will cuddle up and see
     What the weather's like in Key West
On the old-age home TV.

This song was sung coast to coast and became famous from the dark Maine woods to Texas's shining gulf. It was responsible for a statistical increase in visitors to old-age homes by the apprehensive middle-aged and the astonished young.

A Conversation with My Father

My father is eighty-six years old and in bed. His heart, that bloody motor, is equally old and will not do certain jobs anymore. It still floods his head with brainy light. But it won't let his legs carry the weight of his body around the house. Despite my metaphors, this muscle failure is not due to his old heart, he says, but to a potassium shortage. Sitting on one pillow, leaning on three, he offers last-minute advice and makes a request.

"I would like you to write a simple story just once more," he says, "the kind Maupassant wrote, or Chekhov, the kind you used to write. Just recognizable people and then write down what happened to them next."

I say, "Yes, why not? That's possible." I want to please him, though I don't remember writing that way. I *would* like to try to tell such a story, if he means the kind that begins: "There was a woman . . ." followed by plot, the absolute line between two points which I've always despised. Not for literary reasons, but because it takes all hope away. Everyone, real or invented, deserves the open destiny of life.

Finally I thought of a story that had been happening for a couple of years right across the street. I wrote it down, then read it aloud. "Pa," I said, "how about this? Do you mean something like this?"

> Once in my time there was a woman and she had a son. They lived nicely, in a small apartment in Manhattan. This boy at about fifteen became a junkie, which is not unusual in our neighborhood. In order to maintain her close friendship with him, she became a junkie too. She said it was part of the youth culture, with which she felt very much at home. After a while, for a number of reasons, the boy gave it all up and left the city and his mother in disgust. Hopeless and alone, she grieved. We all visit her.

"O.K., Pa, that's it," I said, "an unadorned and miserable tale."

"But that's not what I mean," my father said. "You misunderstood me on purpose. You know there's a lot more to it. You know that. You left everything out. Turgenev wouldn't do that. Chekhov wouldn't do that. There are in fact Russian writers you never heard of, you don't have an inkling of, as good as anyone, who can write a plain ordinary story, who would not leave out what you have left out. I object not to facts but to people sitting in trees talking senselessly, voice from who knows where . . ."

"Forget that one, Pa, what have I left out now? In this one?"

"Her looks, for instance."

"Oh. Quite handsome, I think. Yes."

"Her hair?"

"Dark, with heavy braids, as though she were a girl or a foreigner."

"What were her parents like, her stock? That she became such a person. It's interesting, you know."

"From out of town. Professional people. The first to be divorced in their county. How's that? Enough?" I asked.

"With you, it's all a joke," he said. "What about the boy's father? Why didn't you mention him? Who was he? Or was the boy born out of wedlock?"

"Yes," I said. "He was born out of wedlock."

"For godsakes, doesn't anyone in your stories get married? Doesn't anyone have the time to run down to City Hall before they jump into bed?"

"No," I said. "In real life, yes. But in my stories, no."

"Why do you answer me like that?"

"Oh, Pa, this is a simple story about a smart woman who came to N.Y.C. full of interest love trust excitement very up-to-date, and about her son, what a hard time she had in this world. Married or not, it's of small consequence."

"It is of great consequence," he said.

"O.K.," I said.

"O.K. O.K. yourself," he said, "but listen. I believe you that she's good-looking, but I don't think she was so smart."

"That's true," I said. "Actually that's the trouble with stories. People start out fantastic. You think they're extraordinary, but it turns out as the work goes along, they're just average with a good education. Sometimes the other way around, the person's a kind of dumb innocent, but he outwits you and you can't even think of an ending good enough."

"What do you do then?" he asked. He had been a doctor for a couple of decades and then an artist for a couple of decades and he's still interested in details, craft, technique.

"Well, you just have to let the story lie around till some agreement can be reached between you and the stubborn hero."

"Aren't you talking silly, now?" he asked. "Start again," he said. "It so happens I'm not going out this evening. Tell the story again. See what you can do this time."

"O.K.," I said. "But it's not a five-minute job." Second attempt:

Once, across the street from us, there was a fine handsome woman, our neighbor. She had a son whom she loved because she'd known him since birth (in helpless chubby infancy, and in the wrestling, hugging ages, seven to ten, as well as earlier and later). This boy, when he fell into the fist of adolescence, became a junkie. He was not a hopeless one. He was in fact hopeful, an ideologue and successful converter. With his busy brilliance, he wrote persuasive articles for his high-school newspaper. Seeking a wider audience, using important connections, he drummed into Lower Manhattan newsstand distribution a periodical called *Oh! Golden Horse!*

In order to keep him from feeling guilty (because guilt is the stony heart of nine-tenths of all clinically diagnosed cancers in America today, she said), and because she had always believed in giving bad habits room at home where one could keep an eye on them, she too became a junkie. Her kitchen was famous for a while—a center for intellectual addicts who knew what they were doing. A few felt artistic like Coleridge and others were scientific and revolutionary like Leary. Although she was often high herself, certain good mothering reflexes remained, and she saw to it that there was lots of orange juice around and honey and milk and vitamin pills. However, she never cooked anything but chili, and that no more than once a week. She explained, when we talked to her, seriously, with a neighborly concern, that it was her part in the youth culture and she would rather be with the young, it was an honor, than with her own generation.

One week, while nodding through an Antonioni film, this boy was severely jabbed by the elbow of a stern and proselytizing girl, sitting beside him. She offered immediate apricots and nuts for his sugar level, spoke to him sharply, and took him home.

She had heard of him and his work and she herself published, edited, and wrote a competitive journal called *Man Does Live by Bread Alone*. In the organic heat of her continuous presence he could not help but become interested once more in his muscles, his arteries and nerve connections. In fact he began to love them, treasure them, praise them with funny little songs in *Man Does Live . . .*

> the fingers of my flesh transcend
> my transcendental soul
> the tightness in my shoulders end
> my teeth have made me whole

To the mouth of his head (that glory of will and determination) he brought hard apples, nuts, wheat germ, and soybean oil. He said to his old friends, From now on, I guess I'll keep my wits about me. I'm going on the natch. He said he was about to begin a spiritual deep-breathing journey. How about you too, Mom? he asked kindly.

His conversation was so radiant, splendid, that neighborhood kids his age began to say that he had never been a real addict at all, only a journalist along for the smell of the story. The mother tried several times to give up what had become without her son and his friends a lonely habit. This effort only brought it to supportable levels. The boy and his girl took their electronic mimeograph and moved to the bushy edge of another borough. They were very strict. They said they would not see her again until she had been off drugs for sixty days.

At home alone in the evening, weeping, the mother read and reread the seven issues of *Oh! Golden Horse!* They seemed to her as truthful as ever. We often crossed the street to visit and console. But if we mentioned any of our children who were at college or in the hospital or dropouts at home, she would cry out, My baby! My baby! and burst into terrible, face-scarring, time-consuming tears. The End.

First my father was silent, then he said, "Number One: You have a nice sense of humor. Number Two: I see you can't tell a plain story. So don't waste time." Then he said sadly, "Number Three: I suppose that means she was alone, she was left like that, his mother. Alone. Probably sick?"

I said, "Yes."

"Poor woman. Poor girl, to be born in a time of fools, to live among fools. The end. The end. You were right to put that down. The end."

I didn't want to argue, but I had to say, "Well, it is not necessarily the end, Pa."

"Yes," he said, "what a tragedy. The end of a person."

"No, Pa," I begged him. "It doesn't have to be. She's only about forty. She could be a hundred different things in this world as time goes on. A teacher or a social worker. An ex-junkie! Sometimes it's better than having a master's in education."

"Jokes," he said. "As a writer that's your main trouble. You don't want to recognize it. Tragedy! Plain tragedy! Historical tragedy! No hope. The end."

"Oh, Pa," I said. "She could change."

"In your own life too you have to look it in the face." He took a couple of nitroglycerin. "Turn to five," he said, pointing to the dial on the oxygen tank. He inserted the tubes into his nostrils and breathed deep. He closed his eyes and said, "No."

I had promised the family to always let him have the last word when arguing, but in this case I had a different responsibility. That woman lives across the street. She's my knowledge and my invention. I'm sorry for her. I'm not going to leave her there in that house crying. (Actually neither would Life, which unlike me has no pity.)

Therefore: She did change. Of course her son never came home again. But right now, she's the receptionist in a storefront community clinic in the East Village. Most of the customers are young people, some old friends. The head doctor has said to her, "If we only had three people in this clinic with your experiences . . ."

"The doctor said that?" My father took the oxygen tubes out of his nostrils and said, "Jokes. Jokes again."

"No, Pa, it could really happen that way, it's a funny world nowadays."

"No," he said. "Truth first. She will slide back. A person must have character. She does not."

"No, Pa," I said. "That's it. She's got a job. Forget it. She's in that storefront working."

"How long will it be?" he asked. "Tragedy! You too. When will you look it in the face?"

The Long-Distance Runner

One day, before or after forty-two, I became a long-distance runner. Though I was stout and in many ways inadequate to this desire, I wanted to go far and fast, not as fast as bicycles and trains, not as far as Taipei, Hingwen, places like that, islands of the slant-eyed cunt, as sailors in bus stations say when speaking of travel, but round and round the county from the seaside to the bridges, along the old neighborhood streets a couple of times, before old age and urban renewal ended them and me.

I tried the country first, Connecticut, which being wooded is always full of buds in spring. All creation is secret, isn't that true? So I trained in the wide-zoned suburban hills where I wasn't known. I ran all spring in and out of dogwood bloom, then laurel.

People sometimes stopped and asked me why I ran, a lady in silk shorts halfway down over her fat thighs. In training, I replied and rested only to answer if closely questioned. I wore a white sleeveless undershirt as well, with excellent support, not to attract the attention of old men and prudish children.

Then summer came, my legs seemed strong. I kissed the kids

goodbye. They were quite old by then. It was near the time for parting anyway. I told Mrs. Raftery to look in now and then and give them some of that rotten Celtic supper she makes.

I told them they could take off any time they wanted. To lead your private life, I said. Only leave me out of it.

A word to the wise . . . said Richard.

You're depressed Faith, Mrs. Raftery said. Your boyfriend Jack, the one you think's so hotsy-totsy, hasn't called and you're as gloomy as a tick on Sunday.

Cut the folkshit with me, Raftery, I muttered. Her eyes filled with tears because that's who she is: folkshit from bunion to top-knot. That's how she got liked by me, loved, invented, and endured.

When I walked out the door they were all reclining before the television set, Richard, Tonto, and Mrs. Raftery, gazing at the news. Which proved with moving pictures that there *had* been a voyage to the moon and Africa and South America hid in a furious whorl of clouds.

I said, Goodbye. They said, Yeah, O.K., sure.

If that's how it is, forget it, I hollered and took the Independent subway to Brighton Beach.

At Brighton Beach I stopped at the Salty Breezes Locker Room to change my clothes. Twenty-five years ago my father invested $500 in its future. In fact he still clears about $3.50 a year, which goes directly (by law) to the Children of Judea to cover their deficit.

No one paid too much attention when I started to run, easy and light on my feet. I ran on the boardwalk first, past my mother's leafleting station—between a soft-ice-cream stand and degenerated dune. There she had been assigned by her comrades to halt the tides of cruel American enterprise with simple socialist sense.

I wanted to stop and admire the long beach. I want to stop in order to think admiringly about New York. There aren't many rotting cities so tan and sandy and speckled with citizens at their salty edges. But I had already spent a lot of life lying down or standing and staring. I had decided to run.

After about a mile and a half I left the boardwalk and began to trot into the old neighborhood. I was running well. My breath was long and deep. I was thinking pridefully about my form.

Suddenly I was surrounded by about three hundred blacks.

Who you?

Who that?

Look at her! Just look! When you seen a fatter ass?

Poor thing. She ain't right. Leave her, you boys, you bad boys.

I used to live here, I said.

Oh yes, they said, in the white old days. That time too bad to last.

But we loved it here. We never went to Flatbush Avenue or Times Square. We loved our block.

Tough black titty.

I like your speech, I said. Metaphor and all.

Right on. We get that from talking.

Yes my people also had a way of speech. And don't forget the Irish. The gift of gab.

Who they? said a small boy.

Cops.

Nowadays, I suggested, there's more than Irish on the police force.

You right, said two ladies. More more, much much more. They's French Chinamen Russkies Congoleans. Oh missee, you too right.

I lived in that house, I said. That apartment house. All my life. Till I got married.

Now that *is* nice. Live in one place. My mother live that way in South Carolina. One place. Her daddy farmed. She said. They ate. No matter winter war bad times. Roosevelt. Something! Ain't that wonderful! And it weren't cold! Big trees!

That apartment. I looked up and pointed. There. The third floor.

They all looked up. So what! You blubrous devil! said a dark young man. He wore horn-rimmed glasses and had that intelligent look that City College boys used to have when I was eighteen and first looked at them.

He seemed to lead them in contempt and anger, even the littlest ones who moved toward me with dramatic stealth singing, Devil, Oh Devil. I don't think the little kids had bad feeling because they poked a finger into me, then laughed.

Still I thought it might be wise to keep my head. So I jumped right in with some facts. I said, How many flowers' names do you know? Wildflowers, I mean. My people only knew two. That's what they say now anyway. Rich or poor, they only had two flowers' names. Rose and violet.

Daisy, said one boy immediately.

Weed, said another. That *is* a flower, I thought. But everyone else got the joke.

Saxifrage, lupine, said a lady. Viper's bugloss, said a small Girl Scout in medium green with a dark green sash. She held up a *Handbook of Wildflowers*.

How many you know, fat mama? a boy asked warmly. He wasn't against my being a mother or fat. I turned all my attention to him.

Oh sonny, I said, I'm way ahead of my people. I know in yellows alone: common cinquefoil, trout lily, yellow adder's-tongue, swamp buttercup and common buttercup, golden sorrel, yellow or hop clover, devil's-paintbrush, evening primrose, black-eyed Susan, golden aster, also the yellow pickerelweed growing down by the water if not in the water, and dandelions of course. I've seen all these myself. Seen them.

You could see China from the boardwalk, a boy said. When it's nice.

I know more flowers than countries. Mostly young people these days have traveled in many countries.

Not me. I ain't been nowhere.

Not me either, said about seventeen boys.

I'm not allowed, said a little girl. There's drunken junkies.

But *I! I!* cried out a tall black youth, very handsome and well dressed. I am an African. My father came from the high stolen plains. *I* have been everywhere. I was in Moscow six months, learning machinery. I was in France, learning French. I was in Italy, observing the peculiar Renaissance and the people's sweetness. I was in England, where I studied the common law and the urban blight. I was at the Conference of Dark Youth in Cuba to understand our passion. I am now here. Here am I to become an engineer and return to my people, around the Cape of Good Hope in a Norwegian sailing vessel. In this way I will learn the fine old art of sailing in case the engines of the new society of my old inland country should fail.

We had an extraordinary amount of silence after that. Then one old lady in a black dress and high white lace collar said to another old lady dressed exactly the same way, Glad tidings when someone got brains in the head not fish juice. Amen, said a few.

Whyn't you go up to Mrs. Luddy living in your house, you lady, huh? The Girl Scout asked this.

Why she just groove to see you, said some sarcastic snickerer.

She got palpitations. Her man, he give it to her.

That ain't all, he a natural gift-giver.

I'll take you, said the Girl Scout. My name is Cynthia. I'm in Troop 355, Brooklyn.

I'm not dressed, I said, looking at my lumpy knees.

You shouldn't wear no undershirt like that without no runnin number or no team writ on it. It look like a undershirt.

Cynthia! Don't take her up there, said an important boy. Her head strange. Don't you take her. Hear?

Lawrence, she said softly, you tell me once more what to do I'll wrap you round that lamppost.

Git! she said, powerfully addressing *me*.

In this way I was led into the hallway of the whole house of my childhood.

The first door I saw was still marked in flaky gold, 1A. That's where the janitor lived, I said. He was a Negro.

How come like that? Cynthia made an astonished face. How come the janitor was a black man?

Oh Cynthia, I said. Then I turned to the opposite door, first floor front, 1B. I remembered. Now, here, this was Mrs. Goreditsky, very very fat lady. All her children died at birth. Born, then one, two, three. Dead. Five children, then Mr. Goreditsky said, I'm bad luck on you Tessie and he went away. He sent $15 a week for seven years. Then no one heard.

I know her, poor thing, said Cynthia. The city come for her summer before last. The way they knew, it smelled. They wropped her up in a canvas. They couldn't get through the front door. It scraped off a piece of her. My Uncle Ronald had to help them, but he got disgusted.

Only two years ago. She was still here! Wasn't she scared?

So we all, said Cynthia. White ain't everything.

Who lived up here, she asked, 2B? Right now, my best friend Nancy Rosalind lives here. She got two brothers, and her sister married and got a baby. She very light-skinned. Not her mother. We got all colors amongst us.

Your best friend? That's funny. Because it was *my* best friend. Right in that apartment. Joanna Rosen.

What become of her? Cynthia asked. She got a running shirt too?

Come on Cynthia, if you really want to know, I'll tell you. She married this man, Marvin Steirs.

Who's he?

I recollected his achievements. Well, he's the president of a big corporation, JoMar Plastics. This corporation owns a steel company, a radio station, a new Xerox-type machine that lets you do twenty-five different pages at once. This corporation has a foundation. The JoMar Fund for Research in Conservation. Capitalism is like that, I added, in order to be politically useful.

How come you know? You go over their house a lot?

No. I happened to read all about them on the financial page, just last week. It made me think: a different life. That's all.

Different spokes for different folks, said Cynthia.

I sat down on the cool marble steps and remembered Joanna's cousin Ziggie. He was older than we were. He wrote a poem which told us we were lovely flowers and our legs were petals, which nature would force open no matter how many times we said no.

Then I had several other interior thoughts that I couldn't share with a child, the kind that give your face a blank or melancholy look.

Now you're not interested, said Cynthia. No you're not gonna say a thing. Who lived here, 2A? Who? Two men lives here now. Women coming and women going. My mother says, Danger sign: Stay away, my darling, stay away.

I don't remember, Cynthia. I really don't.

You got to. What'd you come for, anyways?

Then I tried. 2A. 2A. Was it the twins? I felt a strong obligation as though remembering was in charge of the *existence* of the past. This is not so.

Cynthia, I said, I don't want to go any further. I don't even want to remember.

Come on, she said, tugging at my shorts, don't you want to see Mrs. Luddy, the one lives in your old house? That be fun, no?

No. No, I don't want to see Mrs. Luddy.

Now you shouldn't pay no attention to those boys downstairs. She will like you. I mean, she is kind. She don't like most white people, but she might like you.

No Cynthia, it's not that, but I don't want to see my father and mother's house now.

I didn't know what to say. I said, Because my mother's dead. This was a lie, because my mother lives in her own room with my father in the Children of Judea. With her hand over her socialist heart, she reads the paper every morning after breakfast. Then she says sadly to my father, Every day the same. Dying . . . dying, dying from killing.

My mother's dead Cynthia. I can't go in there.

Oh . . . oh, the poor thing, she said, looking into my eyes. Oh if my mother died, I don't know what I'd do. Even if I was old as you. I could kill myself. Tears filled her eyes and started down her cheeks. If my mother died, what would I do? She is my protector, she won't let the pushers get me. She hold me tight. She gonna hide me in the cedar box if my Uncle Rudford comes try to get me back. She *can't* die, my mother.

Cynthia—honey—she won't die. She's young. I put my arm out to comfort her. You could come live with me, I said. I got two boys, they're nearly grown up. I missed it, not having a girl.

What? What you mean now, live with you and boys. She pulled away and ran for the stairs. Stay away from me, honky lady. I know them white boys. They just gonna try and jostle my black woman-hood. My mother told me about that, keep you white honky devil boys to your devil self, you just leave me be you old bitch you. Some-body help me, she started to scream, you hear. Somebody help. She gonna take me away.

She flattened herself to the wall, trembling. I was too frightened by her fear of me to say, Honey, I wouldn't hurt you, it's me. I heard her helpers, the voices of large boys crying, We coming, we com-ing, hold your head up, we coming. I ran past her fear to the stairs and up them two at a time. I came to my old own door. I knocked like the landlord, loud and terrible.

Mama not home, a child's voice said. No, no, I said. It's me! a lady! Someone's chasing me, let me in. Mama not home, I ain't allowed to open up for nobody.

It's me! I cried out in terror. Mama! Mama! let me in!

The door opened. A slim woman whose age I couldn't invent looked at me. She said, Get in and shut that door tight. She took a hard pinching hold on my upper arm. Then she bolted the door herself. Them hustlers after you. They make me pink. Hide this white lady now, Donald. Stick her under your bed, you got a high bed.

Oh that's O.K. I'm fine now, I said. I felt safe and at home.

You in my house, she said. You do as I say. For two cents, I throw you out.

I squatted under a small kid's pissy mattress. Then I heard the knock. It was tentative and respectful. My mama don't allow me to open. Donald! someone called. Donald!

Oh no, he said. Can't do it. She gonna wear me out. You know her. She already tore up my ass this morning once. Ain't *gonna* open up.

I lived there for about three weeks with Mrs. Luddy and Donald and three little baby girls nearly the same age. I told her a joke about Irish twins. Ain't Irish, she said.

Nearly every morning the babies woke us at about 6:45. We gave them all a bottle and went back to sleep till 8:00. I made coffee and she changed diapers. Then it really stank for a while. At this time I usually said, Well listen, thanks really, but I've got to go I guess. I guess I'm going. She'd usually say, Well, guess again. *I* guess you ain't. Or if she was feeling disgusted she'd say, Go on now! Get! You wanna go, I guess by now I have snorted enough white lady stink to choke a horse. Go on!

I'd get to the door and then I'd hear voices. I'm ashamed to say I'd become fearful. Despite my wide geographical love of mankind, I would be attacked by local fears.

There was a sentimental truth that lay beside all that going and not going. It *was* my house where I'd lived long ago my family life. There was a tile on the bathroom floor that I myself had broken, dropping a hammer on the toe of my brother Charles as he stood dreamily shaving, his prick halfway up his undershorts. Astonishment and knowledge first seized me right there. The kitchen was the same. The table was the enameled table common to our class, easy to clean, with wooden undercorners for indigent and old cock-roaches that couldn't make it to the kitchen sink. (However, it was not the same table, because I have inherited that one, chips and all.)

The living room was something like ours, only we had less plas-tic. There may have been less plastic in the world at that time. Also, my mother had set beautiful cushions everywhere, on beds and chairs. It was the way she expressed herself, artistically, to embroi-der at night or take strips of flowered cotton and sew them across ordinary white or blue muslin in the most delicate designs, the way women have always used materials that live and die in hunks and tatters to say: This is my place.

Mrs. Luddy said, Uh huh!

Of course, I said, men don't have that outlet. That's how come they run around so much.

Till they drunk enough to lay down, she said.

Yes, I said, on a large scale you can see it in the world. First they make something, then they murder it. Then they write a book about how interesting it is.

You got something there, she said. Sometimes she said, Girl, you don't know *nothing*.

We often sat at the window looking out and down. Little tufts of breeze grew on that windowsill. The blazing afternoon was around the corner and up the block.

You say men, she said. Is that men? she asked. What you call— a Man?

Four flights below us, leaning on the stoop, were about a dozen people and around them devastation. Just a minute, I said. I had seen devastation on my way, running, gotten some of the pebbles of it in my running shoe and the dust of it in my eyes. I had thought with the indignant courtesy of a citizen, This is a disgrace to the City of New York, which I love and am running through.

But now, from the commanding heights of home, I saw it clearly. The tenement in which Jack my old and present friend had come to gloomy manhood had been destroyed, first by fire, then by demolition (which is a swinging ball of steel that cracks bedrooms and kitchens). Because of this work, we could see several blocks wide and a block and a half long. That weird guy Eddy—his house still stood, famous 1510 gutted, with black window frames, no glass, open laths. The stubbornness of the supporting beams! Some persons or families still lived on the lowest floors. In the lots between, a couple of old sofas lay on their fat faces, their springs sticking up into the air. Just as in wartime a half dozen ailanthus trees had already found their first quarter inch of earth and begun a living attack on the dead yards. At night, I knew animals roamed the place, squalling and howling, furious New York dogs and street cats and mighty rats. You would think you were in Bear Mountain Park, the terror of venturing forth.

Someone ought to clean that up, I said.

Mrs. Luddy said, Who you got in mind? Mrs. Kennedy?—

Donald made a stern face. He said, That just what I gonna do when I get big. Gonna get the Sanitary Man in and show it to him. You see that, you big guinea you, you clean it up right now! Then he stamped his feet and fierced his eyes.

Mrs. Luddy said, Come here, you little nigger. She kissed the top of his head and gave him a whack on the backside all at one time.

Well, said Donald, encouraged, look out there now you all! Go on I say, look! Though we had already seen, to please him we looked. On the stoop men and boys lounged, leaned, hopped about, stood on one leg, then another, took their socks off, and scratched their toes, talked, sat on their haunches, heads down, dozing.

Donald said, Look at them. They ain't got self-respect. They got Afros *on* their heads, but they don't know they black *in* their heads.

I thought he ought to learn to be more sympathetic. I said, There are reasons that people are that way.

Yes, ma'am, said Donald.

Anyway, how come you never go down and play with the other kids, how come you're up here so much?

My mama don't like me do that. Some of them is bad. Bad. I might become a dope addict. I got to stay clear.

You just a dope, that's a fact, said Mrs. Luddy.

He ought to be with kids his age more, I think.

He see them in school, miss. Don't trouble your head about it if you don't mind.

Actually, Mrs. Luddy didn't go down into the street either. Donald did all the shopping. She let the welfare investigator in, the meterman came into the kitchen to read the meter. I saw him from the back room, where I hid. She did pick up her check. She cashed it. She returned to wash the babies, change their diapers, wash clothes, iron, feed people, and then in free half hours she sat by that window. She was waiting.

I believed she was watching and waiting for a particular man. I wanted to discuss this with her, talk lovingly like sisters. But before I could freely say, Forget about that son of a bitch, he's a pig, I did have to offer a few solid facts about myself, my kids, about fathers, husbands, passersby, evening companions, and the life of my father and mother in this room by this exact afternoon window.

I told her, for instance, that in my worst times I had given myself one extremely simple physical pleasure. This was cream cheese for breakfast. In fact, I insisted on it, sometimes depriving the children of very important articles and food.

Girl, you don't know nothing, she said.

Then for a little while she talked gently as one does to a person who is innocent and insane and incorruptible because of stupidity. She had had two such special pleasures for hard times, she said. The first, men, but they turned rotten, white women had ruined the best, give them the idea their dicks made of solid gold. The second pleasure she had tried was wine. She said, I do like wine. You *has* to have something just for yourself by yourself. Then she said, But you can't raise a decent boy when you liquor-dazed every night.

White or black, I said, returning to men, they did think they were bringing a rare gift, whereas it was just sex, which is common like bread, though essential.

Oh, you can do without, she said. There's folks does without.

I told her Donald deserved the best. I loved him. If he had flaws, I hardly noticed them. It's one of my beliefs that children do not have flaws, even the worst do not.

Donald was brilliant—like my boys except that he had an easier disposition. For this reason I decided, almost the second moment of my residence in that household, to bring him up to reading level at once. I told him we would work with books and newspapers. He went immediately to his neighborhood library and brought some hard books to amuse me. *Black Folktales* by Julius Lester and *The Pushcart War*, which is about another neighborhood but relevant.

Donald always agreed with me when we talked about reading and writing. In fact, when I mentioned poetry, he told me he knew all about it, that David Henderson, a known black poet, had visited his second-grade class. So Donald was, as it turned out, well ahead of my nosy tongue. He was usually very busy shopping. He also had to spend a lot of time making faces to force the little serious baby girls into laughter. But if the subject came up, he could take *the* poem right out of the air into which language and event had just gone.

An example: That morning, his mother had said, Whew, I just got too much piss and diapers and wash. I wanna just sit down by that window and rest myself. He wrote a poem:

> *Just got too much pissy diapers*
> *and wash and wash*
> *just wanna sit down by that window*
> *and look out*
> > *ain't nothing there.*

Donald, I said, you are plain brilliant. I'm never going to forget you. For godsakes don't you forget me.

You fool with him too much, said Mrs. Luddy. He already don't even remember his grandma, you never gonna meet someone like her, a curse never come past her lips.

I do remember, Mama, I remember. She lying in bed, right there. A man standing in the door. She say, Esdras, I put a curse on you head. You worsen tomorrow. How come she said like that?

Gomorrah, I believe Gomorrah, she said. She know the Bible inside out.

Did she live with you?

No. No, she visiting. She come up to see us all, her children, how we doing. She come up to see sights. Then she lay down and died. She was old.

I remained quiet because of the death of mothers. Mrs. Luddy looked at me thoughtfully, then she said:

My mama had stories to tell, she raised me on. *Her* mama was a little thing, no sense. Stand in the door of the cabin all day, sucking her thumb. It was slave times. One day a young field boy come storming along. He knock on the door of the first cabin hollering, Sister, come out, it's freedom. She come out. She say, Yeah? When? He say, Now! It's freedom now! Then he knock at the next door and say, Sister! It's freedom! Now! From one cabin he run to the next cabin, crying out, Sister, it's freedom now!

Oh I remember that story, said Donald. Freedom now! Freedom now! He jumped up and down.

You don't remember nothing boy. Go on, get Eloise, she want to get into the good times.

Eloise was two but undersized. We got her like that, said Donald. Mrs. Luddy let me buy her ice cream and green vegetables. She was waiting for kale and chard, but it was too early. The kale liked cold. You not about to be here November, she said. No, no. I turned away, lonesomeness touching me, and sang our Eloise song:

> *Eloise loves the bees*
> *the bees they buzz*
> *like Eloise does*

Then Eloise crawled all over the splintery floor, buzzing wildly.
Oh you crazy baby, said Donald, buzz buzz buzz.

Mrs. Luddy sat down by the window.

You all make a lot of noise, she said sadly. You just right on noisy.
The next morning Mrs. Luddy woke me up.

Time to go, she said.

What?

Home.

What? I said.

Well, don't you think your little spoiled boys crying for you?
Where's Mama? They standing in the window. Time to go lady. This
ain't Free Vacation Farm. Time we was by ourself a little.

Oh Ma, said Donald, she ain't a lot of trouble. Go on, get Eloise,
she hollering. And button up your lip.

She didn't offer me coffee. She looked at me strictly all the time.
I tried to look strictly back, but I failed because I loved the sight
of her.

Donald was teary, but I didn't dare turn my face to him, until
the parting minute at the door. Even then, I kissed the top of his
head a little too forcefully and said, Well, I'll see you.

On the front stoop there were about half a dozen mid-morning
family people and kids arguing about who had dumped garbage
out of which window. They were very disgusted with one another.

Two young men in handsome dashikis stood in counsel and
agreement at the street corner. They divided a comment. How come
white womens got rotten teeth? And look so old? A young woman
waiting at the light said, Hush . . .

I walked past them and didn't begin my run till the road opened
up somewhere along Ocean Parkway. I was a little stiff because my
way of life had used only small movements, an occasional stretch to
put a knife or teapot out of reach of the babies. I ran about ten,
fifteen blocks. Then my second wind came, which is classical, famous among runners, it's the beginning of flying.

In the three weeks I'd been off the street, jogging had become popular. It seemed that I was only one person doing her thing, which happened like most American eccentric acts to be the most "in" thing I could have done. In fact, two young men ran alongside of me for nearly a mile. They ran silently beside me and turned off at Avenue H. A gentleman with a mustache, running poorly in the opposite direction, waved. He called out, Hi, señora.

Near home I ran through our park, where I had aired my children on weekends and late-summer afternoons. I stopped at the northeast playground, where I met a dozen young mothers intelligently handling their little ones. In order to prepare them, meaning no harm, I said, In fifteen years, you girls will be like me, wrong in everything.

At home it was Saturday morning. Jack had returned looking as grim as ever, but he'd brought cash and a vacuum cleaner. While the coffee perked, he showed Richard how to use it. They were playing ticktacktoe on the dusty wall.

Richard said, Well! Look who's here! Hi!

Any news? I asked.

Letter from Daddy, he said. From the lake and water country in Chile. He says it's like Minnesota.

He's never been to Minnesota, I said. Where's Anthony?

Here I am, said Tonto, appearing. But I'm leaving.

Oh yes, I said. Of course. Every Saturday he hurries through breakfast or misses it. He goes to visit his friends in institutions. These are well-known places like Bellevue, Hillside, Rockland State, Central Islip, Manhattan. These visits take him all day and sometime half the night.

I found some chocolate-chip cookies in the pantry. Take them, Tonto, I said. I remember nearly all his friends as little boys and girls always hopping, skipping, jumping, and cookie-eating. He was annoyed. He said, No! Chocolate cookies is what the commissaries are full of. How about money?

Jack dropped the vacuum cleaner. He said, No! They have parents for that.

I said, Here, five dollars for cigarettes, one dollar each.

Cigarettes! said Jack. Goddamnit! Black lungs and death! Cancer! Emphysema! He stomped out of the kitchen, breathing. He took the bike from the back room and started for Central Park, which has been closed to cars but opened to bicycle riders. When he'd been gone about ten minutes, Anthony said, It's really open only on Sundays.

Why didn't you say so? Why can't you be decent to him? I asked. It's important to me.

Oh Faith, he said, patting me on the head because he'd grown so tall, all that air. It's good for lungs. And his muscles! He'll be back soon.

You should ride too, I said. You don't want to get mushy in your legs. You should go swimming once a week.

I'm too busy, he said. I have to see my friends.

Then Richard, who had been vacuuming under his bed, came into the kitchen. You still here, Tonto?

Going going gone, said Anthony, don't bat your eye.

Now listen, Richard said, here's a note. It's for Judy, if you get as far as Rockland. Don't forget it. Don't open it. Don't read it. I know he'll read it.

Anthony smiled and slammed the door.

Did I lose weight? I asked. Yes, said Richard. You look O.K. You never look too bad. But where were you? I got sick of Raftery's boiled potatoes. Where were you, Faith?

Well! I said. Well! I stayed a few weeks in my old apartment, where Grandpa and Grandma and me and Hope and Charlie lived, when we were little. I took you there long ago. Not so far from the ocean where Grandma made us very healthy with sun and air.

What are you talking about? said Richard. Cut the baby talk.

Anthony came home earlier than expected that evening because some people were in shock therapy and someone else had run away. He listened to me for a while. Then he said, I don't know what she's talking about either.

Neither did Jack, despite understanding often produced by love after absence. He said, Tell me again. He was in a good mood. He said, You can even tell it to me twice.

I repeated the story. They all said, What?

Because it isn't usually so simple. Have you known it to happen much nowadays? A woman inside the steamy energy of middle age runs and runs. She finds the houses and streets where her childhood happened. She lives in them. She learns as though she was still a child what in the world is coming next.

FROM *Later the Same Day*

Friends

To put us at our ease, to quiet our hearts as she lay dying, our dear friend Selena said, Life, after all, has not been an unrelieved horror—you know, I *did* have many wonderful years with her.

She pointed to a child who leaned out of a portrait on the wall—long brown hair, white pinafore, head and shoulders forward.

Eagerness, said Susan. Ann closed her eyes.

On the same wall three little girls were photographed in a schoolyard. They were in furious discussion; they were holding hands. Right in the middle of the coffee table, framed, in autumn colors, a handsome young woman of eighteen sat on an enormous horse—aloof, disinterested, a rider. One night this young woman, Selena's child, was found in a rooming house in a distant city, dead. The police called. They said, Do you have a daughter named Abby?

And with *him* too, our friend Selena said. We had good times, Max and I. You know that.

There were no photographs of *him*. He was married to another woman and had a new, stalwart girl of about six, to whom no harm would ever come, her mother believed.

Our dear Selena had gotten out of bed. Heavily but with a comic dance, she soft-shoed to the bathroom, singing, "Those were the days, my friend . . ."

Later that evening, Ann, Susan, and I were enduring our five-hour train ride to home. After one hour of silence and one hour of coffee and the sandwiches Selena had given us (she actually stood, leaned her big soft excavated body against the kitchen table to make those sandwiches), Ann said, Well, we'll never see *her* again.

Who says? Anyway, listen, said Susan. Think of it. Abby isn't the only kid who died. What about that great guy, remember Bill Dalrymple—he was a non-cooperator or a deserter? And Bob Simon. They were killed in automobile accidents. Matthew, Jeannie, Mike. Remember Al Lurie—he was murdered on Sixth Street—and that little kid Brenda, who O.D.'d on your roof, Ann? The tendency, I suppose, is to forget. You people don't remember them.

What do you mean, "you people"? Ann asked. You're talking to *us*.

I began to apologize for not knowing them all. Most of them were older than my kids, I said.

Of course, the child Abby was exactly in my time of knowing and in all my places of paying attention—the park, the school, our street. But oh! It's true! Selena's Abby was not the only one of that beloved generation of our children murdered by cars, lost to war, to drugs, to madness.

Selena's main problem, Ann said—you know, she didn't tell the truth.

What?

A few hot human truthful words are powerful enough, Ann thinks, to steam all God's chemical mistakes and society's slimy lies out of her life. We all believe in that power, my friends and I, but sometimes . . . the heat.

Anyway, I always thought Selena had told us a lot. For instance, we knew she was an orphan. There were six, seven other children. She was the youngest. She was forty-two years old before someone informed her that her mother had *not* died in childbirthing her. It was some terrible sickness. And she had lived close to her mother's body—at her breast, in fact—until she was eight months old. Whew! said Selena. What a relief! I'd always felt I was the one who'd killed her.

Your family stinks, we told her. They really held you up for grief.

Oh, people, she said. Forget it. They did a lot of nice things for me too. Me and Abby. Forget it. Who has the time?

That's what I mean, said Ann. Selena should have gone after them with an ax.

More information: Selena's two sisters brought her to a Home. They were ashamed that at sixteen and nineteen they could not take care of her. They kept hugging her. They were sure she'd cry. They took her to her room—not a room, a dormitory with about eight beds. This is your bed, Lena. This is your table for your things. This little drawer is for your toothbrush. All for me? she asked. No one else can use it? Only me. That's all? Artie can't come? Franky can't come? Right?

Believe me, Selena said, those were happy days at Home.

Facts, said Ann, just facts. Not necessarily the *truth*.

I don't think it's right to complain about the character of the dying or start hustling all their motives into the spotlight like that. Isn't it amazing enough, the bravery of that private inclusive intentional community?

It wouldn't help not to be brave, said Selena. You'll see.

She wanted to get back to bed. Susan moved to help her.

Thanks, our Selena said, leaning on another person for the first time in her entire life. The trouble is, when I stand, it hurts me here all down my back. Nothing they can do about it. All the chemotherapy. No more chemistry left in me to therapeut. Ha! Did you know before I came to New York and met you I used to work in that hospital? I was supervisor in gynecology. Nursing. They were my friends, the doctors. They weren't so snotty then. David Clark, big surgeon. He couldn't look at me last week. He kept saying, Lena . . .

Lena . . . Like that. We were in North Africa the same year—'44, I think. I told him, Davy, I've been around a long enough time. I haven't missed too much. He knows it. But I didn't want to make him look at me. Ugh, my damn feet are a pain in the neck.

Recent research, said Susan, tells us that it's the neck that's a pain in the feet.

Always something new, said Selena, our dear friend.

On the way back to the bed, she stopped at her desk. There were about twenty snapshots scattered across it—the baby, the child, the young woman. Here, she said to me, take this one. It's a shot of Abby and your Richard in front of the school—third grade? What a day! The show those kids put on! What a bunch of kids! What's Richard doing now?

Oh, who knows? Horsing around someplace. Spain. These days, it's Spain. Who knows where he is? They're all the same.

Why did I say that? I knew exactly where he was. He writes. In fact, he found a broken phone and was able to call every day for a week—mostly to give orders to his brother but also to say, Are you O.K., Ma? How's your new boyfriend, did he smile yet?

The kids, they're all the same, I said.

It was only politeness, I think, not to pour my boy's light, noisy face into that dark afternoon. Richard used to say in his early mean teens, You'd sell us down the river to keep Selena happy and innocent. It's true. Whenever Selena would say, I don't know, Abby has some peculiar friends, I'd answer for stupid comfort, You should see Richard's.

Still, he's in Spain, Selena said. At least you know that. It's probably interesting. He'll learn a lot. Richard is a wonderful boy, Faith. He acts like a wise guy but he's not. You know the night Abby died, when the police called me and told me? That was my first night's sleep in two years. I *knew* where she was.

Selena said this very matter-of-factly—just offering a few informative sentences.

But Ann, listening, said, Oh!—she called out to us all, Oh!—

and began to sob. Her straightforwardness had become an arrow and gone right into her own heart.

Then a deep tear-drying breath: I want a picture too, she said.

Yes. Yes, wait, I have one here someplace. Abby and Judy and that Spanish kid Victor. Where is it? Ah. Here!

Three nine-year-old children sat high on that long-armed syca-more in the park, dangling their legs on someone's patient head—smooth dark hair, parted in the middle. Was that head Kitty's?

Our dear friend laughed. Another great day, she said. Wasn't it? I remember you two sizing up the men. I *had* one at the time—I thought. Some joke. Here, take it. I have two copies. But you ought to get it enlarged. When this you see, remember me. Ha-ha. Well, girls—excuse me, I mean ladies—it's time for me to rest.

She took Susan's arm and continued that awful walk to her bed.

We didn't move. We had a long journey ahead of us and had expected a little more comforting before we set off.

No, she said. You'll only miss the express. I'm not in much pain. I've got lots of painkiller. See?

The tabletop was full of little bottles.

I just want to lie down and think of Abby.

It was true, the local could cost us an extra two hours at least. I looked at Ann. It had been hard for her to come at all. Still, we couldn't move. We stood there before Selena in a row. Three old friends. Selena pressed her lips together, ordered her eyes into cold distance.

I know that face. Once, years ago, when the children were children, it had been placed modestly in front of J. Hoffner, the principal of the elementary school.

He'd said, No! Without training you cannot tutor these kids. There are real problems. You have to know *how to teach*.

Our P.T.A. had decided to offer some one-to-one tutorial help for the Spanish kids, who were stuck in crowded classrooms with exhausted teachers among little middle-class achievers. He had said, in a written communication to show seriousness and then in personal confrontation to *prove* seriousness, that he could not allow it. And the Board of Ed. itself had said no. (All this no-ness was to lead to some terrible events in the schools and neighborhoods of our poor yes-requiring city.) But most of the women in our P.T.A. were independent—by necessity and disposition. We were, in fact, the soft-speaking tough souls of anarchy.

I had Fridays off that year. At about 11 a.m. I'd bypass the principal's office and run up to the fourth floor. I'd take Robert Figueroa to the end of the hall, and we'd work away at storytelling for about twenty minutes. Then we would write the beautiful letters of the alphabet invented by smart foreigners long ago to fool time and distance.

That day, Selena and her stubborn face remained in the office for at least two hours. Finally, Mr. Hoffner, besieged, said that because she was a nurse, she would be allowed to help out by taking the littlest children to the modern difficult toilet. Some of them, he said, had just come from the barbarous hills beyond Maricao. Selena said O.K., she'd do that. In the toilet she taught the little girls which way to wipe, as she had taught her own little girl a couple years earlier. At three o'clock she brought them home for cookies and milk. The children of that year ate cookies in her kitchen until the end of the sixth grade.

Now, what did we learn in that year of my Friday afternoons off? The following: Though the world cannot be changed by talking to one child at a time, it may at least be known.

Anyway, Selena placed into our eyes for long remembrance that useful stubborn face. She said, No. Listen to me, you people. Please. I don't have lots of time. What I want . . . I want to lie down and think about Abby. Nothing special. Just think about her, you know.

In the train Susan fell asleep immediately. She woke up from time to time, because the speed of the new wheels and the resistance of the old track gave us some terrible jolts. Once, she opened her eyes wide and said, You know, Ann's right. You don't get sick like that for nothing. I mean, she didn't even mention him.

Why should she? She hasn't even seen him, I said. Susan, you still have him-itis, the dread disease of females.

Yeah? And you don't? Anyway, he *was* around quite a bit. He was there every day, nearly, when the kid died.

Abby. I didn't like to hear "the kid." I wanted to say "Abby" the way I've said "Selena"—so those names can take thickness and strength and fall back into the world with their weight.

Abby, you know, was a wonderful child. She was in Richard's classes every class till high school. Good-hearted little girl from the beginning, noticeably kind—for a kid, I mean. Smart.

That's true, said Ann, very kind. She'd give away Selena's last shirt. Oh yes, they were all wonderful little girls and wonderful little boys.

Chrissy *is* wonderful, Susan said.

She *is*, I said.

Middle kids aren't supposed to be, but she is. She put herself through college—I didn't have a cent—and now she has this fellowship. And, you know, she never did take any crap from boys. She's something.

Ann went swaying up the aisle to the bathroom. First she said, Oh, all of them—just wohunderful.

I loved Selena, Susan said, but she never talked to me enough. Maybe she talked to you women more, about things. Men.

Then Susan fell asleep.

Ann sat down opposite me. She looked straight into my eyes with a narrow squint. It often connotes accusation.

Be careful—you're wrecking your laugh lines, I said.

Screw you, she said. You're kidding around. Do you realize I don't know where Mickey is? You know, you've been lucky. You always have been. Since you were a little kid. Papa and Mama's darling.

As is usual in conversations, I said a couple of things out loud and kept a few structured remarks for interior mulling and righteousness. I thought: She's never even met my folks. I thought: What a rotten thing to say. Luck—isn't it something like an insult?

I said, Annie, I'm only forty-eight. There's lots of time for me to be totally wrecked—if I live, I mean.

Then I tried to knock wood, but we were sitting in plush and leaning on plastic. Wood! I shouted. Please, some wood! Anybody here have a matchstick?

Oh, shut up, she said. Anyway, death doesn't count.

I tried to think of a couple of sorrows as irreversible as death. But truthfully nothing in my life can compare to hers: a son, a boy of fifteen, who disappears before your very eyes into a darkness or a light behind his own, from which neither hugging nor hitting can bring him. If you shout, Come back, come back, he won't come. Mickey, Mickey, Mickey, we once screamed, as though he were twenty miles away instead of right in front of us in a kitchen chair; but he refused to return. And when he did, twelve hours later, he left immediately for California.

Well, some bad things have happened in my life, I said.

What? You were born a woman? Is that it?

She was, of course, mocking me this time, referring to an old discussion about feminism and Judaism. Actually, on the prism of isms, both of those do have to be looked at together once in a while.

Well, I said, my mother died a couple of years ago and I still feel it. I think *Ma* sometimes and I lose my breath. I miss her. You understand that. Your mother's seventy-six. You have to admit it's nice still having her.

She's very sick, Ann said. Half the time she's out of it.

I decided not to describe my mother's death. I could have done so and made Ann even more miserable. But I thought I'd save that for her next attack on me. These constrictions of her spirit were coming closer and closer together. Probably a great enmity was about to be born.

Susan's eyes opened. The death or dying of someone near or

dear often makes people irritable, she stated. (She's been taking a course in relationships *and* interrelationships.) The real name of my seminar is Skills: Personal Friendship and Community. It's a very good course despite your snide remarks.

While we talked, a number of cities passed us, going in the opposite direction. I had tried to look at New London through the dusk of the windows. Now I was missing New Haven. The conductor explained, smiling: Lady, if the windows were clean, half of you'd be dead. The tracks are lined with sharpshooters.

Do you believe that? I hate people to talk that way.

He may be exaggerating, Susan said, but don't wash the window.

A man leaned across the aisle. Ladies, he said, I do believe it. According to what I hear of this part of the country, it don't seem unplausible.

Susan turned to see if he was worth engaging in political dialogue.

You've forgotten Selena already, Ann said. All of us have. Then you'll make this nice memorial service for her and everyone will stand up and say a few words and then we'll forget her again—for good. What'll you say at the memorial, Faith?

It's not right to talk like that. She's not dead yet, Annie.

Yes, she is, said Ann.

We discovered the next day that give or take an hour or two, Ann had been correct. It was a combination—David Clark, surgeon, said—of being sick unto real death and having a tabletop full of little bottles.

Now, why are you taking all those hormones? Susan had asked Selena a couple of years earlier. They were visiting New Orleans. It was Mardi Gras.

Oh, they're mostly vitamins, Selena said. Besides, I want to be young and beautiful. She made a joking pirouette.

Susan said, That's absolutely ridiculous.

But Susan's seven or eight years younger than Selena. What did she know? Because: People *do* want to be young and beautiful. When they meet in the street, male or female, if they're getting older they look at each other's face a little ashamed. It's clear they want to say, Excuse me, I didn't mean to draw attention to mortality and gravity all at once. I didn't want to remind you, my dear friend, of our coming eviction, first from liveliness, then from life. To which, most of the time, the friend's eyes will courteously reply, My dear, it's nothing at all. I hardly noticed.

Luckily, I learned recently how to get out of that deep well of melancholy. Anyone can do it. You grab at roots of the littlest future, sometimes just stubs of conversation. Though some believe you miss a great deal of depth by not sinking down down down.

Susan, I asked, you still seeing Ed Flores?

Went back to his wife.

Lucky she didn't kill you, said Ann. I'd never fool around with a Spanish guy. They all have tough ladies back in the barrio.

No, said Susan, she's unusual. I met her at a meeting. We had an amazing talk. Luisa is a very fine woman. She's one of the office-worker organizers I told you about. She only needs him two more years, she says. Because the kids—they're girls—need to be watched a little in their neighborhood. The neighborhood is definitely not good. He's a good father but not such a great husband.

I'd call that a word to the wise.

Well, you know me—I don't want a husband. I like a male person around. I hate to do without. Anyway, listen to this. She, Luisa, whispers in my ear the other day, she whispers, Suzie, in two years you still want him, I promise you, you got him. Really, I may still want him then. He's only about forty-five now. Still got a lot of spunk. I'll have my degree in two years. Chrissy will be out of the house.

Two years! In two years we'll all be dead, said Ann.

I know she didn't mean all of us. She meant Mickey. That boy of hers would surely be killed in one of the drugstores or whorehouses of Chicago, New Orleans, San Francisco. I'm in a big beautiful city, he said when he called last month. Makes New York look like a garbage tank.

Mickey! Where?

Ha-ha, he said, and hung up.

Soon he'd be picked up for vagrancy, dealing, small thievery, or simply screaming dirty words at night under a citizen's window. Then Ann would fly to the town or not fly to the town to disentangle him, depending on a confluence of financial reality and psychiatric advice.

How *is* Mickey? Selena had said. In fact, that was her first sentence when we came, solemn and embarrassed, into her sunny front room that was full of the light and shadow of windy courtyard trees. We said, each in her own way, How are you feeling, Selena? She said, O.K., first things first. Let's talk about important things. How's Richard? How's Tonto? How's John? How's Chrissy? How's Judy? How's Mickey?

I want to talk about Mickey, said Ann.

Oh, let's talk about him, talk about him, Selena said, taking Ann's hand. Let's all think before it's too late. How did it start? Oh, for godsakes talk about him.

Susan and I were smart enough to keep our mouths shut.

Nobody knows, nobody knows anything. Why? Where? Everybody has an idea, theories, and writes articles. Nobody knows.

Ann said this sternly. She didn't whine. She wouldn't lean too far into Selena's softness, but listening to Selena speak Mickey's name, she could sit in her chair more easily. I watched. It was interesting. Ann breathed deeply in and out the way we've learned in our Thursday-night yoga class. She was able to rest her body a little bit.

We were riding the trails of the trough called Park-Avenue-in-the-Bronx. Susan had turned from us to talk to the man across the aisle. She was explaining that the war in Vietnam was not yet over and would not be, as far as she was concerned, until we repaired the dikes we'd bombed and paid for some of the hopeless ecological damage. He didn't see it that way. Fifty thousand American lives, our own boys—we'd paid, he said. He asked us if we agreed with Susan. Every word, we said.

You don't look like hippies. He laughed. Then his face changed. As the resident face-reader, I decided he was thinking: Adventure. He may have hit a mother lode of late counterculture in three opinionated left-wing ladies. That was the nice part of his face. The other part was the sly out-of-town-husband-in-New-York look.

I'd like to see you again, he said to Susan.

Oh? Well, come to dinner day after tomorrow. Only two of my kids will be home. You ought to have at least one decent meal in New York.

Kids? His face thought it over. Thanks. Sure, he said. I'll come.

Ann muttered, She's impossible. She did it again.

Oh, Susan's O.K., I said. She's just right in there. Isn't that good? This is a long ride, said Ann.

Then we were in the darkness that precedes Grand Central.

We're irritable, Susan explained to her new pal. We're angry with our friend Selena for dying. The reason is, we want her to be present when we're dying. We all require a mother or mother-surrogate to fix our pillows on that final occasion, and we were counting on her to be that person.

I know just what you mean, he said. You'd like to have someone around. A little fuss, maybe.

Something like that. Right, Faith?

It always takes me a minute to slide under the style of her public-address system. I agreed. Yes.

The train stopped hard, in a grinding agony of opposing technologies.

Right. Wrong. Who cares? Ann said. She didn't have to die. She really wrecked everything.

Oh, Annie, I said.

Shut up, will you? Both of you, said Ann, nearly breaking our knees as she jammed past us and out of the train.

Then Susan, like a New York hostess, began to tell that man all our private troubles—the mistake of the World Trade Center, Westway, the decay of the South Bronx, the rage in Williamsburg. She rose with him on the escalator, gabbing into evening friendship and, hopefully, a happy night.

At home Anthony, my youngest son, said, Hello, you just missed Richard. He's in Paris now. He had to call collect.

Collect? From Paris?

He saw my sad face and made one of the herb teas used by his peer group to calm their overwrought natures. He does want to improve my pretty good health and spirits. His friends have a book that says a person should, if properly nutritioned, live forever. He wants me to give it a try. He also believes that the human race, its brains and good looks, will end in his time.

At about 11:30 he went out to live the pleasures of his eighteen-year-old nighttime life.

At 3 a.m. he found me washing the floors and making little apartment repairs.

More tea, Mom? he asked. He sat down to keep me company. O.K., Faith. I know you feel terrible. But how come Selena never realized about Abby?

Anthony, what the hell do I realize about you?

Come on, you had to be blind. I was just a little kid, and *I* saw. Honest to God, Ma.

Listen, Tonto. Basically Abby was O.K. She was. You don't know yet what their times can do to a person.

Here she goes with her goody-goodies—everything is so groovy wonderful far-out terrific. Next thing, you'll say people are darling and the world is *so* nice and round that Union Carbide will never blow it up.

I have never said anything as hopeful as that. And why to all our knowledge of that sad day did Tonto at 3 a.m. have to add the fact of the world?

The next night Max called from North Carolina. How's Selena?

I'm flying up, he said. I have one early-morning appointment. Then I'm canceling everything.

At 7 a.m. Annie called. I had barely brushed my morning teeth. It was hard, she said. The whole damn thing. I don't mean Selena. All of us. In the train. None of you seemed real to me.

Real? Reality, huh? Listen, how about coming over for breakfast?—I don't have to get going until after nine. I have this neat sourdough rye?

No, she said. Oh Christ, no. No!

I remember Ann's eyes and the hat she wore the day we first looked at each other. Our babies had just stepped howling out of the sandbox on their new walking legs. We picked them up. Over their sandy heads we smiled. I think a bond was sealed then, at least as useful as the vow we'd all sworn with husbands to whom we're no longer married. Hindsight, usually looked down upon, is probably as valuable as foresight, since it does include a few facts.

Meanwhile, Anthony's world—poor, dense, defenseless thing—rolls round and round. Living and dying are fastened to its surface and stuffed into its softer parts.

He was right to call my attention to its suffering and danger. He was right to harass my responsible nature. But I was right to invent for my friends and our children a report on these private deaths and the condition of our lifelong attachments.

Mother

One day I was listening to the AM radio. I heard a song: "Oh, I long to See My Mother in the Doorway." By God! I said, I understand that song. I have often longed to see my mother in the doorway. As a matter of fact, she did stand frequently in various doorways looking at me. She stood one day, just so, at the front door, the darkness of the hallway behind her. It was New Year's Day. She said sadly, If you come home at 4 a.m. when you're seventeen, what time will you come home when you're twenty? She asked this question without humor or meanness. She had begun her worried preparations for death. She would not be present, she thought, when I was twenty. So she wondered.

Another time she stood in the doorway of my room. I had just issued a political manifesto attacking the family's position on the Soviet Union. She said, Go to sleep for godsakes, you damn fool, you and your Communist ideas. We saw them already, Papa and me, in 1905. We guessed it all.

At the door of the kitchen she said, You never finish your lunch. You run around senselessly. What will become of you?

Then she died.

Naturally for the rest of my life I longed to see her, not only in doorways, in a great number of places—in the dining room with my aunts, at the window looking up and down the block, in the country garden among zinnias and marigolds, in the living room with my father.

They sat in comfortable leather chairs. They were listening to Mozart. They looked at one another amazed. It seemed to them that they'd just come over on the boat. They'd just learned the first English words. It seemed to them that he had just proudly handed in a 100 percent correct exam to the American anatomy professor. It seemed as though she'd just quit the shop for the kitchen.

I wish I could see her in the doorway of the living room.

She stood there a minute. Then she sat beside him. They owned an expensive record player. They were listening to Bach. She said to him, Talk to me a little. We don't talk so much anymore.

I'm tired, he said. Can't you see? I saw maybe thirty people today. All sick, all talk talk talk talk. Listen to the music, he said. I believe you once had perfect pitch. I'm tired, he said.

Then she died.

Ruthy and Edie

One day in the Bronx two small girls named Edie and Ruthy were sitting on the stoop steps. They were talking about the real world of boys. Because of this, they kept their skirts pulled tight around their knees. A gang of boys who lived across the street spent at least one hour of every Saturday afternoon pulling up girls' dresses. They needed to see the color of a girl's underpants in order to scream outside the candy store, Edie wears pink panties.

Ruthy said, anyway, she liked to play with those boys. They did more things. Edie said she hated to play with them. They hit and picked up her skirt. Ruthy agreed. It *was* wrong of them to do this. But, she said, they ran around the block a lot, had races, and played war on the corner. Edie said it wasn't *that* good.

Ruthy said, Another thing, Edie, you could be a soldier if you're a boy.

So? What's so good about that?

Well, you could fight for your country.

Edie said, I don't want to.

What? Edie! Ruthy was a big reader and most interesting

reading was about bravery—for instance Roland's Horn at Ron-
cevaux. Her father had been brave and there was often a lot of discussion about this at suppertime. In fact, he sometimes modestly
said, Yes, I suppose I was brave in those days. And so was your
mother, he added. Then Ruthy's mother put his boiled egg in front
of him where he could see it. Reading about Roland, Ruthy learned
that if a country wanted to last, it would require a great deal of
bravery. She nearly cried with pity when she thought of Edie and
the United States of America.

You don't want to? she asked.

No.

Why, Edie, why?

I don't feel like.

Why, Edie? How come?

You always start hollering if I don't do what you tell me. I don't
always have to say what you tell me. I can say whatever I like.

Yeah, but if you love your country you have to go fight for it.
How come you don't want to? Even if you get killed, it's worth it.

Edie said, I don't want to leave my mother.

Your mother? You must be a baby. Your mother?

Edie pulled her skirt very tight over her knees. I don't like it
when I don't see her a long time. Like when she went to Springfield to my uncle. I don't like it.

Oh boy! said Ruthy. Oh boy! What a baby! She stood up. She
wanted to go away. She just wanted to jump from the top step, run
down to the corner, and wrestle with someone. She said, You know,
Edie, this is *my* stoop.

Edie didn't budge. She leaned her chin on her knees and felt
sad. She was a big reader too, but she liked *The Bobbsey Twins* or
Honey Bunch at the Seashore. She loved that nice family life. She tried
to live it in the three rooms on the fourth floor. Sometimes she
called her father Dad, or even Father, which surprised him. Who?
he asked.

I have to go home now, she said. My cousin Alfred's coming.

She looked to see if Ruthy was still mad. Suddenly she saw a dog. Ruthy, she said, getting to her feet. There's a dog coming. Ruthy turned. There *was* a dog about three-quarters of the way down the block between the candy store and the grocer's. It was an ordinary middle-sized dog. But it *was* coming. It didn't stop to sniff at curbs or pee on the house fronts. It just trotted steadily along the middle of the sidewalk.

Ruthy watched him. Her heart began to thump and take up too much space inside her ribs. She thought speedily, Oh, a dog has teeth! It's large, hairy, strange. Nobody can say what a dog is thinking. A dog is an animal. You could talk to a dog, but a dog couldn't talk to you. If you said to a dog, STOP! a dog would just keep going. If it's angry and bites you, you might get rabies. It will take you about six weeks to die and you will die screaming in agony. Your stomach will turn into a rock and you will have lockjaw. When they find you, your mouth will be paralyzed wide open in your dying scream.

Ruthy said, I'm going right now. She turned as though she'd been directed by some far-off switch. She pushed the hall door open and got safely inside. With one hand she pressed the apartment bell. With the other she held the door shut. She leaned against the glass door as Edie started to bang on it. Let me in, Ruthy, let me in, please. Oh, Ruthy!

I can't. Please, Edie, I just can't.

Edie's eyes rolled fearfully toward the walking dog. It's coming. Oh, Ruthy, please, please.

No! No! said Ruthy.

The dog stopped right in front of the stoop to hear the screaming and banging. Edie's heart stopped too. But in a minute he decided to go on. He passed. He continued his easy steady pace.

When Ruthy's big sister came down to call them for lunch, the two girls were crying. They were hugging each other and their hair was a mess. You two are nuts, she said. If I was Mama, I wouldn't let you play together so much every single day. I mean it.

Many years later in Manhattan it was Ruthy's fiftieth birthday. She had invited three friends. They waited for her at the round kitchen table. She had been constructing several pies so that this birthday could be celebrated in her kitchen during the day by any gathered group without too much trouble. Now and then one of the friends would say, Will you sit down, for godsakes! She would sit immediately. But in the middle of someone's sentence or even one of her own, she'd jump up with a look of worry beyond household affairs to wash a cooking utensil or wipe crumbs of flour off the Formica counter.

Edie was one of the women at the table. She was sewing, by neat hand, a new zipper into an old dress. She said, Ruthy, it wasn't like that. We both ran in and out a lot.

No, said Ruth. You would never have locked me out. You were an awful sissy, sweetie, but you would never, never have locked me out. Just look at yourself. Look at your life!

Edie glanced, as people will, when told to do that. She saw a chubby dark-haired woman who looked like a nice short teacher, someone who stood at the front of the schoolroom and said, History is a wonderful subject. It's all stories. It's where we come from, who we are. For instance, where do you come from, Juan? Where do your parents and grandparents come from?

You know that, Mizz Seiden. Porto Rico. You know that a long-o time-o, Juan said, probably in order to mock both languages. Edie thought, Oh, to whom would he speak?

For Christsakes, this is a party, isn't it? said Ann. She was patting a couple of small cases and a projector on the floor next to her chair. Was she about to offer a slide show? No, she had already been prevented from doing this by Faith, who'd looked at the clock two or three times and said, I don't have the time, Jack is coming tonight. Ruth had looked at the clock too. Next week, Ann? Ann said O.K. O.K. But Ruthy, I want to say you have to quit knocking yourself. I've seen you do a million good things. If you were such a dud, why'd I write it down in my will that if anything happened to me, you and Joe were the ones who'd raise my kids.

You were just plain wrong. I couldn't even raise my own right.

Ruthy, really, they're pretty much raised. Anyway, how can you say an awful thing like that? Edie asked. They're wonderful beautiful brilliant girls. Edie knew this because she had held them in her arms the third or fourth day of life. Naturally, she became the friend called aunt.

That's true. I don't have to worry about Sara anymore, I guess.

Why? Because she's a married mommy? Faith asked. What an insult to Edie!

No, that's O.K., said Edie.

Well, I do worry about Rachel. I just can't help myself. I never know where she is. She was supposed to be here last night. She does usually call. Where the hell is she?

Oh, probably in jail for some stupid little sit-in or something, Ann said. She'll get out in five minutes. Why she thinks that kind of thing works is a mystery to me. You brought her up like that and now you're surprised. Besides which, I don't want to talk about the goddamn kids, said Ann. Here I've gone around half of most of the nearly socialist world and nobody asks me a single question. I have been a witness of events! she shouted.

I do want to hear everything, said Ruth. Then she changed her mind. Well, I don't mean everything. Just say one good thing and one bad thing about every place you've been. We only have a couple of hours. (It was four o'clock. At six, Sara and Tomas with Letty, the first grandchild, standing between them would be at the door. Letty would probably think it was her own birthday party. Someone would say, What curly hair! They would all love her new shoes and her newest sentence, which was Remember dat? Because for such a long time there had been only the present full of milk and looking. Then one day, trying to dream into an afternoon nap, she sat up and said, Gramma, I boke your cup. Remember dat? In this simple way the lifelong past is invented, which, as we know, thickens the present and gives all kinds of advice to the future.) So, Ann, I mean just a couple of things about each country.

That's not much of a discussion, for Christsake.

It's a party, Ann, you said it yourself.

Well, change your face, then.

Oh. Ruth touched her mouth, the corners of her eyes. You're right. Birthday! she said.

Well, let's go, then, said Ann. She stated two good things and one bad thing about Chile (an earlier visit), Rhodesia, the Soviet Union, and Portugal.

You forgot about China. Why don't you tell them about our trip to China?

I don't think I will, Ruthy; you'd only contradict every word I say.

Edie, the oldest friend, stripped a nice freckled banana she'd been watching during Ann's talk. The thing is, Ruth, you never simply say yes. I've told you so many times, *I* would have slammed the door on you, admit it, but it was your house, and that slowed me down.

Property, Ann said. Even among poor people, it begins early.

Poor? asked Edie. It was the Depression.

Two questions—Faith believed she'd listened patiently long enough. I love that story, but I've heard it before. Whenever you're down in the dumps, Ruthy. Right?

I haven't, Ann said. How come, Ruthy? Also, will you please sit with us.

The second question: What about this city? I mean, I'm kind of sick of these big international reports. Look at this place, looks like a toxic waste dump. A war. Nine million people.

Oh, that's true, Edie said, but Faith, the whole thing *is* hopeless. Top to bottom, the streets, those kids, dumped, plain dumped. That's the correct word, "dumped." She began to cry.

Cut it out, Ann shouted. No tears, Edie! No! Stop this minute! I swear, Faith said, you'd better stop that! (They were all, even

Edie, ideologically, spiritually, and on puritanical principle against despair.)

Faith was sorry to have mentioned the city in Edie's presence. If you said the word "city" to Edie, or even the cool adjective "municipal," specific children usually sitting at the back of the room appeared before her eyes and refused to answer when she called on them. So Faith said, O.K. New subject: What do you women think of the grand juries they're calling up all over the place?

All over what place? Edie asked. Oh, Faith, forget it, they're going through something. You know you three lead such adversarial lives. I hate it. What good does it do? Anyway, those juries will pass.

Edie, sometimes I think you're half asleep. You know that woman in New Haven who was called? I know her personally. She wouldn't say a word. She's in jail. They're not kidding.

I'd never open my mouth either, said Ann. Never. She clamped her mouth shut then and there.

I believe you, Ann. But sometimes, Ruth said, I think, Supposed I was in Argentina and they had my kid. God, if they had our Sara's Letty, I'd maybe say anything.

Oh, Ruth, you've held up pretty well, once or twice, Faith said.

Yes, Ann said, in fact we were all pretty good that day, we were sitting right up against the horses' knees at the draft board—were you there, Edie? And then the goddamn horses started to rear and the cops were knocking people on their backs and heads—remember? And, Ruthy, I was watching you. You just suddenly plowed in and out of those monsters. You should have been trampled to death. And you grabbed the captain by his gold buttons and you hollered, You bastard! Get your goddamn cavalry out of here. You shook him and shook him.

He ordered them, Ruth said. She set one of her birthday cakes, which was an apple plum pie, on the table. I saw him. He was the responsible person. I saw the whole damn operation. I'd begun to run—the horses—but I turned because I was the one supposed to be in front and I saw him give the order. I've never honestly been so angry.

Ann smiled. Anger, she said. That's really good.

You think so? Ruth asked. You sure?

Buzz off, said Ann.

Ruth lit the candles. Come on, Ann, we've got to blow this out together. And make a wish. I don't have the wind I used to have.

But you're still full of hot air, Edie said. And kissed her hard. What did you wish, Ruthy? she asked.

Well, a wish, some wish, Ruth said. Well, I wish that this world wouldn't end. This world, this world, Ruth said softly.

Me too, I wished exactly the same. Taking action, Ann hoisted herself up onto a kitchen chair, saying, ugh my back, ouch my knee. Then: Let us go forth with fear and courage and rage to save the world.

Bravo, Edie said softly.

Wait a minute, said Faith . . .

Ann said, Oh, you . . . you . . .

But it was six o'clock and the doorbell rang. Sara and Tomas stood on either side of Letty, who was hopping or wiggling with excitement, hiding behind her mother's long skirt or grabbing her father's thigh. The door had barely opened when Letty jumped forward to hug Ruth's knees. I'm gonna sleep in your house, Gramma.

I know, darling, I know.

Gramma, I slept in your bed with you. Remember dat?

Oh sure, darling, I remember. We woke up around five and it was still dark and I looked at you and you looked at me and you had a great big Letty smile and we just burst out laughing and you laughed and I laughed.

I remember dat, Gramma. Letty looked at her parents with shyness and pride. She was still happy to have found the word "remember," which could name so many pictures in her head.

And then we went right back to sleep, Ruth said, kneeling now to Letty's height to kiss her little face.

Where's my Aunt Rachel? Letty asked, hunting among the crowd of unfamiliar legs in the hallway.

I don't know.

She's supposed to be here, Letty said. Mommy, you promised. She's really supposed.

Yes, said Ruth, picking Letty up to hug her and then hug her again. Letty, she said as lightly as she could, She *is* supposed to be here. But where can she be? She certainly is supposed.

Letty began to squirm out of Ruth's arms. Mommy, she called, Gramma is squeezing. But it seemed to Ruth that she'd better hold her even closer, because, though no one else seemed to notice— Letty, rosy and soft-cheeked as ever, was falling, already falling, falling out of her brand-new hammock of world-inventing words onto the hard floor of man-made time.

Zagrowsky Tells

I was standing in the park under that tree. They call it the Hanging Elm. Once upon a time it made a big improvement on all kinds of hooligans. Nowadays if, once in a while . . . No. So this woman comes up to me, a woman minus a smile. I said to my grandson, Uh oh, Emanuel. Here comes a lady, she was once a beautiful customer of mine in the pharmacy I showed you.

Emanuel says, Grandpa, who?

She looks O.K. now, but not so hot. Well, what can you do, time takes a terrible toll off the ladies.

This is her idea of a hello: Iz, what are you doing with that black child? Then she says, Who is he? Why are you holding on to him like that? She gives me a look like God in judgment. You could see it in famous paintings. Then she says, Why are you yelling at that poor kid?

What yelling? A history lesson about the park. This is a tree in guidebooks. How are you by the way, Miss . . . Miss . . . I was embarrassed. I forgot her name absolutely.

Well, who is he? You got him pretty scared.

Me? Don't be ridiculous. It's my grandson. Say hello Emanuel, don't put on an act.

Emanuel shoves his hand in my pocket to be a little more glued to me. Are you going to open your mouth sonny yes or no?

She says, Your grandson? Really, Iz, your grandson? What do you mean, your grandson?

Emanuel closes his eyes tight. Did you ever notice children get all mixed up? They don't want to hear about something, they squinch up their eyes. Many children do this.

Now listen Emanuel, I want you to tell this lady who is the smartest boy in kindergarten.

Not a word.

Goddamnit, open your eyes. It's something new with him. Tell her who is the smartest boy—he was just five, he can already read a whole book by himself.

He stands still. He's thinking. I know his little cute mind. Then he jumps up and down yelling, Me me me. He makes a little dance. His grandma calls it his smartness dance. My other ones (three children grown up for some time already) were also very smart, but they don't hold a candle to this character. Soon as I get a chance, I'm gonna bring him to the city to Hunter for gifted children; he should get a test.

But this Miss . . . Miss . . . she's not finished with us yet. She's worried. Whose kid is he? You adopt him?

Adopt? At my age? It's Cissy's kid. You know my Cissy? I see she knows something. Why not? I had a public business. No surprise.

Of course I remember Cissy. She says this, her face is a little more ironed out.

So my Cissy, if you remember, she was a nervous girl.

I'll *bet* she was.

Is that a nice way to answer? Cissy *was* nervous . . . The nervousness, to be truthful, ran in Mrs. Z's family. Ran? Galloped . . . tarum tarum tarum.

When we were young I used to go over there to visit, and while me and her brother and uncles played pinochle, in the kitchen the three aunts would sit drinking tea. Everything was Oi! Oi! Oi! What for? Nothing to oi about. They got husbands . . . Perfectly fine gentlemen. One in business, two of them real professionals. They just got in the habit somehow. So I said to Mrs. Z., one oi out of you and it's divorce.

I remember your wife very well, this lady says. *Very* well. She puts on the same face like before; her mouth gets small. Your wife *is* a beautiful woman.

So . . . would I marry a mutt?

But she was right. My Nettie when she was young, she was very fair, like some Polish Jews you see once in a while. Like for instance maybe some big blond peasant made a pogrom on her great-grandma.

So I answered her, Oh yes, very nice-looking; even now she's not so bad, but a little bit on the grouchy side.

O.K., she makes a big sigh like I'm a hopeless case. What did happen to Cissy?

Emanuel, go over there and play with those kids. No? No.

Well, I'll tell you, it's the genes. The genes are the most important. Environment is O.K. But the genes . . . that's where the whole story is written down. I think the school had something to do with it also. She's more an artist like your husband. Am I thinking of the right guy? When she was a kid you should of seen her. She's a nice-looking girl now, even when she has an attack. But then she was something. The family used to go to the mountains in the summer. We went dancing, her and me. What a dancer. People were surprised. Sometimes we danced until 2 a.m.

I don't think that was good, she says. I wouldn't dance with my son all night . . .

Naturally, you're a mother. But "good," who knows what's good? Maybe a doctor. I could have been a doctor, by the way. Her brother-in-law in business would of backed me. But then what? You don't have the time. People call you day and night. I cured more people in a day than a doctor in a week. Many an M.D. called me, said Zagrowsky, does it work . . . that Parke-Davis medication they put out last month, or it's a fake? I got immediate experience and I'm not too stuck up to tell.

Oh, Iz, you are, she said. She says this like she means it but it makes her sad. How do I know this? Years in a store. You observe. You watch. The customer is always right, but plenty of times you know he's wrong and also a goddamn fool.

All of a sudden I put her in a certain place. Then I said to myself, Iz, why are you standing here with this woman? I looked her straight in the face and I said, Faith? Right? Listen to me. Now you listen, because I got a question. Is it true, no matter what time you called, even if I was closing up, I came to your house with the penicillin or the tetracycline later? You lived on the fourth-floor walk-up. Your friend what's-her-name, Susan, with the three girls next door? I can see it very clear. Your face is all smeared up with crying, your kid got 105°, maybe more, burning up, you didn't want to leave him in the crib screaming, you're standing in the hall, it's dark. You were living alone, am I right? So young. Also your husband, he comes to my mind, very jumpy fellow, in and out, walking around all night. He drank? I betcha. Irish? Imagine you didn't get along so you got a divorce. Very simple. You kids knew how to live.

She doesn't even answer me. She says . . . you want to know what she says? She says, Oh shit! Then she says, Of course I remember. God, my Richie was sick! Thanks, she says, thanks, god-almighty thanks.

I was already thinking something else: The mind makes its own business. When she first came up to me, I couldn't remember. I knew her well, but where? Then out of no place, a word, her bossy face maybe, exceptionally round, which is not usual, her dark apartment, the four flights, the other girls—all once lively, young . . . you could see them walking around on a sunny day, dragging a couple kids, a carriage, a bike, beautiful girls, but tired from all day, mostly divorced, going home alone? Boyfriends? Who knows how that type lives? I had a big appreciation for them. Sometimes, five o'clock I stood in the door to see them. They were mostly the way models *should* be. I mean not skinny—round, like they were made of little cushions and bigger cushions, depending on where you looked; young mothers. I hollered a few words to them, they hollered back. Especially I remember her friend Ruthy—she had two little girls with long black braids, down to here. I told her, In a couple of years, Ruthy, you'll have some beauties on your hands. You better keep an eye on them. In those days the women always answered you in a pleasant way, not afraid to smile. Like this: They said, You really think so? Thanks, Iz.

But this is all used-to-be and in that place there is not only good but bad and the main fact in regard to *this* particular lady: I did her good but to me she didn't always do so much good.

So we stood around a little. Emanuel says, Grandpa, let's go to the swings. Go yourself—it's not so far, there's kids, I see them. No, he says, and stuffs his hand in my pocket again. So don't go— Ach, what a day, I said. Buds and everything. She says, That's a catalpa tree over there. No kidding! I say. What do you call that one, doesn't have a single leaf? Locust, she says. Two locusts, I say.

Then I take a deep breath: O.K.—you still listening? Let me ask you, if I did you so much good including I saved your baby's life, how come you did *that*? You know what I'm talking about. A perfectly nice day. I look out the window of the pharmacy and I see four customers, that I seen at least two in their bathrobes crying to me in the middle of the night, Help help! They're out there with signs. ZAGROWSKY IS A RACIST. YEARS AFTER ROSA PARKS, ZA-GROWSKY REFUSES TO SERVE BLACKS. It's like an etching right *here*. I point out to her my heart. I know exactly where it is.

She's naturally very uncomfortable when I tell her. Listen, she says, we were right.

I grab on to Emanuel. You?

Yes, we wrote a letter first, did you answer it? We said, Zagrowsky, come to your senses. Ruthy wrote it. We said we would like to talk to you. We tested you. At least four times, you kept Mrs. Green and Josie, our friend Josie, who was kind of Spanish black . . . she lived on the first floor in our house . . . you kept them waiting a long time till everyone ahead of them was taken care of. Then you were very rude, I mean nasty, you can be extremely nasty, Iz. And then Josie left the store, she called you some pretty bad names. You remember?

No, I happen not to remember. There was plenty of yelling in the store. People *really* suffering; come in yelling for codeine or what to do their mother was dying. That's what I remember, not some crazy Spanish lady hollering.

But listen, she says—like all this is not in front of my eyes, like the past is only a piece of paper in the yard—you didn't finish with Cissy.

Finish? *You* almost finished my business and don't think that Cissy didn't hold it up to me. Later when she was so sick.

Then I thought, Why should I talk to this woman. I see myself: how I was standing that day how many years ago?—like an idiot behind the counter waiting for customers. Everybody is peeking in past the picket line. It's the kind of neighborhood, if they see a picket line, half don't come in. The cops say they have a right. To destroy a person's business. I was disgusted but I went into the street. After all, I knew the ladies. I tried to explain, Faith, Ruthy, Mrs. Kratt—a stranger comes into the store, naturally you have to serve the old customers first. Anyone would do the same. Also, they sent in black people, brown people, all colors, and to tell the truth I didn't like the idea my pharmacy should get the reputation of being a cut-rate place for them. They move into a neighborhood . . . I did what everyone did. Not to insult people too much, but to discourage them a little, they shouldn't feel so welcome. They could just move in because it's a nice area.

All right. A person looks at my Emanuel and says, Hey! he's not altogether from the white race, what's going on? I'll tell you what: life is going on. You have an opinion. I have an opinion. Life don't have no opinion.

I moved away from this Faith lady. I didn't like to be near her. I sat down on the bench. I'm no spring chicken. Cock-a-doodle-do, I only holler once in a while. I'm tired, I'm mostly the one in charge of our Emanuel. Mrs. Z. stays home, her legs swell up. It's a shame.

In the subway once she couldn't get off at the right stop. The door opens, she can't get up. She tried (she's a little overweight). She says to a big guy with a notebook, a big colored fellow, Please help me get up. He says to her, You kept me down three hundred years, you can stay down another ten minutes. I asked her, Nettie, didn't you tell him we're raising a little boy brown like a coffee bean. But he's right, says Nettie, we done that. We kept them down.

We? We? My two sisters and my father were being fried up for Hitler's supper in 1944 and you say we?

Nettie sits down. Please bring me some tea. Yes, Iz, I say: *We*.

I can't even put up the water I'm so mad. You know, my Mrs., you are crazy like your three aunts, crazy like our Cissy. Your whole family put in the genes to make it for sure that she wouldn't have a chance. Nettie looks at me. She says, Ai ai. She doesn't say oi anymore. She got herself assimilated into ai . . . That's how come she also says "we" done it. Don't think this will make you an American, I said to her, that you included yourself in with Robert E. Lee. Naturally it was a joke, only what is there to laugh?

I'm tired right now. This Faith could even see I'm a little shaky. What should she do, she's thinking. But she decides the discussion ain't over so she sits down sideways. The bench is damp. It's only April.

What about Cissy? Is she all right?

It ain't your business how she is.

O.K. She starts to go.

Wait wait! Since I seen you in your nightgown a couple of times when you were a handsome young woman . . . She really gets up this time. I think she must be a woman's libber, they don't like remarks about nightgowns. Bathrobes, she didn't mind. Let her go! The hell with her . . . but she comes back. She says, Once and for all, cut it out, Iz. I really *want* to know. Is Cissy all right?

You want. She's fine. She lives with me and Nettie. She's in charge of the plants. It's an all-day job.

But why should I leave her off the hook. Oh boy, Faith, I got to say it, what you people put on me! And you want to know how Cissy is. *You!* Why? Sure. You remember you finished with the picket lines after a week or two. I don't know why. Tired? Summer maybe, you got to go away, make trouble at the beach. But I'm stuck there. Did I have air conditioning yet? All of a sudden I see Cissy outside. She has a sign also. She must've got the idea from you women. A big sandwich board, she walks up and down. If someone talks to her, she presses her mouth together.

I don't remember that, Faith says.

Of course, you were already on Long Island or Cape Cod or someplace—the Jersey shore.

No, she says, I was not. I was not. (I see this is a big insult to her that she should go away for the summer.)

Then I thought, Calm down, Zagrowsky. Because for a fact I didn't want her to leave, because, since I already began to tell, I have to tell the whole story. I'm not a person who keeps things in. Tell! That opens up the congestion a little—the lungs are for breathing, no secrets. My wife never tells, she coughs, coughs. All night. Wakes up. Ai, Iz, open up the window, there's no air. You poor woman, if you want to breathe, you got to tell.

So I said to this Faith, I'll tell you how Cissy is but you got to hear the whole story how we suffered. I thought, O.K. Who cares! Let her get on the phone later with the other girls. They should know what they started.

How we took our own Cissy from here to there to the biggest doctor—I had good contacts from the pharmacy. Dr. Francis O'Connel, the heavy Irishman over at the hospital, sat with me and

Mrs. Z. for two hours, a busy man. He explained that it was one of the most great mysteries. They were ignoramuses, the most brilliant doctors were dummies in this field. But still, in my place, I heard of this cure and that one. So we got her massaged fifty times from head to toe, whatever someone suggested. We stuffed her with vitamins and minerals—there was a real doctor in charge of this idea.

If she would take the vitamins—sometimes she shut her mouth. To her mother she said dirty words. We weren't used to it. Meanwhile, in front of my place every morning, she walks up and down. She could of got minimum wage, she was so regular. Her afternoon job is to follow my wife from corner to corner to tell what my wife done wrong to her when she was a kid. Then after a couple months, all of a sudden she starts to sing. She has a beautiful voice. She took lessons from a well-known person. On Christmas week, in front of the pharmacy she sings half of the *Messiah* by Handel. You know it? So that's nice, you think. Oh, that's beautiful. But where were you you didn't notice that she don't have on a coat. You didn't see she walks up and down, her socks are falling off? Her face and hands are like she's the super in the cellar. She sings! she sings! Two songs she sings the most: one is about the Gentiles will see the light and the other is, Look! a virgin will conceive a son. My wife says, Sure, naturally, she wishes she was a married woman just like anyone. Baloney. She could of. She had plenty of dates. Plenty. She sings, the idiots applaud, some skunk yells, Go, Cissy, go. What? Go where? Some days she just hollers.

Hollers what?

Oh, I forgot about you. Hollers anything. Hollers, Racist! Hollers, He sells poison chemicals! Hollers, He's a terrible dancer, he got three left legs! (Which isn't true, just to insult me publicly, plain silly.) The people laugh. What'd she say? Some didn't hear so well; hollers, You go to whores. Also not true. She met me once with a woman actually a distant relative from Israel. Everything is in her head. It's a garbage pail.

One day her mother says to her, Cissile, comb your hair, for godsakes, darling. For this remark, she gives her mother a sock in the face. I come home I see a woman not at all young with two black eyes and a bloody nose. The doctor said, Before it's better with your girl, it's got to be worse. That much he knew. He sent us to a beautiful place, a hospital right at the city line—I'm not sure if it's Westchester or the Bronx, but thank God, you could use the subway. That's how I found out what I was saving up my money for. I thought for retiring in Florida to walk around under the palm trees in the middle of the week. Wrong. It was for my beautiful Cissy, she should have a nice home with other crazy people.

So little by little, she calms down. We can visit her. She shows us the candy store, we give her a couple of dollars; soon our life is this way. Three times a week my wife goes, gets on the subway with delicious foods (no sugar, they're against sugar); she brings something nice, a blouse or a kerchief—a present, you understand, to show love; and once a week I go, but she don't want to look at me. So close we were, like sweethearts—you can imagine how I feel. Well, you have children so you know, little children little troubles, big children big troubles—it's a saying in Yiddish. Maybe the Chinese said it too.

Oh, Iz. How could it happen like that? All of a sudden. No signs?

What's with this Faith? Her eyes are full of tears. Sensitive I suppose. I see what she's thinking. Her kids are teenagers. So far they look O.K. but what will happen? People think of themselves. Human nature. At least she doesn't tell me it's my wife's fault or mine. I did something terrible! I loved my child. I know what's on people's minds. I know psychology *very* well. Since this happened to us, I read up on the whole business.

Oh, Iz . . .

She puts her hand on my knee. I look at her. Maybe she's just a nut. Maybe she thinks I'm plain old (I almost am). Well, I said it before. Thank God for the head. Inside the head is the only place you got to be young when the usual place gets used up. For some reason she gives me a kiss on the cheek. A peculiar person.

Faith, I still can't figure it out why you girls were so rotten to me.

But we were right.

Then this lady Queen of Right makes a small lecture. She don't remember my Cissy walking up and down screaming bad language but she remembers: After Mrs. Kendrick's big fat snotty maid walked out with Kendrick's allergy order, I made a face and said, Ho ho! the great lady! That's terrible? She says whenever I saw a couple walk past on the block, a black-and-white couple, I said, Ugh—disgusting! It shouldn't be allowed! She heard this remark from me a few times. So? It's a matter of taste. Then she tells me about this Josie, probably Puerto Rican, once more—the one I didn't serve in time. Then she says, Yeah, and really, Iz, what about Emanuel?

Don't you look at Emanuel, I said. Don't you dare. He has nothing to do with it.

She rolls her eyes around and around a couple of times. She got more to say. She also doesn't like how I talk to women. She says I called Mrs. Z. a grizzly bear a few times. It's my wife, no? That I was winking and blinking at the girls, a few pinches. A lie . . . maybe I patted, but I never pinched. Besides, I know for a fact a couple of them loved it. She says, No. None of them liked it. Not one. They only put up with it because it wasn't time yet in history to holler. (An American-born girl has some nerve to mention history.)

But, she says, Iz, forget all that. I'm sorry you have so much trouble now. She really is sorry. But in a second she changes her mind. She's not so sorry. She takes her hand back. Her mouth makes a little O.

Emanuel climbs up on my lap. He pats my face. Don't be sad, Grandpa, he says. He can't stand if he sees a tear on a person's face. Even a stranger. If his mama gets a black look, he's smart, he doesn't go to her anymore. He comes to my wife. Grandma, he says, my poor mama is very sad. My wife jumps up and runs in. Worried. Scared. Did Cissy take her pills? What's going on? Once, he went to Cissy and said, Mama, why are you crying? So this is her answer to her little boy: she stands up straight and starts to bang her head on the wall. Hard.

My mama! he screams. Lucky I was home. Since then he goes straight to his grandma for his troubles. What will happen? We're not so young. My oldest son is doing extremely well—only he lives in a very exclusive neighborhood in Rockland County. Our other boy—well, he's in his own life, he's from that generation. He went away.

She looks at me, this Faith. She can't say a word. She sits there. She opens her mouth almost. I know what she wants to know. How did Emanuel come into the story. When?

Then she says to me exactly those words. Well, where does Emanuel fit in?

He fits, he fits. Like a golden present from Nasser.

Nasser?

O.K., Egypt, not Nasser—he's from Isaac's other son, get it? A close relation. I was sitting one day thinking, Why? why? The answer: To remind us. That's the purpose of most things.

It was Abraham, she interrupts me. He had two sons, Isaac and Ishmael. God promised him he would be the father of generations; he was. But you know, she says, he wasn't such a good father to those two little boys. Not so unusual, she has to add on.

You see! That's what they make of the Bible, those women; because they got it in for men. Of *course* I meant Abraham. Abraham. Did I say Isaac? Once in a while I got to admit it, she says something true. You remember one son he sent out of the house altogether, the other he was ready to chop up if he only heard a noise in his head saying, Go! Chop!

But the question is, Where did Emanuel fit. I didn't mind telling. I wanted to tell. I explained that already.

So it begins. One day my wife goes to the administration of

Cissy's hospital and she says, What kind of a place you're running here. I have just looked at my daughter. A blind person could almost see it. My daughter is pregnant. What goes on here at night? Who's the supervisor? Where is she this minute?

Pregnant? they say it like they never heard of it. And they run around and the regular doctor comes and says, Yes, pregnant. Sure. You got more news? my wife says. And then: meetings with the weekly psychiatrist, the day-by-day psychologist, the nerve doctor, the social worker, the supervising nurse, the nurse's aide. My wife says, Cissy knows. She's not an idiot, only mixed up and depressed. She *knows* she has a child in her womb inside of her like a normal woman. She likes it, my wife said. She even said to her, Mama, I'm having a baby, and she gave my wife a kiss. The first kiss in a couple of years. How do you like that?

Meanwhile, they investigated thoroughly. It turns out the man is a colored fellow. One of the gardeners. But he left a couple months ago for the Coast. I could imagine what happened. Cissy always loved flowers. When she was a little girl she was planting seeds every minute and sitting all day in front of the flower pot to see the little flower cracking up the seed. So she must of watched him and watched him. He dug up the earth. He put in the seeds. She watches.

The office apologized. Apologized? An accident. The supervisor was on vacation that week. I could sue them for a million dollars. Don't think I didn't talk to a lawyer. That time, then, when I heard, I called a detective agency to find him. My plan was to kill him. I would tear him limb from limb. What to do next. They called them all in again. The psychiatrist, the psychologist, they only left out the nurse's aide.

The only hope she could live a half-normal life—not in the institutions: she must have this baby, she could carry it full term. No, I said, I can't stand it. I refuse. Out of my Cissy, who looked like a piece of gold, would come a black child. Then the psychologist says, Don't be so bigoted. What nerve! Little by little my wife figured out a good idea. O.K., well, we'll put it out for adoption. Cissy doesn't even have to see it in person.

You are laboring under a misapprehension, says the boss of the place. They talk like that. What he meant, he meant we got to take that child home with us and if we really loved Cissy . . . Then he gave us a big lecture on this baby: it's Cissy's connection to life; also, it happens she was crazy about this gardener, this son of a bitch, a black man with a green thumb.

You see I can crack a little joke because look at this pleasure. I got a little best friend here. Where I go, he goes, even when I go down to the Italian side of the park to play a little bocce with the old goats over there. They invite me if they see me in the supermarket: Hey, Iz! Tony's sick. You come on an' play, O.K.? My wife says, Take Emanuel, he should see how men play games. I take him, those old guys they also seen plenty in their day. They think I'm some kind of a do-gooder. Also, a lot of those people are ignorant. They think the Jews are a little bit colored anyways, so they don't look at him too long. He goes to the swings and they make believe they never even seen him.

I didn't mean to get off the subject. What is the subject? The subject is how we took the baby. My wife, Mrs. Z., Nettie, she plain forced me. She said, We got to take this child on us. I will move out of here into the project with Cissy and be on welfare. Iz, you better make up your mind. Her brother, a top social worker, he encouraged her, I think he's a Communist also, the way he talks the last twenty, thirty years . . .

He says: You'll live, Iz. It's a baby, after all. It's got your blood in it. Unless of course you want Cissy to rot away in that place till you're so poor they don't keep her anymore. Then they'll stuff her into Bellevue or Central Islip or something. First she's a zombie, then she's a vegetable. That's what you want, Iz?

After this conversation I get sick. I can't go to work. Meanwhile, every night Nettie cries. She don't get dressed in the morning. She walks around with a broom. Doesn't sweep up. Starts to sweep, bursts into tears. Puts a pot of soup on the stove, runs into the bedroom, lies down. Soon I think I'll have to put her away too.

I give in.

My listener says to me, Right, Iz, you did the right thing. What else could you do?

I feel like smacking her. I'm not a violent person, just very excitable, but who asked her?—Right, Iz. She sits there looking at me, nodding her head from rightness. Emanuel is finally in the playground. I see him swinging and swinging. He could swing for two hours. He likes that. He's a regular swinger.

Well, the bad part of the story is over. Now is the good part. Naming the baby. What should we name him? Little brown baby. An intermediate color. A perfect stranger.

In the maternity ward, you know where the mothers lie, with the new babies, Nettie is saying, Cissy, Cissile darling, my sweetest heart (this is how my wife talked to her, like she was made of gold—or eggshells), my darling girl, what should we name this little child?

Cissy is nursing. On her white flesh is this little black curly head. Cissy says right away: Emanuel. Immediately. When I hear this, I say, Ridiculous. Ridiculous, such a long Jewish name on a little baby. I got old uncles with such names. Then they all get called Manny. Uncle Manny. Again she says—Emanuel!

David is nice, I suggest in a kind voice. It's your grandpa's, he should rest in peace. Michael is nice too, my wife says. Joshua is beautiful. Many children have these beautiful names nowadays. They're nice modern names. People like to say them.

No, she says, Emanuel. Then she starts screaming, Emanuel Emanuel. We almost had to give her extra pills. But we were careful on account of the milk. The milk could get affected.

O.K., everyone hollered. O.K. Calm yourself, Cissy. O.K. Emanuel. Bring the birth certificate. Write it down. Put it down. Let her see it. Emanuel . . . In a few days, the rabbi came. He raised up his eyebrows a couple times. Then he did his job, which is to make the bris. In other words, a circumcision. This is done so the child will be a man in Israel. That's the expression they use. He isn't the first colored child. They tell me long ago we were mostly dark. Also, now I think of it, I wouldn't mind going over there to Israel. They say there are plenty black Jews. It's not unusual over there at all. They ought to put out more publicity on it. Because I have to think where he should live. Maybe it won't be so good for him here. Because my son, his fancy ideas . . . ach, forget it.

What about the building, your neighborhood, I mean where you live now? Are there other black people in the community?

Oh yeah, but they're very snobbish. Don't ask what they got to be so snobbish.

Because, she says, he should have friends his own color, he shouldn't have the burden of being the only one in school.

Listen, it's New York, it's not Oshkosh, Wisconsin. But she gets going, you can't stop her.

After all, she says, he should eventually know his own people. It's their life he'll have to share. I know it's a problem to you, Iz, I know, but that's the way it is. A friend of mine with the same situation moved to a more integrated neighborhood.

Is that a fact? I say, Where's that?

Oh, there are . . .

I start to tell her, Wait a minute, we live thirty-five years in this apartment. But I can't talk. I sit very quietly for a while, I think and think. I say to myself, Be like a Hindu, Iz, calm like a cucumber. But it's too much. Listen, Miss, Miss Faith—do me a favor, don't teach me.

I'm not teaching you, Iz, it's just . . .

Don't answer me every time I say something. Talking talking. It's true. What for? To whom? Why? Nettie's right. It's our business. She's telling me Emanuel's life.

You don't know nothing about it, I yell at her. Go make a picket line. Don't teach me.

She gets up and looks at me kind of scared. Take it easy, Iz.

Emanuel is coming. He hears me. He got his little worried face. She sticks out a hand to pat him, his grandpa is hollering so loud.

But I can't put up with it. Hands off, I yell. It ain't your kid. Don't lay a hand on him. And I grab his shoulder and push him through the park, past the playground and the big famous arch. She runs after me a minute. Then she sees a couple friends. Now she has what to talk about. There, four women. They make a little bunch. They talk. They turn around, they look. One waves. Hiya, Iz.

This park is full of noise. Everybody got something to say to the next guy. Playing this music, standing on their heads, juggling— someone even brought a piano, can you believe it, some job.

I sold the store four years ago. I couldn't put in the work no more. But I wanted to show Emanuel my pharmacy, what a beautiful place it was, how it sent three children to college, saved a couple lives—imagine: one store!

I tried to be quiet for the boy. You want ice cream, Emanuel? Here's a dollar, sonny. Buy yourself a Good Humor. The man's over there. Don't forget to ask for the change. I bend down to give him a kiss. I don't like that he heard me yell at a woman and my hand is still shaking. He runs a few steps, he looks back to make sure I didn't move an inch.

I got my eye on him too. He waves a chocolate popsicle. It's a little darker than him. Out of that crazy mob a young fellow comes up to me. He has a baby strapped on his back. That's the style now. He asks like it's an ordinary friendly question, points to Emanuel. Gosh what a cute kid. Whose is he? I don't answer. He says it again, Really some cute kid.

I just look in his face. What does he want? I should tell him the story of my life? I don't need to tell. I already told and told. So I said very loud—no one else should bother me—how come it's your business, mister? Who do you think he is? By the way, whose kid you got on your back? It don't look like you.

He says, Hey there buddy, be cool be cool. I didn't mean anything. (You met anyone lately who meant something when he opened his mouth?) While I'm hollering at him, he starts to back away. The women are gabbing in a little clutch by the statue. It's a considerable distance, lucky they got radar. They turn around sharp like birds and fly over to the man. They talk very soft. Why are you bothering this old man, he got enough trouble? Why don't you leave him alone?

The fellow says, I wasn't bothering him. I just asked him something.

Well, he thinks you're bothering him, Faith says.

Then her friend, a woman maybe forty, very angry, starts to holler, How come you don't take care of your own kid? She's crying. Are you deaf? Naturally the third woman makes a remark, doesn't want to be left out. She taps him on his jacket: I seen you around here before, buster, you better watch out. He walks away from them backwards. They start in shaking hands.

Then this Faith comes back to me with a big smile. She says, Honestly, some people are a pain, aren't they, Iz? We sure let him have it, didn't we? And she gives me one of her kisses. Say hello to Cissy—O.K.? She puts her arms around her pals. They say a few words back and forth, like cranking up a motor. Then they burst out laughing. They wave goodbye to Emanuel. Laughing. Laughing. So long, Iz . . . see you . . .

So I say, What is going on, Emanuel, could you explain to me what just happened? Did you notice anywhere a joke? This is the first time he doesn't answer me. He's writing his name on the sidewalk. EMANUEL. Emanuel in big capital letters.

And the women walk away from us. Talking. Talking.

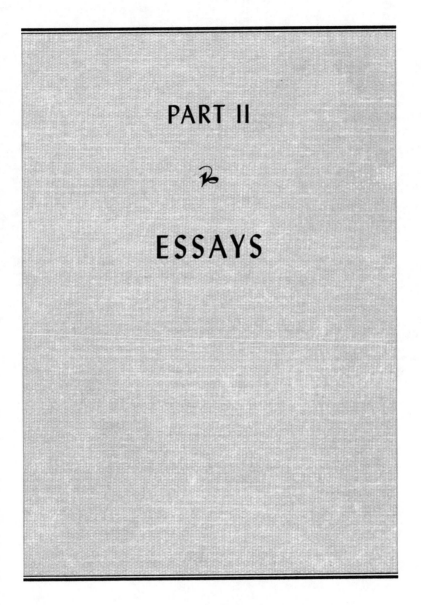

PART II

ESSAYS

FROM *Just As I Thought*

Injustice

When I was about nine years old, I was a member of an organization called the Falcons. We were Socialist youths under twelve. We wore blue shirts and red kerchiefs. We met once a week (or was it once a month?). To the tune of "Maryland, My Maryland," we sang:

> *The workers' flag is deepest red*
> *it shrouded oft our martyr'd dead.*

With the Socialist ending, not the Communist one, we sang the "Internationale." We were warned that we would be tempted to sing the Communist ending, because at our occasional common demonstrations there were more of them singing. They would try, with their sneaky politics, to drown us out.

At our meetings we learned about real suffering, which was due to the Great Depression through which we were living that very year. Of course many of my friends already had this information. Their fathers weren't working. Their mothers had become so grouchy you couldn't ask them for the least little thing. Every day in our neighborhood there were whole apartments, beds, bureaus, kitchen tables out on the street. We understood that this was because of capitalism, which didn't care that working people had no work and no money for rent.

We also studied prejudice—now known as racism. Prejudice was particularly sad, since it meant not liking people for no reason at all, except the color of their skin. That color could happen to anyone if they'd been born to some other parents on another street. We ourselves had known prejudice—well, not us exactly. In Europe, that godforsaken place, our parents and grandparents had known it well. From a photograph over my grandmother's bed, my handsome uncle, killed at seventeen because of prejudice, looked calmly at me when I sought him for reminder's sake. Despite its adherence to capitalism, prejudice, and lynching, my father said we were lucky to be here in this America. We sometimes sang "America the Beautiful" at our meetings. Parents were divided on that.

At each meeting we paid 5 cents or 10 cents—not so much to advance Socialism as to be able to eat cookies at four o'clock. One day at cookie-eating time, our comrade counselor teacher, a young woman about eighteen years old, announced that we were going to do a play. There would be a party too. It would include singing and maybe dancing. We began to rehearse immediately. She had been thinking about all this for a couple of weeks. The idea had matured into practical action.

Our play was simple, a kind of agitprop in which a father comes home; he says "Well, Sarah, the shop closed down today. No more work! And without warning!" The mother is in despair. How to feed the children! The children's breakfast bowls are empty. Some boys carry the furniture (lots of chairs from the meeting room) out to the hall. Eviction! In the second act, the neighbors meet to drag the furniture back, proving working-class solidarity. They then hold a rally and march to City Hall at the back of the room, singing the "Internationale" all the way. The event would have to take place in the evening after supper in case some father or mother still had a job.

I was one of the little empty-bowl children. Every day after school I worked in the bathroom mirror at the creation of a variety of heartrending expressions. But my sweetest contribution would be the song

> One dark night when we were all in bed
> Old mother Leary took a candle to the shed
> and when the cow tipped it over
> she winked her eye and said
> There'll be a hot time in the old town tonight.

This song had been chosen to show we had fun too; our childhood was being respected.

Before supper that important night, I decided to sing for my mother. When I finished, she said gently, lovingly, "Gracie darling, you can't sing. You know you can't hold the tune. The teacher in school, she even said you were a listener. Try again—a little softer . . ."

"I can so sing," I said. "I was picked. I wouldn't of been picked if I couldn't sing." I sang the song once more.

"No no," my mother said. "That girl Sophie, Mrs. Greenberg's Sophie? She has no idea. She has no ear. Maybe deaf even. No no, you can't sing. You'll make a fool of yourself. People will laugh. For Sophie maybe, the more laughing the better."

"I don't care. I have to go. I have to go in a half hour. I have two parts!"

"What? And I'm supposed to sit in the audience and see how your feelings are hurt when they laugh at you. When Papa hears— well, he wouldn't go anyway. That Sophie, she's just a kid herself."

"But, Mama, I have to go."

"No no," she said. "No. You're not going. Just to be a fool. They'll have to figure out what to do."

Guiltless, but full of shame, I never returned to the Falcons. In fact, in sheer spite I gave up my work for Socialism for at least three years.

Fifty years later I told my sister this story. She said, "I can't believe that of Mama—that she would prevent you from singing—especially if you had an obligation. She wasn't like that."

Well, I had developed a kind of class analysis, an explanation which I think is pretty accurate. Our parents, remarkable people, were also a couple of ghetto Jews struggling with hard work and intensive education up the famous American ladder. At a certain rung in that ladder during my childhood they appeared to have climbed right into the professional middle class. At that comfortable rung (probably upholstered), embarrassed panic would be the response to possible exposure.

"Exposure to what? What are you talking about?" my sister asked. "You forget, really. Mama had absolutely perfect pitch. For a person like that your wandering all over the scale must have been torture. I mean real physical pain. To her, you were just screeching. In fact," my sister said, "although you've improved, you still sound that way to me."

My sister has continued to be fourteen years older than I. Neither of us has recovered from that hierarchical fact. So I said, "Okay, Jeanne."

But she had not—when she was nine—been a political person and she had never been a listener. She took singing lessons, then sang. She and my brother practiced the piano like sensible children. In fact, in their eighties they have as much musical happiness in their fingertips as in their heads.

As for my mother—though I had no ear and clearly could not sing, she thought I might try the piano. After all, we had one. There were notes on paper inside a nice yellow book that said *Inventions by Bach* on its cover. Since I was a big reader, I might be able to accomplish *something*. I had no gift. That didn't mean I must be a deprived person. Besides, why had the Enlightenment poured its seductive light all across the European continent right into the poor endangered households of Ukrainian Jews? Probably, my mother thought, so that a child, any child (even a tone deaf one), could be given a chance despite genetic deficiency to become, in my mother's embarrassed hopeful world, a whole person.

(1995)

The Illegal Days

It was the late thirties, and we all knew that birth control existed, but we also knew it was impossible to get. You had to be older and married. You couldn't get anything in drugstores, unless you were terribly sick and had to buy a diaphragm because your womb was falling out. The general embarrassment and misery around getting birth control were real.

There was Margaret Sanger at that time, and she had a clinic right here in Manhattan in a beautiful house on Sixteenth Street; I still walk past and look at it. As brave as the Margaret Sanger people were, they were under very tough strictures. It was scary to go there. I was eighteen, and it was 1940 when I tiptoed in to get a diaphragm. I said I was married.

When I was young, it really angered me that birth control was so hard to get. Kids who were not as sophisticated as we Bronx kids just didn't know what to do. But I never felt that this was happening just to me. I had a very good social sense then from my own political family. I also had a lot of good girl friends, and we used to talk about it together. We had in common this considerable disgust and anger at the whole situation.

I grew up in the Bronx in a puritanical, socialist, Jewish family. My mother was particularly puritanical, and all that sex stuff was very hard for her to talk about—so she didn't. My father was a doctor, but we still didn't talk about such things. I really never felt terribly injured by all that. It just seemed to be the way it was with all my friends. We considered ourselves freethinkers—in advance of our parents.

Most of my friends married early. I married when I was nineteen; then my husband went overseas during the Second World War. I would have loved it if I had had a child when he went overseas, but we had decided against it.

When he came back, I was in my late twenties, and in the next couple of years, I had two children. When the children were one and a half and three, I got pregnant again. I don't remember if my birth control failed . . . I wasn't the most careful person in the world. Something in me did want to have more children, but since I had never gotten pregnant until I really wanted to—I was twenty-six and a half when I had my first child—I had assumed that the general mode would continue.

I knew I couldn't have another child. I was exhausted with these two tiny little kids; it was just about all I could do to take care of them. As a child, I had been sick a lot, and people were always thinking I was anemic . . . I was having bouts of that kind. I was just very tired, all the time. I knew something was wrong because my whole idea in my heart had always been to have five, six children—I *loved* the idea of having children—but I knew I couldn't have this kid.

Seeing the state I was in, even my father said, "You must not have another child." That gives you an idea of my parents' view. They didn't feel you had to just keep having babies if you had a lot to do, small children, and not a lot of money.

And my husband and I were having hard times. It was really rough. My husband was not that crazy about having children anyway; it was very low on his list of priorities. We lived where the school is now, right next door, and were supers of the rooming house. He was just beginning his career. He eventually made documentary films, but he'd come back from the Army and was getting it all together, like a lot of those guys. So anyway, it was financially hard. But it was mostly the psychological aspect of it that would have been hard for him.

In the 1930s, my late teens, I really didn't know a lot of people who had had abortions, but then later on—not much later, when I was a young married woman in the 1940s—I heard much more. People would talk about it. By then, women were traveling everywhere—to this famous guy in Pennsylvania, to Puerto Rico. And you were always hearing about somebody who once did abortions but wasn't there doing them anymore.

I didn't ask my father for help. I wasn't really a kid, stuck and pregnant and afraid that the world would fall down on me. I was a woman with two small children, trying to be independent. I didn't want to distress him. He already wasn't feeling very well; he had a bad heart. And he really couldn't travel; he lived in the North Bronx, and I was living on Eleventh Street—it would have been a terrible subway trip. I just didn't want to bother him.

I talked the situation over with the women in the park where I used to hang out with the kids. None of them thought having an abortion was a terrible thing to do. You would say, "I can't have a kid now . . . I can't do it," and everybody was perfectly sympathetic. They said to me, "Ask So-and-so. She had one recently." I did, and I got a name. The woman didn't say anything about the guy; she just said, "Call." I assumed he was a real doctor, and he was. That may have been luck.

My abortion was a very clean and decent affair, but I didn't know until I got there that it would be all right. The doctor's office was in Manhattan, on West End Avenue. I went during the day, and I went with my husband. The doctor had two or three rooms. My husband sat and waited in one of them. There were other people waiting for other kinds of care, which is how this doctor did it; he did a whole bunch of things. He saw someone ahead of me, and when he put me in another room to rest for a few minutes afterwards, I heard him talking to other patients.

The nurse was there during the procedure. He didn't give me an anesthetic; he said, "If you want it, I'll give it to you, but it will be much safer and better if I don't." It hurt, but it wasn't that painful. So I don't have anything traumatic to say about it. I was angry that I had to become a surreptitious person, and I was in danger, but the guy was very clean, and he was very good, and he was arrested within the next year. He went to jail.

I didn't feel bad about the abortion. I didn't have the feelings that people are always describing. I may have hidden some of the feelings, but having had a child at that time would have been so much worse for me. I was certainly scared, and it's not something you want necessarily to do, but I don't see it in that whole ethical or moral framework. I guess I really didn't think of the fetus as a child until it really was a child.

But you'll hear plenty of abortion stories. I will tell you what happened next after that was over, which is what I really want to talk about. I became pregnant again a couple of years later. I wanted to have the child, but my husband didn't. It was very hard; I didn't know what to do. I was kind of in despair.

I got three or four addresses, again from women in the park. My husband wasn't going to come with me. Partly I didn't want him to come; I probably was mad at him. I had this good friend, and she said, "You're not going alone." I was very grateful to her. She said, "I'll go with you," and she did.

I remember very clearly traveling to those places—to the end of Long Island and the end of Queens and the end of Brooklyn. I went to each one of these guys, but they wouldn't do it. One guy said, "Look, if you weren't married, I would risk it, but you're married and maybe you just have to make do." He felt I didn't need an abortion that much. I'll never forget. The only person we could find was some distance away, and didn't sound very good to me at all. I was frightened . . . terribly frightened.

A week or two later, I remember, it was a freezing night; I was visiting people, and I ran home very fast. I was distraught and terrified because I was going to have to go either to Puerto Rico or someplace else. It was late in the pregnancy; it might have been the second trimester. That night I ran home at top speed—I can't tell you—in the cold, crying, from about eight blocks away. I ran all the way home and just fell into bed. I remember I had a terrible bellyache from the running.

When I woke up the next morning, I was bleeding fiercely. It seemed to me I was having a miscarriage. I'd had another miscarriage, and both my children were born early, so it was not a weird thing that this would happen to me.

So I called this doctor I'd been to several times before, and he said to me, "Did you do something?" I said, "No! It's just like the last time I had a miscarriage. I'm bleeding." And he said, "Call somebody in your family. Get some ergot [a drug that stops uterine contractions]." I said, "Don't you want me to come over?" and he said, "*No! Don't come.*"

By this time my father had had a serious heart attack, so I didn't tell him anything about it. I continued to bleed. I bled and bled, for three days, four days. I was really in terrible shape, and I couldn't get anyone to take care of me. On about the third or fourth day, my doctor finally said, "Come over." He had to do a D&C.

Sometime after that, when I spoke to my father about it, he said, "That doctor was being watched. There's no other explanation. He was a kind guy. He knew you. He must have recently done something, and he was scared."

These things are not talked about a lot, this kind of criminalization of the medical profession, the danger these doctors were in. It meant that they could not take care of you. It's not even about abortion.

A good friend had an even clearer experience with this. She also was bleeding at the wrong time and it didn't stop. She went to the emergency room here at a Catholic hospital, and they refused to take care of her. They just flatly refused. They said she had to have a rabbit test to see if she was pregnant and the results would take a couple of days. They would not touch her because she *might* be pregnant, and they *might* disturb the child. She continued to bleed, and they would not take care of her. She was a little skinny woman; she didn't have that much blood. Well, she wasn't pregnant. It turned out she had a tumor. It was an emergency—she had to be operated on immediately.

Your life, a woman's life, was simply not the first thing that hospital had on its mind at all. Not only that: Even if the doctor had compassion—as in my friend's case, one of the doctors was very anxious about her—they couldn't do anything unless they were willing to risk a great deal.

I think women died all the time when abortions were illegal. The horrible abortions were one way; the other was the refusal of institutions—medical, church, and state—to care for you, their willingness to let you die.

It's important to be public about the issue, and I have been for years. I helped organize one of the first abortion speak-outs in the country, which was held at the Washington Square Methodist Church in New York City back in the late sixties.

But I'll be very truthful. I never liked the slogan "Abortion on demand," and most of my friends hated it. We'd go on marches and we could never say it. It's such a trivialization of the experience. It's like "Toothpaste on demand." If somebody said there should be birth control on demand, I would say yes. That would make a lot of sense. If I ask for a diaphragm, if I ask for a condom, I should just get it right off the bat.

But an abortion . . . After all, it's a surgical procedure and really a very serious thing to undertake. It's not a small matter. Just because I didn't suffer a lot around my abortion, suffering is not the only thing that makes something important. I didn't suffer but it was important. And when you say "on demand," it ignores the real question, which is: where are you in your pregnancy? If you're in your sixth month, it's probably not wise, not good for you, even dangerous. Not that I think if a woman goes to a clinic and wants to have an abortion, she shouldn't have it when she needs it. It's just that there's a lot to think about.

The last demonstration that I went to was in Montpelier, Vermont (Mobilization for Women's Lives, November 12, 1989). There were about twenty-five hundred women and men. The governor spoke, a woman governor, Madeleine Kunin; and, one of the great highlights, an older woman—older than me, even (I'm sixty-seven)—from Catholics for a Free Choice spoke; and I spoke.

I said that abortion is only the tip of the iceberg. These guys who run at the clinics—and by the way, our Burlington clinic was really raided, with people knocked down—are point men who make the noise and false, hypocritical statements about human life, which they don't much care about, really. What they really want to do is take back ownership of women's bodies. They want to return us to a time when even our children weren't our own; we were simply the receptacles to have these children. The great novels of the nineteenth and early twentieth centuries were often about women who knew that if they took one wrong step, their children would be taken away from them.

And another point I made is that abortion isn't what they're thinking about; they're really thinking about sex. They're really thinking about love and reducing it to its most mechanical aspects—that is to say, the mechanical fact of intercourse as a specific act to make children in this world, and thinking of its use in any other way as wrong and wicked. They are determined to reduce women's normal sexual responses, to end them, really, when we've just had a couple of decades of admitting them.

My generation—and only in our later years—and the one right after mine have been the only ones to really enjoy any sexual freedom. The kids have to know that it's not just the right to abortion which is essential; it's their right to a sexual life.

(1991)

Obviously, the AIDS epidemic had not yet assaulted that next generation when I spoke/wrote this piece.

Jobs

These are the jobs I've had in the last thirty years. Some before the war, some after. (When I say "the war," I mean the Second World War, because if people of my generation were going to die in a war, that would be the war.)

This was the first job: door opener and telephone answerer for a doctor. All I had to say afternoon and evening was: Please come in and sit down. Also: Thank you, but call back at 6:30.

Of all the jobs I was ever to have, that one had the most thank you's.

Second job: This was an important and serious job for the Central Elevator Company. Six days a week, because the five-day week hadn't been invented yet. (Working people had heard of it and thought it was probably a good idea but the employers didn't see how it could be useful.) I typed bills at this important job and I answered simple letters. Nobody gave me anything too hard to do because they could see I felt stupid. I was younger than everybody. They and I thought that meant extreme stupidity.

The fact is, I did make at least one mistake a week. I had to figure out the payroll. Each week I underpaid or overpaid at least one worker. Whoever this man was—usually one of the elevator mechanics—he would be kind and try to help me cover the error. Whoever the man happened to be, he would usually say, "Don't feel bad, honey. You'll get smarter. It takes time."

(I have a friend in charge of payrolls right now. She is in charge of one big IBM-type machine and 12,000 paychecks for 12,000 people. She makes a mistake only once a year or maybe once in two years. Of course when that mistake is made, 12,000 men and women are overpaid or underpaid. Machines do things in a more efficient way.)

Then I was a telephone answerer again.

Then it was 1942, a year that happened before most people were born. I married a soldier and went down South with him to keep him company while he was training.

That was in time for the fourth job. I was a babysitter for a Southern family named Grimm, whose father was missing in action. I learned how to make hominy grits for the babies and corn mush. I have never made them since.

Then I was a 5&10 salesgirl, but not for long. The pay was 35 cents an hour. There weren't enough hours.

The next job was the best I ever have had. I was the secretary to the fire chief on the Army post and in on all the fires. Most of them were brush and continued all summer in the North Carolina grass. An important part of my job was the ringing of the fire bell at noon. In order to ring it at the right time, I had to call the post switchboard operator at about ten or eleven. I asked her for the *absolutely* correct time. One day I called her and said, "Elle, how do you know what the correct time is? Who tells *you*?" "Oh," she said, "I set my clock every day by the twelve noon fire bell."

Then the war ended, and everything since has happened very quickly. Life starts off slow but gets faster and faster. I had the following jobs:

1. Secretary to a reinsurance company. They insured insurance companies. Anybody can go broke, that proves.
2. Secretary to the Southern Conference for Human Welfare. They raised money to educate black and white Southerners to a little understanding of each other.
3. Secretary to New York Tenants Association, which did just that—got tenants together for more hot water and hotter heat.
4. Superintendent in a rooming house, in charge of linens.
5. Part-time secretary to the professors of zirconium and titanium at Columbia University.
6. Then finally I was a teacher.

But during all those jobs, once I was married and after I had children, most of the day I was a housewife. That is the poorest paying job a woman can hold. But most women feel gypped by life if they don't get a chance at it. And all during those jobs and all the time I was a housewife, I was a writer. The whole meaning of my life, which was jammed until midnight with fifteen different jobs and places, was writing. It took me a long time to know that, but I know it now.

(mid-1960s)

Six Days: Some Rememberings

I was in jail. I had been sentenced to six days in the Women's House of Detention, a fourteen-story prison right in the middle of Greenwich Village, my own neighborhood. This happened during the American war in Vietnam, I have forgotten which important year of the famous sixties. The civil disobedience for which I was paying a small penalty probably consisted of sitting down to impede or slow down some military parade.

I was surprised at the sentence. Others had been given two days or dismissed. I think the judge was particularly angry with me. After all, I was not a kid. He thought I was old enough to know better, a forty-five-year-old woman, a mother and teacher. I ought to be too busy to waste time on causes I couldn't possibly understand.

I was herded with about twenty other women, about 90 percent black and Puerto Rican, into the bullpen, an odd name for a women's holding facility. There, through someone else's lawyer, I received a note from home telling me that since I'd chosen to spend the first week of July in jail, my son would probably not go to summer camp, because I had neglected to raise the money I promised. I read this note and burst into tears, real running-down-the-cheek tears. It was true: thinking about other people's grown boys, I had betrayed my little son. The summer, starting that day, July 1, stood up before me day after day, steaming the city streets, the after-work crowded city pool.

I guess I attracted some attention. You—you white girl you—you never been arrested before? A black woman about a head taller than I put her arm on my shoulder. It ain't so bad. What's your time, sugar? I gotta do three years. You huh?

Six days.

Six days? What the fuck for?

I explained, sniffling, embarrassed.

You got six days for sitting down front of a horse? Cop on the horse? Horse step on you? Jesus in hell, cops gettin crazier and stupider and meaner. Maybe we get you out.

No, no, I said. I wasn't crying because of that. I didn't want her to think I was scared. I wasn't. She paid no attention. Shoving a couple of women aside—Don't stand in front of me, bitch. Move over. What you looking at?—she took hold of the bars of our cage, commenced to bang on them, shook them mightily, screaming, Hear me now, you motherfuckers, you grotty pigs, get this housewife out of here! She returned to comfort me. —Six days in this low-down hole for sitting front of a horse!

Before we were distributed among our cells, we were dressed in a kind of nurse's-aide scrub uniform, blue or green, a little too large or a little too small. We had to submit to a physical in which all our hiding places were investigated for drugs. These examinations were not too difficult, mostly because a young woman named Andrea Dworkin had fought them, refused a grosser, more painful examination some months earlier. She had been arrested protesting the war in front of the U.S. mission to the UN. I had been there too, but I don't think I was arrested that day. She was mocked for that determined struggle at the Women's House, as she has been for other braveries, but according to the women I questioned, certain humiliating, perhaps sadistic customs had ended—for that period at least.

My cellmate was a beautiful young woman, twenty-three years old, a prostitute who'd never been arrested before. She was nervous, but she had been given the name of an important long-termer. She explained in a businesslike way that she *was* beautiful and would need protection. She'd be okay once she'd found that woman. In the two days we spent together, she tried *not* to talk to the other women in our cell block. She said they were mostly street whores and addicts. She would never be on the street. Her man wouldn't allow it anyway.

I slept well for some reason, probably the hard mattress. I don't seem to mind where I am. Also, I must tell you, I could look out the window at the end of our corridor and see my children or their friends on their way to music lessons or Greenwich House pottery. Looking slantwise I could see right into Sutter's Bakery, then on the corner of Tenth Street. These were my neighbors at coffee and cake.

Sometimes the cell block was open, but not our twelve cells. Other times the reverse. Visitors came by: they were prisoners, detainees not yet sentenced. They seemed to have a strolling freedom, though several, unsentenced, unable to make bail, had been there for months. One woman peering into the cells stopped when she saw me. Grace! Hi! I knew her from the neighborhood, maybe the park, couldn't really remember her name.

What are you in for? I asked.

Oh nothing—well, a stupid drug bust. I don't even use—oh well, forget it. I've been here six weeks. They keep putting the trial off. Are you okay?

Then I complained. I had planned not to complain about anything while living among people who'd be here in these clanging cells a long time; it didn't seem right. But I said, I don't have anything to read and they took away my pen and I don't have paper.

Oh, you'll get all that eventually, she said. Keep asking.

Well, they have all my hairpins. I'm a mess.

No no, she said, you're okay. You look nice.

(A couple of years later, the war continuing, I was arrested in Washington. My hair was still quite long. I wore it in a kind of bun on top of my head. My hairpins gone, my hair straggled wildly every which way. Muriel Rukeyser, arrested that day along with about thirty other women, made the same generous sisterly remark. No no, Grace, love you with your hair down, you really ought to always wear it this way.)

The very next morning, my friend brought me *The Collected Stories of William Carlos Williams.* —These okay?

God! Okay. —Yes!

My trial is coming up tomorrow, she said. I think I'm getting off with time already done. Overdone. See you around?

That afternoon, my cellmate came for her things. —I'm moving to the fourth floor. Working in the kitchen. Couldn't be better. We were sitting outside our cells, she wanted me to know something. She'd already told me, but said it again: I still can't believe it. This creep, this guy, this cop, he waits, he just waits till he's fucked and fine, pulls his pants up, pays me, and arrests me. It's not legal. It's not. My man's so mad, he's like to kill *me*, but he's not that kind of— he's not a criminal type, *my* man. She never said the word "pimp." Maybe no one did. Maybe that was our word.

I had made friends with some of the women in cells across the aisle. How can I say "made friends"? I just sat and spoke when spoken to, I was at school. I answered questions—simple ones. Why would I do such a fool thing on purpose? How old were my children? My man any good? Then: you live around the corner? That was a good idea, Evelyn said, to have a prison in your own neighborhood, so you could keep in touch, yelling out the window.

As in fact we were able to do right here and now, calling and being called from Sixth Avenue, by mothers, children, boyfriends.

About the children: One woman took me aside. Her daughter was brilliant, she was in Hunter High School, had taken a test. No, she hardly ever saw her, but she wasn't a whore—it was the drugs. Her daughter was ashamed; the grandmother, the father's mother, made the child ashamed. When she got out in sixth months it would be different. This made Evelyn and Rita, right across from my cell, laugh. Different, I swear. Different. Laughing. But she *could* make it, I said. Then they really laughed. Their first laugh was a bare giggle compared to these convulsive roars. Change her ways? That dumb bitch. Ha!!

Another woman, Helen, the only other white woman on the cell block, wanted to talk to me. She wanted me to know that she was not only white but Jewish. She came from Brighton Beach. Her father, he should rest in peace, thank God, was dead. Her arms were covered with puncture marks almost like sleeve patterns. But she needed to talk to me because I was Jewish. (I'd been asked by Rita and Evelyn—was I Irish? No, Jewish. Oh, they answered.) She walked me to the barred window at the end of the corridor, the window that looked down on West Tenth Street. She said, How come you so friends with those black whores? You don't hardly talk to me. I said I liked them, but I liked her too. She said, If you knew them for true, you wouldn't like them. They nothing but street whores. You know, once I was friends with them. We done a lot of things together, I knew them fifteen years, Evy and Rita maybe twenty, I been in the streets with them, side by side, Amsterdam, Lenox, West Harlem; in bad weather we covered each other. Then one day along came Malcolm X and they don't know me no more, they ain't talking to me. You too white. I ain't all that white. Twenty years, they ain't talking.

My friend Myrt called one day, that is, called from the street, called, Grace Grace. I heard and ran to the window. A policeman, a regular beat cop, was addressing her. She looked up, then walked away before I could yell my answer. Later on she told me that he'd said, I don't think Grace would appreciate you calling her name out like that.

What a mistake! For years, going to the park with my children, or simply walking down Sixth Avenue on a summer night past the Women's House, we would often have to thread our way through whole families calling up—bellowing, screaming to the third, seventh, tenth floor, to figures, shadows behind bars and screened windows, How you feeling? Here's Glena. She got big. Mami mami, you like my dress? We gettin you out baby. New lawyer come by.

And the replies, among which I was privileged to live for a few days, shouted down: —You looking beautiful. What he say? Fuck you, James. I got a chance? Bye-bye. Come next week.

Then the guards, the heavy clanking of cell doors. Keys. Night.

I still had no pen or paper despite the great history of prison literature. I was suffering a kind of frustration, a sickness in the way claustrophobia is a sickness—this paper-and-penlessness was a terrible pain in the area of my heart, a nausea. I was surprised.

In the evening, at lights-out (a little like the Army, or on a good day a strict, unpleasant camp), women called softly from their cells. Rita hey Rita, sing that song—Come on, sister, sing. A few more importunings and then Rita in the cell diagonal to mine would begin with a ballad. A song about two women and a man. It was familiar to everyone but me. The two women were prison sweethearts. The man was her outside lover. One woman, the singer, was being paroled. The ballad told her sorrow about having been parted from him when she was sentenced, now she would leave her loved woman after three years. There were about twenty stanzas of joy and grief.

Well, I was so angry not to have pen and paper to get some of it down that I lost it all—all but the sorrowful plot. Of course she had this long song in her head, and in the next few nights she sang and chanted others, sometimes with a small chorus.

Which is how I finally understood that I didn't lack pen and paper but my own memorizing mind. It had been given away with a hundred poems, called rote learning, old-fashioned, backward, an enemy of creative thinking, a great human gift disowned.

Now there's a garden where the Women's House of Detention once stood. A green place, safely fenced in, with protected daffodils and tulips; roses bloom in it too, sometimes into November.

The big women's warehouse and its barred blind windows have been removed from Greenwich Village's affluent throat. I was sorry when it happened; the bricks came roaring down, great trucks carried them away.

I have always agreed with Rita and Evelyn that if there are prisons, they ought to be in the neighborhood, near a subway—not way out in the distant suburbs, where families have to take cars, buses, ferries, trains, and the population that considers itself innocent forgets, denies, chooses to never know that there is a whole huge country of the bad and the unlucky and the self-hurters, a country with a population greater than that of many nations in our world.

(1994)

Cop Tales

At the Wall Street Action last October, the police were on one side of the sawhorses. We were on the other. We were blocking Wall Street workers. The police were blocking us. One of them was very interested in solar housing. Our solar expert explained the science and economics of it all. Another cop from Long Island worried a lot about the Shoreham nuclear power plant. "Can't do anything about it," he said. "They'll build it. I hate it. I live there. What am I going to do?"

That could be a key to the police, I thought. They have no hope. Cynical. They're mad at us because we have a little hope in the midst of our informed worries.

Then he said, looking at the Bread and Puppet Theater's stilt dancers, "Look at that, what's going on here? People running around in the street dancing. They're going every which way. It ain't organized." We started to tell him how important the dancers were. "No, no, that's okay," he said. "The anti-war demonstrators were like this at first, mixed up, but they got themselves together.

You'll get yourself together too. In a couple of years you'll know how to do it better."

Earlier, about 6 a.m., two cops wearing blue hardhats passed. One of them looked behind him. "Here come the horses," he said. "Let's get the hell out of here!" And they moved at top casual walking speed in the opposite direction.

Also at 6 a.m., but about fifteen years ago, we would walk up and down before the White Hall Street Induction Center wearing signs that said I SUPPORT DRAFT REFUSAL. It wouldn't take more than a couple of hours for the system to gather up its young victims, stuff them into wagons, and start them off on their terrible journey. At 9:30 on one of those mornings, about twenty women sat down all across the street to prevent the death wagons from moving. They sat for about thirty minutes. Then a plainclothesman approached an older gray-haired woman: "Missus, you don't want to get arrested." "I have to," she said. "My grandson's in Vietnam." Gently they removed her. Then with billy clubs, a dozen uniformed men moved up and down that line of young women, dragging them away, by their arms, their hair, beating them, I remember (and Norma Becker* remembers), mostly in the breast.

Last May at the rainy Armed Forces Day Parade, attended by officers, their wives, and Us, some of Us were arrested by a couple of Cops for Christ. At the desk, as they took our names, smiling, they gave us "Cops for Christ" leaflets. We gave "Disarm for Human Life" leaflets.

Another year, one of the first really large antidraft actions— also at the Induction Center at dawn. We were to surround the building. The famous people, or *Notables* as the Vietnamese used to say, sat down to bar the front entrance. That's where the TV cameras were. Our group of regulars went around to the back of the center and sat down. Between us and the supply entrance sat a solid

* Chair of the War Resisters League.

line of huge horses and their solemn police riders. We sat cross-legged, speaking softly as the day brightened. Sometimes someone would joke and someone else would immediately say, Be serious. Off to one side, a captain watched us and the cavalry. Suddenly the horses reared, charged us as we sat, smashing us with their great bodies, scattering our supporting onlookers. People were knocked down, ran this way and that, but the horses were everywhere, rearing—until at a signal from the captain, which I saw, they stopped, settled down, and trotted away. That evening the papers and TV reported that a couple of thousand had demonstrated. Hundreds had been peacefully arrested.

At Wall Street too: A gentleman with a Wall Street attaché case tried to get through our line. The police, who were in the middle of a discussion about Arabian oil, said, "Why not try down there, mister. You can get through down there." The gentleman said he wanted to get through right here and right now, and began to knee through our line. The cop on the other side of the sawhorse said, "You heard us. Down there, mister. How about it?" The gentleman said, "Damnit, what are you here for?" He began to move away, calling back in fury, "What the hell are you cops here for anyway?" "Just role-playing," the cop called in reply.

There were several cheerful police at the Trident nuclear submarine demonstration last year. One officer cheerily called out to the Trident holiday visitors to be careful as they trod on the heads of the demonstrators blocking the roadway. "They're doing what they believe in." He asked us to step back, but not more than six inches. He told a joke. He said he hated war, always had. Some young state troopers arrived—more help was needed. They were tall and grouchy. A black youngster, about twelve, anxious to see what was going on, pushed against the line. One of the state troopers leaned forward and smacked the child hard on the back of the head. "Get back, you little bastard," he said. I reached out to get the attention of the cheery cop, who wore a piece of hierarchical gold on his jacket. "Officer," I said, "you ought to get that trooper out of here, he's dangerous." He looked at me, his face went icy cold. "Lady, be careful," he said. "I just saw you try to strike that officer."

Not too long ago, I saw Finnegan, the plainclothes Red Squad boss. I hadn't seen him in a long time. "Say, Finnegan," I said, "all these years you've been working at one thing and I've been working at the opposite, but look at us. Nothing's prevented either of us from getting gray." He almost answered, but a lot of speedy computations occurred in his brain and he couldn't. It's the business of the armed forces and the armored face to maintain distance at all times.

(1980)

The Seneca Stories: Tales from the Women's Peace Encampment

My friends and I came to the Seneca Women's Peace Encampment from Vermont. No matter what else we saw in those five days of work/action/arrest/talk, we felt the wide eventful sky above us, a blazing place from which sudden thunderstorms attacked. We had driven south out of the Green Mountains, out of the hills where cows pasture on narrow spiraling terraces down to the great flat fields of corn, long, barely sloping acres of soybeans. So much horizon!

We came into a careful, conservative New York area that had once experienced extraordinary history. In the 1590s, the women of the Iroquois nation had met in Seneca to ask the tribes to stop their warfare. In 1848, the first Women's Rights Convention had met in Seneca Falls. During the 1850s Harriet Tubman led slaves north through this country. Her safe house still stands. The towns and countryside of Seneca County seemed to be a geography of American Herstory, where women of color and women of less color once lived powerfully and rebelliously, offering their female leadership in a dream of peace and justice for women—and men too. In fact, the planned encampment was named just that, the Women's Encampment for a Future of Peace and Justice.

There were many greeters when we passed the Amish farm and made a sharp right into the encampment. Women poked their heads into the windows of our car to assure us of a welcome, to tell us where to park, where the "Non-registration" booth was, to tell any men in the car that they would be welcome in the large area around the house and garden but beyond the barn the women wanted privacy and safety. We bumped our car over the terrible corrugations that had once been the earth of a farmer's cornfield. We learned that we were expected to put three hours of work into camp maintenance every day. We contributed seven dollars. We found out quickly that the condition of the soil beyond the parking in the tenting fields was also pretty poor. Corn uses the land up, and it was a hope often expressed that this land could be renewed, returned to the fertility of the green farms of the county.

Because of friends from New York and New England who had camped earlier we knew: Seneca was Stories. The story of the flag; the story of the TV camera crew; the story of the woman who climbed the Army depot tower and painted out the words MISSION FIRST—leaving the words PEOPLE ALWAYS; the story of the astrologers who advised the protesters on what day and what hour to do civil disobedience; the story of the men who apologized; the women who joined us; the story of the woman who wore a shirt saying *Nuke the Bitches Till They Glow*, who was moved a tiny bit, so she removed the words *Till They Glow*, reserving further action for deeper thought; the story of boardwalks and ramps lovingly built to keep us all from twisting our ankles, and all that work—the plumbing and electrical work—done by women; the story of rumor, invention, and absolute factual truth in the lovely combinations that become myth.

Here are some of the stories I lived in or alongside of—and a couple of stories told me so often that I've begun to think I was a part of those stories too.

On Saturday, July 30, 1983, about one hundred women left Seneca Falls to walk twelve miles to the encampment. They carried large cutouts of Susan B. Anthony, Elizabeth Cady Stanton, Harriet Tubman, Sojourner Truth, and other women their walk honored. They intended to show the connections between the everyday killing oppression of women and the battering of our world in the man-made war. They walked peacefully through uninhabited miles of field and scrub and small towns lined with American flags. When they came into Waterloo, they saw a huge sign stretched between two houses. It greeted them: NUKE THEM TILL THEY GLOW. THEN SHOOT THEM IN THE DARK.

They turned the corner to cross the Waterloo bridge and were met by several hundred Waterloo citizens, nearly all holding little and large flags, nearly all screaming foul cries and words they hoped would insult the women: "Commies," "Lezzies," "Kill them," "Nuke them." Many carried flagpoles with pointed tips, and their enraged screams and jabbing terrified our women, who, after brief discussion, decided to sit down. (This is often done in confrontations to show that violence is not intended and also to give the sitters a chance to talk quietly about what to do next.) The sheriff, an elected official who had known all about the walk weeks earlier, had no way to control the infuriated crowd that consisted of his neighbors, who were, after all, voters. He offered a detour, which made sense to some women. But for the women sitting under the barrage of hatred, it seemed foolish to turn their backs. Besides, they felt somewhat stubborn about upholding their right to walk through an American town without vicious abuse. They thought that right was worth a good deal. Many women tried courageously to look into the eyes of the men and women barring their way . . . to somehow change the confrontation into a meeting. Finally, and ironically, the quiet women were arrested for disorderly conduct, while the screamers were allowed to go. One by one, the women were dragged off to become the fifty-four Jane Does who spent five days in the only jail big enough to hold them all—the Interlaken High School.

Among the women arrested was one prominent Waterloo citizen who was horrified by the behavior of the townspeople. Her daughter was one of the first to come to the encampment the next day to inform us that many of her neighbors were ashamed, that the hard screaming knot didn't represent them, though it would be seen again and again—at the Seneca Depot truck gate, at the Interlaken High School, where thirteen brave vigilers who were keeping a watch at night were surrounded by huge trailer trucks, assuring darkness, invisibility, and terror. Here too the flags were used to poke and jab at the circle of women.

The green lawn outside the Interlaken High School was a place where lots of play happened too. In the daylight we pantomimed the August 1 march for our Jane Does watching from distant windows. We played out the fence-climbing arrests, we sang to them and, in fact, sang so well that day by day, the taunters became quieter. If we shouted, they shouted. But when we sang, they listened. I listened myself. We were singing beautifully. And we were saddened for the opposition, which tried a couple of songs, worked on "Jingle Bells," but foundered on "America the Beautiful," which we joyfully took up.

A story: one of the vigilers at the Interlaken High School prison was approached by a man who told her he'd been one of the people at the Waterloo bridge. He hadn't screamed, he said, just waved his flag. He asked what the whole thing was about, for godsakes. She explained the reason for the camp, the historical purpose of the walk. "Oh," he said, "I thought you were all sitting down in the road because the VFW wasn't letting any women be part of *their* parade. And I agreed with them. That's why I was mad."

Two days after the August 1 march, I was a greeter at the camp entrance. A big car turned in. Father and son. The father leaned out the window and said, "We came to say we're sorry about everything. That's all." The son spoke through the far window. "We wanted to ask you women how you do it. Those people were really rotten to you. I heard them. They insult you and they call you names and you're so calm. My father and me—we honor you. We don't understand, but we honor you."

Two young women came up out of darkness to join us in our night circle at Interlaken High School. Someone tells me they own or work in a restaurant near the depot. They sit with us as we go around the circle trying to see who will go home and who will sit the night out with a good chance of arrest. The two young women sit with us for about an hour, listening to us listen to one another, then proudly and deliberately walk past their neighbors on the way down to the car. The words "Traitor, traitor" follow them in a halfhearted way.

A great deal has been written about that hostility at Waterloo, as though a country that refuses to pass something as simple as the Equal Rights Amendment would not have pockets of vicious misogyny, as though a nation with tens of thousands of nuclear bombs, Army bases, weapons factories in the midst of unemployment would not be able to raise a furious patriarchal horde.

From that rage of flags that seemed so pervasive in the towns of Seneca County we must go back to the days before the camp's opening. A Waterloo man came to the already exhausted, worried organizers and maintainers of the camp and said, "Take this flag and put it at the camp entrance, or else we will tell the world, the media, the town, how you refused the American flag." The women met to discuss this—as we were all to meet time and time again in large and in small circles. There was so much strong feeling on either side that a committee of fifteen was charged with resolving the problem: five women in strong opposition, five women in determined support, and five easygoing intermediate mediators. After seven hours under the only shade tree in that part of the camp, it was suggested that women could make their own flags. And many flags *were* made, not national flags, but painted and embroidered banners with pictures and sayings about our lives—also a couple of handsome homemade American flags—and all these were hung on lines in the front yard of the camp, along the road. However, the flag of the provoker was not accepted. As a result, the flag entrepreneurs of Seneca County did an incredible business, as anyone driving through the red-white-and-blue towns will tell.

In the Nicastro Restaurant a couple of miles up the road, the encampment leaflet and vision statement are tacked to the wall right next to two awards to Mr. and Mrs. Nicastro: Parents of the Year. In their guest book we have all written our thanks for the decency of this family to all the women who drank coffee and ate fine celebratory dinners after jail. They allowed the place to be used during the summer for meetings between the campers and the community.

On August 1, about 2,500 women marched from the nearby Sampson State Park to the depot. It was a long, hot walk, stalled by the sheriff every twenty-five feet or so; he was waiting for state troopers. He feared another confrontation. The angry opposition had already entrenched itself and its flags at the truck gate. But this time a band of very brave Waterloo citizens stood with their children not too far away, holding signs that said they'd fight for our rights whether they agreed with us or not.

Once at the gate, women came forward to transform the military steel mesh into an embroidery of banners, dolls, children's photographs, quilts, christening dresses, lovers' photos. Then they stepped back, and the women who planned the civil disobedience came forward. Immediately women began to climb over the high fence. I thought it was rather ridiculous, but as I and my Vermont affinity group of six women looked and looked, it became more interesting. It was the riskiness of the fence. I thought, This may be the last fence I'll be able to climb in my life (I'm sixty and I see a fence shortage ahead), so I joined the others and we climbed that fence that looked to us women—young or old—a lot like the school

fence that encircled girlhood, the one that the boys climbed adven-
turously over again and again. We were carted off by young
soldiers—many of them black and Hispanic—all of them perplexed,
most of them quite kind. There was a physical delight in the climbing act, but I knew and still believe that the serious act was to sit,
as many women did, in little circles through the drenching night
and blazing day on the hot cement in front of the truck gate with
the dwindling but still enraged "Nuke Them Till They Glow"
group screaming "Lesbian bitches" from their flag-enfolded cars.

To this gate the serious citizens of Waterloo or Romulus or
Geneva came. Folks who'd read of this excitement brought their
children and their coolers to watch silently, and sometimes speak,
asking the hard questions again: "What about the Russians?" or
"We have to make a living, don't we?"; and sometimes to say sadly,
"Did you really burn a flag and then urinate on it?" No. No. No.

So we *had* troubled them. And we asked: wouldn't it have been
wonderful if hundreds, thousands of Germans had sat down before
the gates of the Krupp gas-oven plants and troubled the contented
hearts and minds of the good German people? They might also
have asked those first two questions.

On Wednesday, August 3, people gathered at the fairgrounds in
Waterloo outside the big corrugated metal building in which the
trial would be conducted. Lots of visible media—meaning TV.
Our Jane Does had continued their resistance: they were carried
into "court," then back into the yard as the judge tried to conduct
one trial after another. They demanded a common trial and dis-
missal of unjust charges. We, their supporters, were removed from
the building. Singing again. Finally the senselessness of individual
trials became clear. Three women were allowed to speak for the
group. Then the judge dismissed the case and ordered the charges
dropped. He, like the sheriff, was an elected official, but saw the
wind blowing in a different direction. Outside in the terrible heat,
I walked among the men and women, the cameras, the stalwart

youths standing like statues holding enormous flags on thick flag-poles. And found a group of Waterloo women with cardboard signs. WE SUPPORT YOUR RIGHT TO WALK THROUGH OUR TOWN. THE CONSTITUTION SHELTERS YOU. Our Seneca sisters were hugging them, thanking them for their bravery. "Oh," said one woman, surprised and embarrassed, "we didn't think we'd be so important as all that." "You're the most important of all to us," we answered.

There were so many other events that ought to be written about, and I know will be. But briefly . . . the busloads of women that came all the way from Minnesota . . . the women from Greenham Common in England, and Comiso in Italy, and from the Netherlands and Germany who worked so hard to share their experiences with us . . . the religious women who asked if they could pray in the depot chapel, were given permission, then asked to leave when the pacific nature of those prayers was understood . . . the walk to Harriet Tubman's house . . . the civil disobedience actions of Labor Day, when the women chose to dig a hole under the fence instead of climbing over it.

One of the most important events, and I do think of it as an event in itself, was the local news that Seneca encampment became. That news coverage is part of the news I brought home. The combination of stubbornness that is nonviolent action, the peculiar, arduous, delicate process of our constantly public meetings set against the opposition's vituperative rage illuminated the issues. What we talked and acted about was Peace and Justice, and the way we went about it spoke to the word "Future."

One more story: I am waiting to use the phone. There are two phones. I am pretty annoyed with the long, gabby calls of the people on the line in front of me, until I'm finally close enough to hear a couple. One woman is giving information about her entire affinity group to a contact person . . . Someone's dog has to be picked up . . . A mother must be called . . . A job has to be put off. The woman on the other phone is young and in tears. She's saying,

"Mom. Ma, please, it's my world they're gonna blow up." Then some silence. Then: "Ma, please, I have to do it. It's not terrible to get arrested. I'm all right, Ma, please listen, you got married and had us and everything and a house, but they still kept making nuclear bombs." More tears. "Listen, listen please, Ma."

I wanted to take the phone from her and say, "Ma, don't worry, your kid's okay. She's great. Don't you see she's one of the young women who will save my granddaughter's life?"

(1983)

Women's Pentagon
Action Unity Statement

For two years we have gathered at the Pentagon because we fear for our lives. We still fear for the life of this planet, our earth, and the life of the children who are our human future.

We are women who come in most part from the northeastern region of our United States. We are city women who know the wreckage and fear of city streets; we are country women who grieve the loss of the small farm and have lived on the poisoned earth. We are young and older, we are married, single, lesbian. We live in different kinds of households, in groups, families, alone; some are single parents.

We work at a variety of jobs. We are students—teachers—factory workers—office workers—lawyers—farmers—doctors—builders—waitresses—weavers—poets—engineers—homeworkers—electricians—artists—blacksmiths. We are all daughters and sisters.

We came to mourn and rage and defy the Pentagon because it is the workplace of the imperial power which threatens us all. Every day while we work, study, love, the colonels and generals who are planning our annihilation walk calmly in and out the doors of its five sides. They have accumulated over 30,000 nuclear bombs at the rate of three to six bombs every day.

They are determined to produce the billion-dollar MX missile. They are creating a technology called Stealth—the invisible, unperceivable arsenal. They have revived the cruel old killer, nerve gas. They have proclaimed Directive 59, which asks for "small nuclear wars, prolonged but limited." The Soviet Union works hard to keep up with the United States initiatives. We can destroy each other's cities, towns, schools, children many times over. The United States has sent "advisors," money, and arms to El Salvador and Guatemala to enable those juntas to massacre their own people.

The very same men, the same legislative committees that offer trillions of dollars to the Pentagon, have brutally cut day care, children's lunches, battered women's shelters. The same men have concocted the Family Protection Act, which will mandate the strictly patriarchal family and thrust federal authority into the lives we live in our own homes. They are preventing the passage of ERA's simple statement and supporting the Human Life Amendment, which will deprive all women of choice and many women of life itself.

In this environment of contempt and violence, racism, woman hating, and the old European habit of Jew hatred—called anti-Semitism—all find their old roots and grow.

We are in the hands of men whose power and wealth have separated them from the reality of daily life and from the imagination. We are right to be afraid.

At the same time, our cities are in ruins, bankrupt; they suffer the devastation of war. Hospitals are closed, our schools deprived of books and teachers. Our black and Latino youths are without decent work. They will be forced, drafted to become the cannon fodder for the very power that oppresses them. Whatever help the poor receive is cut or withdrawn to feed the Pentagon, which needs about $500 million a day for its murderous health. It extracted

$157 billion last year from our own tax money, $1,800 from a family of four.

With this wealth our scientists have been corrupted; over 40 percent work in government and corporate laboratories that refine the methods for destroying or deforming life.

The lands of the Native American people have been turned to radioactive rubble in order to enlarge the nuclear warehouse. The uranium of South Africa, necessary to the nuclear enterprise, enriches the white minority and encourages the vicious system of racist oppression and war.

The President has just decided to produce the neutron bomb, which kills people but leaves property (buildings like this one) intact.

There is fear among the people, and that fear, created by the industrial militarists, is used as an excuse to accelerate the arms race. "We will protect you," they say, but we have never been so endangered, so close to the end of human time.

We women are gathering because life on the precipice is intolerable.

We want to know what anger in these men, what fear that can only be satisfied by destruction, what coldness of heart and ambition drives their days.

We want to know because we do not want that dominance which is exploitative and murderous in international relations, and so dangerous to women and children at home—we do not want that sickness transferred by the violent society through the fathers to the sons.

What is it that we women need for our ordinary lives, that we want for ourselves and also for our sisters in new nations and old colonies who suffer the white man's exploitation and too often the oppression of their own countrymen?

We want enough good food, decent housing, communities with clean air and water, good care for our children while we work. We want work that is useful to a sensible society. There is a modest technology to minimize drudgery and restore joy to labor. We are determined to use skills and knowledge from which we have been excluded—like plumbing or engineering or physics or composing. We intend to form women's groups or unions that will demand safe workplaces, free of sexual harassment, equal pay for workers of comparable value. We respect the work women have done in caring for the young, their own and others, in maintaining a physical and spiritual shelter against the greedy and militaristic society. In our old age we expect our experience, our skills, to be honored and used.

We want health care which respects and understands our bodies. Physically challenged sisters must have access to gatherings, actions, happy events, work.

We want an education for children which tells the true story of our women's lives, which describes the earth as our home to be cherished, to be fed as well as harvested.

We want to be free from violence in our streets and in our houses. One in every three of us will be raped in her lifetime. The pervasive social power of the masculine ideal and the greed of the pornographer have come together to steal our freedom, so that whole neighborhoods and the life of the evening and night have been taken away from us. For too many women, the dark country road and the city alley have concealed the rapist. We want the night returned, the light of the moon, special in the cycle of our female lives, the stars and the gaiety of the city streets.

We want to have the right or not to have children—we do not want gangs of politicians and medical men to say we must be sterilized for the country's good. We know that this technique is the racist's method for controlling populations. Nor do we want to be prevented from having an abortion when we need one. We think this freedom should be available to poor women, as it always has been to the rich. We want to be free to love whomever we choose. We will live with women or with men or we will live alone. We will not allow the oppression of lesbians. One sex or one sexual preference must not dominate another.

We do not want to be drafted into the Army. We do not want our young brothers drafted. We want *them* equal with *us*.

We want to see the pathology of racism ended in our time. It has been the imperial arrogance of white male power that has separated us from the suffering and wisdom of our sisters in Asia, Africa, South America, and in our own country.

To some women racism has offered privilege and convenience. These women often fail to see that they themselves have lived under the unnatural authority and violence of men in government, at work, at home. Privilege does not increase knowledge or spirit or understanding. There can be no peace while one race dominates another, one people, one nation, one sex despises another.

We must not forget that tens of thousands of American women live much of their lives in cages, away from family, lovers, all the growing years of their children. Most of them were born at the intersection of oppressions: people of color, female, poor. Women on the outside have been taught to fear those sisters. We refuse that separation. We need each other's knowledge and anger in our common struggle against the builders of jails and bombs.

We want the uranium left in the earth, and the earth given back to the people who tilled it. We want a system of energy which is renewable, which does not take resources out of the earth without returning them. We want those systems to belong to the people and their communities, not to the giant corporations which invariably turn knowledge into weaponry. We want the sham of Atoms for Peace ended, all nuclear plants decommissioned, and the construction of new plants stopped. That is another war against the people and the child to be born in fifty years.

We want an end to the arms race. No more bombs. No more amazing inventions for death.

We understand all is connectedness. The earth nourishes us as we with our bodies will eventually feed it. Through us, our mothers connected the human past to the human future. We should know the life and work of animals and plants in seeding, reseeding, and in fact simply inhabiting this planet. Their exploitation and the organized destruction of never-to-be-seen-again species threatens and sorrows us.

With that sense, that ecological right, we oppose the financial connections between the Pentagon and the multinational corporations and banks that the Pentagon serves, what Eisenhower called the military-industrial complex.

Those connections are made of gold and oil.

We are made of blood and bone, we are made of the sweet and finite resource, water.

We will not allow these violent games to continue. If we are here in our stubborn thousands today, we will certainly return in the hundreds of thousands in the months and years to come.

We know there is a healthy, sensible, loving way to live and we intend to live that way in our neighborhoods and our farms in these United States, and among our sisters and brothers in all the countries of the world.

(1982)

Of Poetry and Women and the World

Our panel has kind of an odd definition, and I think the three of us have taken it to mean whatever we want to talk about. And since what I want to talk about partly follows the last panel, it may be a very good way of working our way into other subjects.

I have to begin by saying that as far as I know, and even listening to all the people talking earlier, I have to say that war is manmade. It's made by men. It's their thing, it's their world, and they're terribly injured in it. They suffer terribly in it, but it's made by men. How do they come to live this way? It took me years to understand this. Because when I was a little girl, I was a boy—like a lot of little girls who like to get into things and want to be where the action is, which is up at the corner someplace, where the boys are. And I understood this very well, because that was what really interested me. I could hardly wait to continue being a boy so that I could go to war and do all the other exciting boys' things. And it took my own life, really, for me to begin to change my mind somehow—after a number of years of actually living during the Second World War. I lived a lot in Army camps. And I liked living in those Army camps; I liked them because it was very exciting, and it seemed to be where it was all at, and there were a lot of boys there, one of which, one of the boys, was my husband. The other boys were just gravy, so to speak.

But as time went on in my own life, and as I began to read and think and live inside my own life, and began to work as a writer, I stopped being a boy. At some certain point, I stopped being one, I stopped liking being one, I stopped wanting to be one. I began to think there would be nothing worse in this world than being one. I thought it was a terrible life, a hard life, and a life which would ask of me behavior, feelings, passions, and excitements that I didn't want and that I didn't care about at all. Meanwhile, at the same time, what had happened was that I had begun to live among women. Well, of course I had always lived among women. All people, all girls, live among women, all girls of my time and culture live among mothers, sisters, and aunts—and lots of them too. So I had always lived among them, but I hadn't really thought about it that much. Instead, I had said, "Well, there they are and their boring lives, sitting around the table while the men are playing cards in the other room and yelling at one another. That's pretty exciting, right?" And it wasn't until I began to live among women, which wasn't until I had children, that I began to look at that life and began to be curious about it.

Now, that brings us to writing: how we come to writing and how we come to think about it. When I came to think as a writer, it was because I had begun to live among women. Now, the great thing is that I didn't know them, I didn't know who they were. Which I should have known, since I had all these aunts, right? But I didn't know them, and that, I think, is really where lots of literature comes from. It really comes, not from knowing so much, but from not knowing. It comes from what you're curious about. It comes from what obsesses you. It comes from what you want to know. (A lot of war literature comes from that too, you know—the feeling that Robert Stone had, that "this is it." The reason he felt like this is that it *hadn't been it* at all. So he wondered—but more of that later.) So I wondered about these lives, and these are the lives that interested me.

And when I began to write about them, I saw immediately, since my reading and thinking in my early thirties followed a period of very masculine literature, that I was writing stuff that was trivial, stupid, boring, domestic, and not interesting. However, it began to appear that that was all I could do, and I said, "Okay, this is my limitation, this is my profound interest, this life of women, and this is what I really have to do. I can't help myself. Everybody's going to say that it's trivial, it isn't worth anything, it's boring, you know. Nobody's hitting anybody very much [but later on, I had a few people hitting each other]. And what else can I do?"

I tell that story only for other writers who are young or maybe just young in writing. To tell them that no matter what you feel about what you're doing, if that is really what you're looking for, if that is really what you're trying to understand, if that is really what you're stupid about, if that's what you're dumb about and you're trying to understand it, stay with it, no matter what, and you'll at least live your own truth or be hung for it.

We've talked about whether art is about morality or— I don't even understand some of these words, anyway. But I do understand words like "justice," which are simpler. And one of the things that art is about, for me, is justice. Now, that isn't a matter of opinion, really. That isn't to say, "I'm going to show these people right or wrong" or whatever. But what art is about—and this is what justice is about, although you'll have your own interpretations—is the illumination of what isn't known, the lighting up of what is under a rock, of what has been hidden. And I think people feel like that who are beginning to write. I was just speaking to someone who's a Native American, who was saying that what he was doing was picking up this rock at the mouth of a cave, out there in the desert, picking it up and saying, "I've got to light this up, and add what I find to the weight and life of human experience." That's what justice is about, and that's what art is about, that kind of justice and that kind of experience.

As for me, I didn't say, "Well, I'm going to pick up this rock and see if there are any women under it." I didn't think about it that way. But what I thought to myself was: am I tired of some of these books that I'm reading! Some of them are nice, and some of them are exciting, but really, I've read about this stuff already. And who's this guy Henry Miller? You know, big deal. He's not talking to me. My life's not going to get a lot sexier on account of him. His is, no question about it. Maybe.

So, luckily, I began to understand it. It was just luck or pride or something like that. Or just not being able to accept slurs at myself or my people, women, Jews, or whatever. Even in Shakespeare, it always hurt my feelings. So I didn't really know that that's what I was going to do, but that's what I set out to do, and I did it, and I said, Yes, those lives are what I want to add to the balance of human experience.

We were accused of having been doomstruck the other day. And in a way we should be, why shouldn't we be? Things are rotten. I'm sixty-one and three-quarters years old and I've seen terrible times during the Depression, and I do think the life of the people was worse during the McCarthy period. I just want to throw that in extra. That is to say the everyday life, the fearful life, of Americans was harder in that time than this. But the objective facts of world events right now are worse than at any other time. And we all know that, we can't deny it, and it's also true that it's very hard to look in the faces of our children, and terrifying to look into the faces of our grandchildren. And I cannot look at my granddaughter's face, really, without shading my eyes a little bit and saying, "Well, listen, Grandma's not going to let that happen." But we have to face it, and they have to face it, just as we had to face what was much less frightening.

If I talk about going to the life of women and being interested in that, and pursuing it, and writing about it all the time and not thinking about whether it was interesting or not, and finding by luck—I like to say by luck, you know, it's polite somehow—finding by luck that it was interesting and useful to people, I also need to talk a little about what the imagination is. The word "imagination," as we're given it from childhood on, is really about imagining fantasy. We say, "Oh, that kid has some imagination, you know. Some smart kid; that kid imagined all these devils and goblins, and so forth." But the truth is that—"the truth," you know what I mean: when I say the truth, I mean *some* of the truth—the fact is, the possibility is that what we need right now is to imagine the real. That is where our leaders are falling down and where we ourselves have to imagine the lives of other people. So men—who get very pissed at me sometimes, even though I really like some of them a lot—men have got to imagine the lives of women, of all kinds of women. Of their daughters, of their own daughters, and of the lives that their daughters lead. White people have to imagine the reality, not the invention but the reality, of the lives of people of color. Imagine it, imagine that reality, and understand it. We have to imagine what is happening in Central America today, in Lebanon and South Africa. We have to really think about it and imagine it and call it to mind, not simply refer to it all the time. What happens is that when you just keep referring to things, you lose them entirely. But what if you think in terms of the life of the people, you really have to keep imagining. You have to think of the reality of what is happening down there, and you have to imagine it. When somebody said to Robert Stone, "Isn't there a difference between the life of Pinochet and of you, sir?" you have to imagine that life, and if you begin to imagine it, you know that there's a damn lot of difference between those two lives. There's a lot of difference between my life, there's a lot of difference between my ideas, between my feelings, between what thrills, what excites me, what nauseates me, what disgusts me, what repels me, and what many, many male children and men grownups have been taught to be excited and thrilled and adrenalined by. And it begins in the very beginning. It begins in the sandbox, if you want to put it that way. It begins right down there, at the very beginning of childhood. And I'm happy, for my part, to see among my children and their children changes beginning to happen, and also among a lot of young men—that's one of the things that's most encouraging to me: to think that some of these young guys have been listening, and imagining the lives of their daughters in a new way, and thinking about it, and wanting something different for them. That is what some of imagining is about.

So these are the things I've been thinking about a lot as a writer, both solitary in the world and at my desk. I just want to read you one little piece, and that's how I'll conclude. I probably left something out, but you can't say everything. We're really talking about society and artists, and this was in relation to the question of what was the responsibility of the writer, if there was any. And I thought, Every human being has lots of responsibility, and therefore the poet and the artist also has responsibility, why not? But this is the responsibility of society.

> It is the responsibility of society to let the poet be a poet
> It is the responsibility of the poet to be a woman
> It is the responsibility of the poets to stand on street corners
> giving out poems and beautifully written leaflets
> also leaflets they can hardly bear to look at
> because of the screaming rhetoric
> It is the responsibility of the poet to be lazy, to hang out
> and prophesy
> It is the responsibility of the poet not to pay war taxes
> It is the responsibility of the poet to go in and out of ivory
> towers and two-room apartments on Avenue C
> and buckwheat fields and Army camps
> It is the responsibility of the male poet to be a woman
> It is the responsibility of the female poet to be a woman
> It is the poet's responsibility to speak truth to power, as the
> Quakers say

It is the poet's responsibility to learn the truth from the powerless
It is the responsibility of the poet to say many times: There is no
      freedom without justice and this means economic
      justice and love justice
It is the responsibility of the poet to sing this in all the original
      and traditional tunes of singing and telling poems
It is the responsibility of the poet to listen to gossip and pass it
      on in the way storytellers decant the story of life
There is no freedom without fear and bravery. There is no freedom
      unless earth and air and water continue and children
      also continue
It is the responsibility of the poet to be a woman to keep an eye on
      this world and cry out like Cassandra, but be
      listened to this time.

(1986)

Thinking About Barbara Deming

At the Friends' Meeting House a couple of weeks after Barbara Deming died, we gathered to remember her for one another, to take some comfort and establish her continuity in our bones.

Later our friend Blue gave me two little wool hats assigned to me by Barbara as she worked those last weeks at dying. That work included the distribution of the things of her life, how to be accurate and fair in the giving, how not to omit anyone of that beloved and wide-webbed community. I imagine that when she came to my name she thought, Grace needs wool hats up there in the North where the body's warmth flies up and through the thinning hair of her head. Besides, I've noticed that she likes little wool hats.

"This too," Blue said, and gave me an envelope. In it were shards and stones gathered from the rubble of Vietnamese towns in '67 or '68. On the envelope, these shaky letters were written: "endless love." Nothing personal there, not "*with* endless love." The words were written waveringly, with a dying hand, on paper that covered bits and pieces of our common remembrance and understanding of another people's great suffering. I thought Barbara was saying, Send those words out, out out into the airy rubbly meaty mortal fact of the world, endless love, the dangerous transforming spirit.

Prison Notes is the story of two walks undertaken to help change the world without killing it. Barbara Deming was an important member of both. Twenty years of her brave life lie between them. Both walks were about connectedness, though the first began as a peace walk in 1964—from Quebec to Guantanamo, the American Army base in Cuba. In Georgia, it became impossible to demonstrate for peace without addressing the right of all citizens, black and white, to walk together down any street in any city of this country. Before the events in Albany, Georgia, had ended—the jailing, the fasts, the beatings—the peace movement and the civil-rights movement had come to know themselves deeply related, although there are still people in both movements who do not understand this flesh-and-blood connection.

The second walk, in 1983, began in the city of Seneca, New York. The walk, organized by the Seneca Women's Peace Encampment, continued through upstate towns in order to reach the huge missile base in Romulus. Its purpose was, in fact, to connect the struggles of women against patriarchal oppression at home and at work to the patriarchal oppression which is military power—endless war.

In both cases the walks were bound by nonviolent discipline.

Both walks were interrupted by hatred and rage. The walkers in '64 and again in '83 had to decide whether to continue on their lawful way or accede to the demand of the police chief (or sheriff) to take a different, less visible route; to leave the screaming, cursing men and women with their minds set in a national cement of race hatred, Jew hatred, women hatred, lesbian hatred, or to insist on the citizens' responsibility to use democratic rights—not just talk about them.

In both cases the walkers decided: we will not attack anyone, we will be respectful, we will not destroy anything, we will walk these streets with our nonviolent, sometimes historically informative, signs and leaflets. We may be pacifists, but we are not passivists. In both cases a confrontation occurred. It was not sought by the walkers, but it was accepted by them.

On that first long journey, men and women walked and went to jail together. Women alone took the second shorter walk, and fifty-four were jailed. Barbara was among them. It was her last action, and those who were arrested with her are blessed to have lived beside her strong, informed, and loving spirit for those few days. That difference between the two walks measures a development in movement history and also tells the distance Barbara traveled in those twenty years.

The direction her life took was probably established by the fact that her first important love was another woman, a hard reality that is not discussed in *Prison Notes* (this is probably the reason she insisted that her letter to Norma Becker be included in any reissue of that book). This truth about herself took personal political years in which she wrote stories and poems and she became a fine artist who suffered because she was unable to fully use the one unchangeable fact of her life—that she was a woman who loved women.

As a writer myself, I must believe that Barbara's attention to the "other" (who used to be called the stranger) was an organic part of her life as an artist—the writer's natural business is a long stretch toward the unknown life. All Barbara's "others" (the world's "others" too), the neighbor, the cop, the black woman or man, the Vietnamese, led her inexorably to the shadowed lives of women, and finally to the unknown humiliated lesbian, herself.

It was hard when this knowledge forced her to separate her life and work from other comrades, most of whom believed themselves eternally connected to her. "Why leave us now?" friends cried out in the pages of *WIN* magazine. "Now, just when we have great tasks." She explained: "Because I realize just as the black life is invisible to white America, so I see now my life is invisible to you."

Of course *she* was not the separator. *They* had been, the friends who wrote, saying, "We know it's okay to be a woman," but hated to hear the word "feminist" said again and again. She stubbornly insisted that they recognize Woman, and especially Lesbian, as an oppressed class from which much of the radical world had separated itself—some for ideological reasons, some with a kind of absentminded "We'll get to that later." (And many did.)

Of course, she never separated herself from the struggles against racism and militarism. She integrated them into her thinking. As she lived her life, she made new connections which required new analyses. And with each new understanding, she acted, "clinging to the truth," as she had learned from Gandhi, offering opposition as education and love as a way to patience.

The long letters that Barbara began to write after her terrible automobile accident in '71 have become books. They are studious, relentless in argument; she seems sometimes in these letters to be lifting one straw at a time from a haystack of misunderstanding to get to a needle of perfect communication stuck somewhere at the bottom. At the same time she had developed a style which enabled her to appear to be listening to her correspondent while writing the letter. In our last conversation (by phone), she explained that she had decided to discontinue treatment, the agonizing, useless treatment for her ovarian cancer. She had decided, she said, to die. "I'm happy now, I'm serene and I want to die in that serenity. I don't want to die in a chaos of numbness and nausea."

She left the hospital and went home to Sugarloaf Key to be with her companion, Jane Gapen, and the women of that community. To be present when friends came to visit. They came long distances to say goodbye, to stay a couple of days, to be part of the ceremonies of farewell and passage.

In the end she taught us all something about dying. I thank her for that last lesson, and I have written here in the present tense a few other things I learned from her before those last days.

Learning from Barbara Deming:

First: She's a listener.
So you can learn something about paying attention.

Second: She's stubborn.
So you can learn how to stand, look into the other's face, and
    not run.

Third: She's just.
So you can learn something about patience.

Fourth: She loves us—women, I mean—and speaks to the
    world.
So you can learn how to love women and men.

(1985)

The Gulf War

One Saturday morning in late March 1991: the Gulf War has ended. The Iraqis, retreating, have been bombed and strafed on their road home, having unwisely turned their backs to us. The war is not over.

I am walking with my women friends. They are a group that calls itself WIMPs: Women Indict Military Policies. They're a part of the peace movement that thinks about peace even when the newspapers say there's no war. We're walking single file, led by a solemn drumbeat through the streets of our neighborhood in lower Manhattan. Our postwar signs say IS THE MIDDLE EAST MORE STABLE NOW? One sign has a picture of an Iraqi child. Across his chest the words *Collateral Damage* are superimposed.

We're surprised when people thank us for our flyers and for our presence in the streets. Every now and then, some old-fashioned person says, "Go back to Russia." Or a modern fellow says, "Go kiss Saddam's ass." But we're in New York, where the yellow ribbons that have tied our country into a frightened sentimental knot are not so prevalent.

I've been in the U.S. peace or antiwar movement since before the Vietnam War, the mid-1950s. In fact, the Vietnam War interrupted the work many people were doing in trying to end militarism and prevent nuclear war and nuclear proliferation.

In 1961 I was invited to join a group called the Greenwich Village Peace Center, founded by the American Friends Service Committee, which with its customary wisdom left us alone to figure out the consensus, nonviolence decentralized or direct action. We had come from neighborhood concerns: schools, parks, transport. Many of us had children and were worried about the nuclear tests that were sending radioactivity into the air—particularly strontium 90, which traveled through air, to grass, to cows, to our children's milk. We didn't like the arms race, which, during air-raid drills, forced our children to hide under school desks. We were not so much understanding as experiencing the connections. We had, I suppose, been scratching around furiously under the oppression of McCarthyism and were glad to have come together in an autonomous way that was also sensible and communal.

One day our friend and board member Dr. Otto Nathan* said, "You know, there is the beginning of a war in Southeast Asia in a country, very small, called Vietnam. We are now in there with advisors—all kinds of soldiers. Soon—who knows?—we have to pay attention."

We *did* pay attention a couple of weeks later by holding a meeting and discussion (not called a teach-in yet). Just an educational event at a local church, well attended—and then our slow work began as the war itself slowly gathered its political and military determination to slaughter a million Vietnamese as well as 58,000 Americans.

---

* Dr. Otto Nathan, Einstein's executor, an economist, said sadly to me one day, "You know, it isn't guns *or* butter. If THEY wanted it, the country could have guns *and* butter." When I mentioned this to other smart economists they disagreed. The thirty years of simple American malice since then have inclined me to agree with Dr. Nathan.

Now I will tell you something about the way we organized against this war—how roughly 3,500 events were successfully hidden from other Americans and the world; how it was shaken by the terrible accumulating speed of the Gulf War. It's as though the war itself was one of those smart weapons, tested in vicious electoral campaigns and used in this case to eliminate the peace movement and its national and historical accomplishment, the Vietnam Syndrome. At this moment of triumph, with 300 Americans and 100,000 Iraqis dead, the President announced that he had indeed extinguished the peace movement and the Vietnam Syndrome. Was the main purpose of the Gulf War to bathe the American conscience in blood so as to give it a taste for blood? Well, certainly that was one of its purposes.

The peace movement itself is a valuable old fact, unstable at its broadest constituency, rock-solid at its center. It lives, as many readers know—broad or narrow—in our rich, powerful, somewhat backward, secretly poor, racist, uncomfortably large democratic nation, the United States—which is also cranky and righteous. The elections every four years are considered the final responsibility of citizenship, though usually only about 50 percent of registered voters vote. That's why it takes an awful lot of time and nerve for people to speak up. (That's why a short war is best.) If, on a street corner while giving out flyers, you ask someone why they don't speak up, they are apt to say they don't need to, we're already a democracy. Our two political parties, smiling proudly at one another, enable us to demand lots of pluralism in other countries.*

Now, how should I describe how this war's peace movement happened? There were already women and men innocently joyful about the end of the Cold War (me too), believing we'd come to that moment in our lifetimes when serious expensive internal problems

* Vermont, where I now live, elected an independent socialist, a terrible shock to the U.S. Congress.

could be addressed. The Panama invasion was a bad sign, but if you work in any oppositional movement you will be opposed vigorously. (This surprises some people.) We didn't expect things to be easy, but we had added hope to the personality, if not the character, of our work. The continuing antiwar workers were doing the usual antimilitarism work—opposing the arms budget (much of it hidden in costs of old wars; hidden too in the Energy Department budget), fighting underground testing, conducting classes in nonviolence, anti-recruitment drives in high schools. And a boycott of war toys. It seemed clearer with each administration decision that President Bush and his warrior companions had drawn their first line in the sandbox in a tough school, and they hadn't changed too much—in action or in boy language.

Environmental organizations were doing their important work globally and in village toxic dumps. The Central American networks were dealing with decades of exported U.S. repression and war. Feminist groups—radical, socialist, academic, or traditional—were facing the backlashes that often follow success—the anti-abortion moralities of the anti-sexual right as well as the wishful pronouncements of patriarchy that feminism was dead. Blacks and other people of color also hoped that the inner-city disaster of homelessness and poverty would be reversed somehow, although racism, as the most severe inherited illness of the United States, was continuing its nasty life. Gay groups struggled with discrimination and the grief of AIDS. Middle Eastern organizations suffered indifference and nearly everyone else's ignorance . . . at a time when their role was about to become central.

I've told you all this to show that radical and social justice organizations had plenty to do. But the experience of Vietnam and the work of decades began to pay off. In general, most of the groups I've described saw their connections to one another—were in fact living those connections. Before the coalition (two in some places—three in Seattle, I've been told—at first anyway) there was a lot of overlapping. For instance, many women in Central American work were feminists. They listened to the radio and watched television and heard the drone and confidence of prowar male experts—even more tedious than some of their political brothers. It's hard to believe that fifteen years ago people opposed to nuclear power and anti-nuclear-war activists didn't understand that they had a common agenda. It took long discussions and a couple of years of political argument and mediation to bring them together. Environmentalists had to learn that war made an ecological mess. Oh? First resistance. Then surprise. Then connection.

On August 29, 1990, Jeff Patterson refused to join his unit; he sat down on the airstrip in Hawaii. He had enlisted in the Marine Corps straight out of high school in California—for the same reason most youngsters do: educational opportunities, maybe some adventure. His experience during deployments to Okinawa, South Korea, and the Philippines changed his outlook entirely. He said, "I have, as an artillery controller, directed cannons on Oahu, rained burning white phosphorous and tons of high explosives on the big island, and blasted away at the island of Kahoolawe . . . I can bend no further." In the next few weeks, others were to join him.

On September 12, 1990, one of the first peace meetings in New York was held at the Cooper Union. There were thousands of women and men—the auditorium was full; there were loudspeakers outside. The weather was fine and the plaza around the Cooper Union was packed with intent listeners. I have been living in white Vermont, and as a true New Yorker I became excited once again to see all the colors of the people of my city. And the numbers! A surprise really. Oh, I thought, this war will never happen.

At the literature table I looked at various flyers and petitions, particularly the flyer and petition issued by the coalition that had put this marvelous meeting together, with its twenty to thirty speakers. I thought it was all right—kind of jargony, but not too terrible. This huge meeting was what mattered.

Still, I did say to the young woman at the lit table: "How come you guys left out the fact that Iraq did go into Kuwait? How come?" She said, "That's not really important." "I know what you mean," I said, "but it happens to be true."

I did know what she meant, and I read their explanation a couple of weeks later. It insisted that if the American people were told about the invasion of Kuwait, they would "become confused." It would "obfuscate" the basic facts and actions. Unfortunately, of course, the American people had already been told and continued to be told day and night about this pathetic little country of trillion-aires, and so omitting facts became a lie and did get in the way of organizing people unaccustomed to being held to political lines. It was a stubbornness that hurt work in New York more than elsewhere, but people are used to that, and national—I should say local—organizing all around the country against the frighteningly speedy troop and propaganda buildup continued. Reports of their success vary according to the facts and the disposition of the reporter.

Two coalitions finally had to happen in New York. One was the Coalition to Stop Intervention in the Middle East, which, with its strong cadre of the Workers' World Party, had organized the important New York September 12 meeting; the other became the National Campaign for Peace in the Middle East, with its base in traditional peace and anti-intervention groups. The division was real, a matter of substance, style—and at the same time there were organizations that had simply started to do their anti–Gulf War in one coalition or another—also, it depended on how much they were doing outside the big cities. An example would be Palestinian Aid in the coalition and Palestinian Solidarity in the campaign. The division came to a pointy head over the dates of the major Wash-ington demonstration. The coalition had decided on the nineteenth before a common meeting with the campaign. Reasons for both dates are as good as they were bad. It was good to do it on Martin Luther King's holiday weekend, because . . . Yes, I thought. It was bad to plan it for that weekend because . . . Yes, I thought. In any event, the vote ran extremely high against the nineteenth.

In late December 1990, the campaign proposed a joint state-ment supporting both demonstrations. The coalition said no. Many people went to both. The coalition went ahead, had its demonstra-tion on the nineteenth with good representation of people of color—blacks, Hispanics, and many Middle Eastern Americans. In San Francisco there were about 150,000 demonstrators. The twenty-sixth brought out about 250,000 people in Washington. The tone and the style of these demonstrations were extraordinary. There were more hand-made, non-organizational signs as well as the big ballooning sky-hiding world hoisted above us all by Greenpeace. The Bread and Puppet marched with its huge puppets, its great music and stilt dancers, and its Vermont cadre of a couple of hundred B. and P. lov-ers and activist banner carriers. Some of the signs—culled from my head and *The Nation*: WAR IS GOOD BUSINESS; INVEST YOUR SON OR YOUR DAUGHTER; GEORGE BUSH IS HAVING A WARGASM; A KINDER GENTLER BLOODBATH; GIVE ESTROGEN A CHANCE; READ MY APOCALYPSE.

These impressive demonstrations happened later, after the war had started but before the rage and drive of the air war and its mur-derous preemption of hope taught us to say the word "blitzkrieg" and understand where our civilian and military leaders had gone to school.

I want to say a little more about the opposition to the inevitable war before January 15, 1991. Interesting fact: 73 percent of American women were opposed to the war in the month before it started. Men were split down the middle.

The New York Times printed a letter on August 22, 1990, from Alex Molnar, whose son, a twenty-one-year-old Marine, had been sent to Saudi Arabia. He concluded his letter (to President Bush): "And I'm afraid that as the pressure mounts, you will wager my son's life in a gamble to save your political future . . ." The letter was reprinted many times and created a movement called the Military Families Support Network . . . which by early March 1991 had

chapters in thirty-nine states. MFSN supported the use of economic sanctions, opposed massive deployment of U.S. forces and
the entire military offensive. Their emphasis on the support of troops
has put off a number of columnists. I myself feel that a slogan like
"Support the Troops" has to include the words "by Bringing Them
Home Now."

Actually, in almost every demonstration I've been a part of or
come upon in another city or town, those last words *were* there.
There's a kind of critiquing of the events and actions of that hard
short period that is not criticism but is more like an academic exer-
cise made by people at their desks who are not out on the streets or
engaged in the decision-making processes of any noncentralized
organization.

Journeys, peace missions to Iraq or journeys of inquiry, have
been a part of peace-movement activity from late summer/early
autumn 1990, when they began organizing, into February 1991 and
the war.

In mid-October a peace delegation organized by the Fellowship
of Reconciliation spent two days in Jordan and a week in Iraq. The
main purpose of this mission was to bring medicine to Amman
and especially to Baghdad. David McReynolds, one of the members of the twenty-person team, returned and reported on the lives
of children in Baghdad. I think of one scene he describes: fathers
in a small Iraqi village holding their children up to the windows of
the Americans' bus. I did not see this report in our newspapers.

The Gulf Peace team opened a peace camp on the border of Iraq
and Saudi Arabia. It remained there for ten days and thousands of
sorties of the air war. It was evacuated on January 26, 1991, by the
Iraqis. There were eighty-six witnesses living at the camp, many
from other countries as well as the United States. They saw the
beginning of the environmental destruction by our smart Air Force
and the great suffering of the people. I read their reports in the left
and pacifist press.

Later—in early February, during the war—Ramsey Clark and a

group of well-known photographers and reporters went, including an American Iraqi with family there who was able to bring him into conversation with the ordinary civilians and their experiences— beginning with the bombed road from Jordan into Iraq and the destruction of civilian vehicles—food-and-grain trucks. Also the markets, water stations, schools—all the targets, I guess, of our "stupid" bombs.

To return to prewar actions, statements . . . On November 14 the National Congress of Churches at a conference in Portland, Oregon, condemned U.S. policy in the Gulf: "As Christians . . . we must witness against weak resignation to the illogical logic of militarism and war." The National Conference of Catholic Bishops wrote to President Bush: "In this situation, moving beyond the deployment of military forces in an effort to deter Iraq's aggression to the undertaking of offensive military action could well violate the criteria for a 'just war,' especially the principles of proportionality and last resort."

These strong leadership statements stood, but the churches themselves fell into an awful quietness as the war began. I am reminded here that it is important to say that the religious fellowships, the Catholic and Jewish, the Protestant peace churches as well, did *not* retreat. What happened most to churches and congregations sincerely opposed to the war to begin with is what happened to representatives and senators that swore they'd never back down. The sight of a yellow ribbon unnerved them. They fell before it, just as tyrants and Satans had once fallen before the cross placed before their terrified eyes.

Meanwhile, in the rest of the country, hundreds of meetings, vigils, sit-ins, teach-ins were occurring. By early March 1991, over 3,500 actions had taken place and over 4,000 arrests had been made. In our valley (between New Hampshire and Vermont) perhaps a dozen small towns held regular vigils. A newspaper advertisement was signed by 1,100 people. Who were they? The women and men who drove in and out of dirt roads were probably 1960s folks, now forty or so, with kids—or not—also Vietnam vets. But the signers were often old budget enemies from town meetings, people seen only at the dump or recycling center—or in church. We were amazed— What? She signed! That one! But this was before the war . . . Vigils continued through the weeks of the war. We are going back now to the signers. What will we find?

Full-page advertisements were taken out by SaneFreeze and the Ad Hoc Committee, which also organized teach-ins. Communications from other parts of the country tell the same story—sometimes more original. Seven or eight men or women from Oakland traveled the train system singing funny anti-Bush lyrics. They were applauded and cursed. Here are some quotes from Lucy Lippard's report in *Z* of artists' and just plain creative people's responses to the prospects of war and to the war itself:

> Our street theater piece "The Bushes Take You For A Ride" has George and Barbara in a red cardboard car running out of gas and being "serviced" by a soldier/gas pump—GI José. A hose from his red satin heart is administered by a "Plasmaco nursery" representing Petrolium Multinational. When the soldier collapses, the audience is solicited for more volunteers.
>
> Two of Boulder's most effective cultural groups are satirical. LISP (Ladies in Support of the President) is "an organization of patriotic God-fearing LADIES who deplore nasty war protests" and offer "George is not a wimp" buttons. An offshoot of the local Queer Cosmos, these men in drag haunt recruitment centers and plead prissily at rallies for "all you homosexuals and commies to please go home." A long-standing socialist feminist group (with anti-racist "Klarette" performances and a public "Sodomy Patrol" among their past credits) are polling crowds.
>
> GRIT (Gulf Response Information Team, "a very private research group") are sending the results to the President. Their ques-

tions begin straight, sucking people in, and end with outrageous ones, like "In order to support our troops, how many casualties from your family would be acceptable? (a) 1 (b) 2 (c) 3 or more (d) all of them."

Small groups like GRIT, and individual artists, can be less intimidating and attract less hostility and more dialogue than massive demonstrations, which serve another purpose. For instance, playwright Art Mayers patrolled Maine's state capitol building, in Arab headdress and mask dripping with blood, muttering over and over, "the horror of it, the horror of it." He was eventually arrested for "terrorizing children," but the charges were dropped.

When I stopped at the office of the War Resisters League to pick up some flyers, they were receiving as many as ninety calls a day asking for military counseling, from reservists as well as active-duty men *and* women. A high-school kid who had just enlisted was speaking to Peter Jamieson, a Vietnam vet (he's a counselor.) Michael Marsh, who has organized the work in this office, is down at Camp LeJeune, North Carolina, where seven Marine COs are being court-martialed on charges of desertion. I was given a sheet of paper listing fifteen resisters. In Germany there are American soldiers at U.S. bases who are resisting deployment. A Military Counseling Network has been in place since early autumn—the American Friends Service Committee, the War Resisters League, and the Central Committee of Conscientious Objectors were major networkers.

A fine project (which, with more money, could have got under way earlier) was MADRE's tour of Women of Courage. MADRE, whose major political work had been about Nicaragua, especially the women, their hospitals, and day-care centers, had undertaken to send about twenty women from different Middle Eastern countries on tour through the United States and Canada. While one group spoke in New England, others were in Toronto—and in California cities. Women from Iraq, Turkey, Palestine, Egypt, and Israel were in the group, I heard. Each city or two visited had to add an American mother whose son or daughter was in the desert.

In going over material I'd gathered for this chapter, I found something I'd written to a friend I work and think with at the very beginning of January 1991:

> Another thing I worry about: Resistance to this war is great. So—if we *do* go to war, it will take a lot of hardworking repression to keep that anger in check or turn it around. We better watch out for it. It will only *start* with the suppression of information from the front and continue by hiding our regional and town actions from one another till we think we or our villages or our families are alone.

This is exactly what happened: the pools. According to the Fund for Free Expression, of the 1,400 journalists in the Persian Gulf only 192—including technicians and photographers—were placed in press pools with combat forces. Journalists "apprehended or threatened with detention or detained include E. Schmitt and Kifner of *The New York Times*, Gughliotti of *The Washington Post*, King and Bayles of the Associated Press . . . These are people who did try to break free of government censors . . ." "A French TV crew was forced at gunpoint by U.S. marines to give up videotape it had shot of U.S. wounded in the battle to retake the Saudi town of Khafji."

Almost overnight, once the war started, the silence began. Having lived for sixty-eight years, a surprising number of them in some political consciousness, I must report that I've never experienced the kind of repression that set in once the air war started. It was not like the McCarthy period—that is, there were no personal direct attacks on well-known people of that kind. It was as though a great damp blanket had been laid over our country with little pinholes for American flags to stick up into the public air.

Here is another paragraph from the February 27, 1991, report of the Fund for Free Expression.

There have been several instances of retaliation against journalists who have questioned the propriety of the war. After he wrote approvingly of an antiwar march, *San Francisco Examiner* associate editor and columnist Warren Hinckle was put on a partially paid three-month leave. "I take the position that I was censored," Hinckle says. The editor of the Kutztown, Pennsylvania, *Patriot* was fired after he wrote an editorial calling for peace. *Village Voice* national affairs editor Dan Bischoff was cancelled as a guest on CBS news "Nightwatch" program. The Pentagon refused to produce anyone to appear on the program if the *Voice* was to be represented among the participants. The program's producer recalls a Pentagon representative as objecting on the grounds that "if someone from the *Village Voice* is on, that raised the possibility that there will be a discussion of the merits" of the lawsuit filed by the *Voice* and other media organizations challenging the Pentagon press restrictions. The Public Broadcasting System postponed a rebroadcast of a Bill Moyers "Frontline" program on the Iran-Contra affair because, according to an internal PBS memo, the program's raising of "serious questions about then–Vice President Bush's involvement and actions" make it "journalistically inappropriate" during the war against Iraq, because "the program could be viewed as overtly political by attempting to undermine the President's credibility."

FAIR—Fairness and Accuracy in Reporting—offered the following report on February 22:

About 1.5 percent of nightly news programs . . . were identified as antiwar protests. Only one leader of a peace organization was quoted in broadcasts surveyed. Seven Super Bowl players were sought out to comment on the war. Half of all sources were connected to U.S. or Allied governments, 3 in 10 from the military.

Another report on television—this time by three academic re-searchers, Sut Jhally, Justin Lewis, and Michael Morgan—revealed that there was a correlation between knowledge—information—and opposition to the war. Television viewing was broken down into three groups. The longer people looked at television, the less they knew. The short-time viewers were not well informed, but much better informed than the others. After some protests follow-ing FAIR's exposés, certain programs like the *McNeil-Lehrer News-hour* (daily) finally allowed Noam Chomsky, Erwin Knoll, and Edward Said to speak their dissenting views.

It's not as though media workers on our side didn't fight back. Paper Tiger/Deep Dish produced a Gulf Crisis TV series—seen on public access channels and finally PBS (Public Broadcasting). Tapes were used in university teach-ins.

When peace people (organizers) talked critically of the period, they varied—widely. Frances Crowe, in western Massachusetts, "found a huge antiwar movement waiting to be organized. After ten years of trying to organize around the Middle East, people are ready and willing to learn about the region." Susan Akram asks, "How did the peace movement get so isolated?"

I've tried to describe in these few pages something about what has been happening in the last months in my country. I've left out a lot—by necessity.

If you were part of these events, if you were working in your community, you had a sense of excitement, action, momentum, but at the same time, listening to radio, television news, or reading the daily press darkened you into an unimaginable despair. Not only the sense of a vast damp blanket over the country, but also it seemed that half your neighbors not only didn't know but *wanted not to know*, because if a bit of news squeaked through (the bombing of the Baghdad shelter), there were cries of "Treason!" (the photog-raphers, the anchormen, the television station).

One of the responses to this war that grieved me particularly was the failure of American Jews to see how bad this war was for Israel, how dangerous, how destructive it *had* to be for the hopes for peace and a decent relationship with Palestinians—how it set all that struggle back years and years.

So the war ends—and doesn't end. It never ended for the Vietnamese—all these embargoed years. Not for the Panamanians either, who are worse off than ever. Not for the Middle East, where, as I write, hundreds of thousands of Kurds running, fighting, encouraged by Bush's rhetoric of rebellion, are being slaughtered by Iraq's helicopters and starved and frozen in their tracks. Thousands of Iraqis dead, injured, leave the countryside and the destroyed cities in grief and turmoil. We've learned that *only 7 percent* of our thousands of sorties were so-called smart bombs. The rest were the usual stupid carpet bombs, cluster bombs, etc., used for civilians, ground armies, the earth . . .

Israelis and Palestinians hate each other more than ever—both people having been driven mad: the Israelis by Europeans fifty years ago; the Palestinians by Israelis today. The Palestinians running from the country, Kuwait, which we liberated so that it could continue along its glowing golden road. The oppression of Palestinians in the occupied territories is worse than ever, partly because they made the wrong (foolish) decision to agree with Saddam Hussein, partly because Israel was planning on making it tougher to be a Palestinian anyway.

Why were Bush and friends so determined to jam this war down the originally disinterested throats of allies—the UN and the United States—the American citizenry? We learned—little by little. First everyone said Oil! Of course. Then we learned that we used very little of Kuwait's oil. So we understood next that it was about hegemony—that is, being in charge of everyone else's oil. A major purpose was the great Pentagon need to try out all the new, so far unused trillion dollars' worth of airware. How would they perform?

Many years ago, in 1969, a North Vietnamese said to me as I was leaving Hanoi, "Please tell the great American scientists to stop using us as their laboratory. Your napalm *does* work. So does your improved white phosphorous." Our government also wanted to teach an important lesson: it was possible to move over 400,000 troops in a few weeks halfway round the fattest part of the earth.

It was also a major necessity to wipe out the historical memory of the 1960s, which moved more powerfully than is usually perceived into the 1970s with the rise of the women's movement, the anti-nuclear-power movement, and the science of ecology with its working arm, environmentalism.

I am reminded of a statement made by Donella Meadows at a Dartmouth teach-in. She explained that there was alternative energy for everything in normal comfortable American life—television, air conditioners, light, heat, cars. There was only one enterprise which required such massive infusion of energy for which no alternative to oil could work—and that was war. A tank, she said, could move only seventeen feet on a gallon of gasoline. So this is the final purpose. This has been a war to maintain turmoil in the world (particularly in the Middle East). This has been a war to ensure that Americans can continue to make war, and like it.

(1991)

Report from North Vietnam

Our interpreter Nhan said, "Grace, if you would stay another two weeks, I could teach you the tune of the language. Speaking is singing—a lot of up and down anyway. The word *Hoa* means flower, *Hoa* means harmony. The tune's important. Okay."

Our twenty-one days in Vietnam happened in three parts. The first—Hanoi, the city, the officials, the organizations, useful information, making friends. All necessary to the second part, seven-day, 1,100-kilometer journey to the Ben Hai River, which is the seventeenth parallel, the riverbank of American power. We washed our hands and feet there, a lot of symbolism. Reality too, almost—the roadway was shelled right after we left. American reconnaissance planes which we'd seen above us had noticed a jeep or a movement.

A word about Hanoi. One of our hosts said, from the plane, "Did you see how green we are?" Yes. Old trees, parks, lakes, a beautiful city, old, much of it in bad shape, no new construction in the city. The suburbs had been built for the workers, and bombed flat by us. Hanoi was wildly defended—from the rooftops everywhere—one of seven pilots we talked to said, "Downtown Hanoi, the flak, you don't know what it was like—the air was absolutely black."

As we started from Hanoi on fair roads, immediately the destruction of public buildings, hospitals, schools was apparent. The first city we came to—Phu Ly—totally destroyed. We were not military men, not even people who'd been to wars, we weren't bored by the repetition; we didn't even get used to it. So the destruction we saw happened first to our eyes: the mud and straw huts, and beyond them the cities, where a wall or two of small brick stucco-covered houses remained, and maybe one wall of the larger public buildings. And all the way on National Highway 1, the people—something like Fourteenth Street in Manhattan for about 650 kilometers—going back and forth, about their business of life and repair, carrying on their backs, on bamboo poles, balanced baskets of salt, water spinach, fertilizer, young shoots for transplanting, mud and stones for the roads, firewood for cooking. Bicycles doing the work of trucks. The children—little boys lounging on water buffalo, fishing with nets like sails in the rivers and ponds— and bomb craters. All this life moving on the road, and alongside the road, so that Ching, our driver, who looked like a tough Puerto Rican kid, drove hundreds of miles with his fist on the horn.

"Humans out of the way, here come the Progressive American People, to view the insanity of their countrymen. Let them deal with this disgust and shame."

South—past the Ham Rong Bridge, near Thanh Hoa—another pilot said, "What? It's still standing?" Yes, standing—trucks, cars, bikes, move over it continuously. We note its twisted girders shot with holes.

The Ham Rong Bridge, the pride of the defenders of Thanh Hoa, was the last bridge we saw that withstood the bombing. As we moved farther south along the road, the American intention was clear. The first order was to kill the bridges and destroy transportation. On the reconnaissance maps, a bridge was a bridge in some head, so for a couple of miles every river looked as though maniacs had been let loose by a fool. Hundreds and hundreds of bomb craters—whether the river (and bridge) was 2 feet wide or 1,000 feet wide. The next day, at whatever the small cost—$100 at most—a few planks restored traffic over the mountain streams. The craters—at a couple of thousand per bomb—cost the American taxpayer close to one million dollars.

The larger bridges were more of a problem, but we saw the remains of half a dozen bridges at some rivers. And the repairs varied—on occasion, bound bamboo pontoons; often the riverbed was raised with stones and we drove hubcap-deep across the river. But all along the roads piles of stones were prepared for the next attack of the madmen. Gangs of young girls working and boys too—all of them, for no good reason, cheery and unbelieving at the sight of us.

Wherever we went people said—greeting us hospitably, to put us at ease, guessing our shame—"We distinguish between the American imperialist war maker and the American people." The child in the street believes this. "It is not so hard to explain," Dang Thai Mai, a writer, one of our hosts, said. "After all, General Giap and Diem come from Quangbinh—from the same district."

Okay. So. Trying to be a logical American, I or we think, Well, of course it's a war and they are bombing communication, transportation. It's true, they are overkilling the Vietnamese countryside and the little brooks, but that's America for you, they have overkilled flies, bugs, beetles, trees, fish, rivers, the flowers of their own American fields. They're like overgrown kids who lean on a buddy in kindergarten and kill him.

Then we leave National Highway 1 and move into the villages to live for a few days in a guest house in a small field, which before we left was plowed, manured, and planted with groundnuts up to our door. I guess they expected no immediate guests. The villages. The village Trung Trach was in the Land of Fire. Mr. Tat said, "The Land of Fire for three reasons: first, the fire of the burning heat; second, the fire of continuous *day and night* American bombardment for three years, so that people never left their tunnels; and third, the fires of resistance that burned in the heart of the people."

In all of Quangbinh province, not one brick house stood. This is true of the cities on the main road too. Hoxa, the beautiful city—there's nothing there—grass—some doorsteps. People in Hanoi asked in nostalgic pride, "Did you see Hoxa?" Donghoi—a city of 30,000—something like pictures of Pompeii. A city shaped like New York with its nose in the water, a great outdoor theater whose terraced seats remain, a magnificent blasted Catholic church (the French, in their war, spared the churches). Nobody lives in Donghoi. These cities will not be rebuilt until the Americans leave Vietnam. In the hills a new Donghoi will be built.

I return to the villages. The village Nien Trach Nuc Ninh, Trung Trach, and the village T and D in Vinh Linh Zone at the DMZ. It turned out that these villages far off the roads and highways were military targets too. Each village had a House of Tradition, which kept the artifacts of other victories—the weapons with which they'd fought the French, Japanese, Chinese. Also deactivated CBUs, pellet bombs in one village, the belongings of pilot Dixon, who is buried near the sea—with a cross over his grave—in case his mother should want to come see it after the war. It was in the bombed-out blasted torn-up villages where the entire population had been driven underground to live in tunnels for three years, to suffer in underground hospitals, to study in underground schools. It was into these villages that pilots floated or tumbled out of burning planes.

It's a people's war. The Army and the people are interchangeable in many cases. The Army sometimes works on the roads, the people in the self-defense units: the girls' militia, the old men's militia in the villages take to the artillery, to their rifles, to anything handy. The villages are bombed, restored in mud and thatch, to cultivate the land, to make paths between the craters which in one village had become duck ponds, fisheries, and irrigation sources.

Water spinach, a wonderful vegetable, was planted in some. They could do this because nobody left the land or ran from the Land of Fire. They dug underground and lived in the rooms we saw, and crawled on hands and knees to other rooms and exits through supported tunnels—as we did. The people said, "We could not have held out if we hadn't, in these tunnels, been able to lead a normal life. Normal life is very important, family life, children's education, care of the sick and old, rice cultivation—along with the resistance." Threads were pulled, but the cloth of life mysteriously held. They are naturally proud to have held the greatest power in the world at bay.

I think they hide the cost—they did not, except in two or three cases, introduce us to the severely wounded or ill. The people we saw looked well after six, seven months of no bombing—or very little. The children, hundreds and hundreds, looked well. We did not visit hospitals. Bach Mai was bombed six months later.

So this is what we saw there: the destruction of the cities, roads, and bridges, and finally the villages. Some people do not like the word "genocide" and we leave the word alone; still, in this kind of war, every person takes part, and the next thing a logical military brain hooks into is the fact that every person is a military target, or the mother of a military target, and they live in the same house; since all military targets must be destroyed, it follows that the whole people must be destroyed. And that is what I think was attempted and that is what was absolutely thwarted.

The prisoners. The American war prisoners. This is what we were told about their treatment. When they first fall to the Vietnamese fields or dikes (which they've just bombed), they are taken into the care of the militia or self-defense unit, sometimes a couple of girls or a boy or two of sixteen. No abuse is permitted, and in only one case of seven men we talked to was any attempted.

One of the reasons Captain Wesley Rumble was so sick on the airplane on our return is that the Army doctors loaded him and his stomach was filled with Darvon and Librium for his worries. From what he told us, he was used to traditional Vietnamese medicines for his stomach ailments.

The third fact that emerged from our conversations with these men was the adequacy of the food. Almost all said that they were fed more than their guards—the Vietnamese think the Americans have large frames which must be served. The truth is, the men lost a tremendous amount of weight in the one to three years of imprisonment. The diet is mostly vegetable soup, with a little pork on occasion, and bread and some rice. Monotonous to an American but adequate. On a more varied Vietnamese diet, in three weeks we all lost weight. I lost eleven pounds.

Now, the Vietnamese say they release these men from time to time, as an act of their own humanitarian tradition. They *still* consider these Americans war criminals. They *hope* that some repentance has set in. They bring them news of the world, through occasional radios and books. The Americans all asked questions to show that they were somewhat informed but not well. I wish they could see more American periodicals or papers. The statements of congressmen and the tremendous feeling against the war, as reported in our own establishment press, would be more useful as propaganda. The pilots are sometimes taken to the places they bombed, so they can see the land and the people—who seem only to be things when viewed at 650 miles an hour from a height of thousands of feet.

The three prisoners we brought home were taken to the museums in Hanoi and to the zoo before they left with us.

There's no time and I want to tell two or three things about the prisoners. They said many things I haven't sorted out yet—some of which horrified us, such as, "To be truthful I really liked bombing." I don't understand this remark, and for now I don't intend to. "I wish I'd met you people in '66"—the same man. "I went into this a military man and that's how I'm coming out."

Talking to another Vietnamese military man, one who worked with the prisoners, I said, "You release these men and many of them may make bad propaganda. They say one thing to you, then another thing later on radio or television." "That's all right," he said. "We know they have terrible pressure from the American Army and Navy, but they know the truth." I press forward, because I'm anxious: "Yes, you feel close to them, but they may not say what they feel." He says, "That's all right. We know it. They will go out and say something on radio, they will say something on TV bad, but at night they will go home and whisper the truth to their wife."

(1969)

El Salvador

I wondered what possible contribution I could make to this rich book of facts, this book of women whose lives have been a longing and a struggle for a revolution that would transform their entire country and would include women's lives in that transformation. (This has not always happened in revolutions.)

We were actually on our way to Nicaragua, but stopped in El Salvador. We owed this—the next three days—to our own U.S. government, which did not permit Nica Air to fly from the United States to Nicaragua. Still, the planes of my rich country seem to almost line the skies of the planet—unless some other earth-and-heaven owning nation says, "Not over us! Not just yet!"

In the course of those packed, well-organized days we saw the streets of San Salvador guarded against its own citizens by soldiers dressed in heavy weaponry. We traveled to barbed-wire camps, dusty, full of displaced villagers. We learned from the idealistic and endangered Catholic and Lutheran caretakers that the barbed wire was not so much to keep the peasants in as to prevent the death

squads from easily snatching a hounded mountain villager or a
guerilla's cousin for questioning and torture.

We saw orphanages where an energetic priest tiptoed around
visiting U.S. congressmen. He hoped they would have contacts
with philanthropists who might help pay for the cottage camps so
that little children could have books to learn from and prostheses
to walk with. (Just a few miles from this camp, this orphanage,
on the very same road, four nuns had been killed, removed from the
dangerous occupation of active compassion and prayer by busy kill-
ers.) Walking among these children whose parents were murdered
or imprisoned or in exile, I couldn't help but think of Vietnam,
where first our government created orphans, then decided to adopt,
nurture, and finally educate them, away from the life and history of
their people.

We were able to visit Ilopango prison—the women's prison—a
little while after the fasting, the strikes, the struggles described in *A
Dream Compels Us*. And found, ironically, a somewhat freer environment than we had observed in San Salvador. Young women greeted
us, black-tammed commandantes who had been captured in the mountains. A chorus sang the "Internationale" to us. A theater group made
a play. We met several young women who, having been fruitlessly
interrogated, were shot in the leg to ensure immobility, then raped
and arrested. In Ilopango prison there were many small children—some
the babies of love, some of rape. For the legless young women, sixteen, seventeen years old, there was only one pair of crutches, which
meant that only one woman could get around at a time, making for a
kind of sad listlessness in the others. We called the MADRE* office
in New York (we were members of a tour organized by MADRE),
and they announced this need on the WBAI radio station. Within a
couple of days the office was jammed with crutches, and within two

* MADRE is a New York–based nonprofit organization dedicated to developing
political and material support for the women of Nicaragua and El Salvador.

weeks a group from NACLA* had brought the crutches down to Ilopango. A small shiny pebble in a dirty field of torment, hypocrisy, murder.

Back in San Salvador we visited the Mothers of the Disappeared. Their office had been raided and nearly destroyed a couple of days earlier. The women greeted us generously, as though they didn't know it was our U.S. tax money that was being used to increase and deepen their sorrow. (They knew a great deal.) They had placed two large photograph albums on the table, which we looked at. We could hardly turn the pages, as it would be an act of abandonment of the murdered son or daughter photographed on that page— usually a teacher or health worker, the same dangerous professions attacked by the Contras in Nicaragua.

In San Salvador I

Come   look   they said
here are the photograph albums
these are our children.

We are called the Mothers of the Disappeared
we are also the mothers of those who were seen once more
and then photographed   sometimes parts of them
could not be found

a breast   an eye   an arm is missing
sometimes a whole stomach
that is why we are called   the Mothers
of the Disappeared   although we have these large

---

* The North American Congress on Latin America (NACLA) publishes the bimonthly *Report on the Americas* and sponsors research on political, economic, and social developments in Latin America and the Caribbean.

heavy photograph albums full of beautiful
torn faces

In El Salvador II

Then one woman spoke   About my son
she said   I want to tell you   This
is what happened

I heard a cry   Mother
Mother   keep the door closed   a scream
the high voice of my son   his scream
jumped into my belly   his voice
boiled there and boiled until hot water
ran down my thigh

The following week I waited
by the fire making tortilla   I heard What?
the voice of my second son   Mother quickly
turn your back to the door   turn your back
to the window

And one day of the third week
my third son called me   Oh Mother please
hurry up   hold out our apron   they are
stealing my eyes

And then in the fourth week   my
fourth son   No

No   It was morning   he stood
in the doorway   he was taken right
there   before my eyes the parts of

the body of my son were tormented   are
you listening?   do you understand
this story?   there was only one
child   one boy   like Mary I had
only one son

I have written these few remembrances of a country my country won't leave alone because the faces of the people I saw in those short days do not leave me. I see it clearly right now. The teachers of ANDES—the teachers' union—demonstrating on the steps of the great cathedral, where hundreds, mourning Oscar Romero's murder, had been shot only a couple of years earlier. They held banners and called for decent wages, and an end to disappearances. On those historic steps they seemed naked to the rage of the death squads. I could see how brave they were because their faces were pale and their eyes, searching the quiet crowd, were afraid. Still, they stood there, shouted the demands, and would not be moved.

(1989)

Other People's Children

Our national grief at the thought of Vietnamese children who would be homeless after the American war seemed somehow more bearable during the war, when all our know-how was being used in making orphans. There did exist a history of homeless children and their wars, which could have been helpful, but we paid little attention to it. It was indeed offered to the country during the "babylift" last April, in public newspaper statements by social workers, historians, educators, religious leaders, and doctors, and in political street demonstrations on both coasts.

According to Joseph Reid of the Child Welfare League of America, there were 50,000 homeless children after the Nigerian-Biafran war. The United States (and other countries) thought these children should be offered for adoption. The Nigerians and Biafrans would not permit it. With the help of the International Union for Child Welfare in Geneva, all but twenty-seven of the children were reunited with family or village communities within two years.

Here is another lesson from history: my friend Karen DiGia was a displaced child in Germany after the Second World War.

That is, she was lost in one direction, and her parents, if alive, were lost in another direction, far from home. Here, the Red Cross helped. It took a year and a half before Karen DiGia's living father was found and they were brought together. She was only one child among hundreds of thousands. Had she been adopted away into Italy or the United States or Japan in some well-meaning child-consumers project, her records filed and sealed, they would have never met; she would have become an orphan and he the father of a dead child.

Karen told me that the streets of German cities were full of pictures of children. "Have you seen this child, Anna Marie; she was wearing a blue smock; she wandered away from our camp . . ." Translated for Americans today, whose kind hearts and open purses intend to take Vietnamese children into the finality of adoption, there may well be pictures posted on the walls in Saigon or Danang: "Has anyone seen Phuoung, last seen in a blue smock; she let go of my hand for a minute . . ."

In Vietnam there is a saying: "If mother is lost, there is auntie; if father is lost, there is uncle." The parentless child becomes the child of the large household, the village, old aunts who may not even be blood relatives but who share the natural responsibility of all adults for all the young. This has already happened in North Vietnam, where there is only one "home" for orphans. This is happening now in South Vietnam—grown-up refugees and children in the tens of thousands are returning to their villages in what the Provisional Revolutionary Government called the "Campaign for the Return to the Homelands."

Well, how did the orphan airlift happen, then, considering these histories, these facts? I have to say it coldly. The war in Vietnam, which began in ignorance, self-congratulation, and the slaughter of innocents, ended in much the same way. The orphan airlift in April was a balloon of sentiment that raised some 2,600 Vietnamese children and floated them across 12,000 miles of sky. The groups most responsible for that sky of flying/dying babies were the following:

1. Adoption agencies, with contracts begun in professional

decorum a year earlier. The agencies panicked when it appeared that the war would end and the subject matter of their contracts, Vietnamese children, would disappear, absorbed into the life of their own country. These agencies, determined to meet these contracts, lost their businesslike cool and allowed themselves to be helped by . . .

2. World Airways. Anxious to add love of children to its reputation as one of the world's largest charter airlines, World Airways, in the person of Ed Daly, who owned 81 percent of its stock, leaped into the early-April headlines and news photographs as the first of the baby transporters (although the U.S. government stepped in immediately and halted future World Airways baby flights). World Airways stock rose from 4⅛ to 6½ in one week, Ed Daly held the babies in his arms, and the company applied to the Civil Aeronautics Board for a domestic license to fly coast-to-coast. *The New York Times* tells the story of a $300 million to $400 million fortune amassed during the war years, when, under a contract with the Defense Department, World Airways planes carried cargo while military planes often flew empty.

3. The adoption agencies were also helped by a cynical political decision by the Ford administration to use the children in order to dig military aid for Thieu out of Congress. The language by which the kindness of American families was mocked does exist: U.S. Ambassador to South Vietnam Graham Martin, according to *The New York Times*, told President Thieu's Deputy Prime Minister Phan Quang Dan, "The collective shipment abroad of these orphans should help swing public opinion to the advantage of the Republic of Vietnam."

People who argued in favor of the airlift described the squalid, impoverished, unhealthy conditions of the orphan asylums in wartime Saigon, the possibilities of prejudice against mixed-blood children and handicapped children, and the superior opportunities in the United States in the years to come.

Actually, lovers of children have had every opportunity to help *all* the children of South Vietnam (but without direct ownership)—the

30,000 in orphan homes, the million or so who have lost one or both parents. Legislated aid could have gone from our own Congress to be distributed through international organizations like Medical Aid for Vietnam, the United Nations High Commission on Refugees, American Friends Service Committee, or the International Children's Fund. Private contributions can also be given to these organizations and earmarked for Vietnam. As of this writing, however, despite the fact that the Paris peace accords obligate the United States to provide postwar assistance to the country we devastated, no aid has ever been considered. The destruction of that small country in the last ten years cost Americans, at the government's lowest estimate, $150 billion. Lovers of children, we should be able to persuade Congress to offer one reconstructing billion for food, medicine, hospitals.

Still, it's the iron-hearted god of irony who points out that children who might be subjected to racial prejudice were being sent to the United States, the center of that pathology; that handicapped, war-mutilated children had been taken from a country where it would be the responsibility of family and community to keep them functioning in the ordinary life of the world. They were brought into a society which specializes in institutions, dumping grounds for the handicapped and the old, whose own Vietnam veterans are hidden in the recesses of Veterans Administration hospitals, whose black or handicapped orphans are unadoptable (and there may be as many as 100,000 of these children).

That same iron-hearted god of irony (who usually works in literature) spoke even louder, for we have the moral deafness of self-congratulators. A C5A, a plane that had at other times suffered structural problems (and was actually grounded for these problems in 1971), was stuffed with weapons, howitzers, sent to Vietnam, where it deposited the howitzers intact at the airport, then had its bare compartments filled with Vietnamese babies and older children "orphans," took off for the United States, and crashed in flames.

Years ago—1966 or 1967—people in the peace movement carried a poster of a well-dressed man holding a cigarette against the
arm of a child. On the poster the question was asked: *Would you
burn a child?* In the next poster, the man applied the burning cigarette, and the answer was given: *When necessary.* The third poster
showed a child burned and crippled by American napalm. There
may be a fourth now, that plane crashing, the children burning, the
war ending.

Who are these orphans?

Some *are* orphans, little persons who enter into a normal American procedure planned for the benefit of children, carrying true
papers of orphans. American parents had been waiting for them a
long time. Many of them are already being loved and cuddled behind
the "adoption curtain," as Betty Jean Lifton, writer and author of
Twice Born: Memoirs of an Adopted Daughter, has called it. Their
records are sealed, their past no longer exists.

But some are not orphans at all.

When the first children were flown into San Francisco, they
were kept briefly in the Presidio, an Army base just outside the city.
Two young Vietnamese women and a third who spoke excellent Vietnamese visited the Presidio to talk to the children. These women
were Jane Barton, an AFSC worker who had lived and worked in
hospitals in South Vietnam for three years; Muoi McConnell, who
was a nurse in Danang; and Trang Tuoung Nhu, a Vietnamese
woman born in Hue, who is Indochina coordinator of the International Children's Fund.

I talked with them and to Don Luce of Clergy and Laity Concerned and Doug Hostetter of the United Methodist office of the
United Nations, both of whom had spent years with voluntary organizations in Vietnam and spoke Vietnamese and knew the city
of Saigon. And I understood that the orphan asylums there were
not necessarily full of orphans, but the streets often were.

Children were brought to these institutions during the war
by parents who thought they would be safe. They were brought by

women or men who were unable to care for their babies, and who believed that they would have a better chance at a couple of meals a day in such a place. According to Judith Coburn, a journalist reporting in *The Village Voice*, they were also brought by Saigon bar girls who wanted their mixed-blood kids kept out of the hard life. Or there were children who, at the age of two, were deposited in orphanages by government people, having been taken away from their mothers, who were political prisoners. Any of these parents must have signed papers—papers that were supposed to prove the children's legal availability for adoption, papers that the poor in any country are often persuaded to sign in fear and despair for their kids. All these people might hope or expect to reclaim their kids at the end of the war.

Then there are the children who had not come from orphan asylums, who didn't know how they had been gathered up, or from where, to arrive at what place?—a child who'd survived the C5A crash but lost his mother's map and address; an eleven-year-old who later ran away from his foster parents in California, crying to go home to Vietnam; a boy who'd been in a refugee group from Danang and who had been separated from his mother; and the twenty-nine Cambodian children who arrived, mysteriously and without papers, on the East Coast of the United States. (The hard work of Congresswoman Elizabeth Holtzman [D-N.Y.] and her staff has kept those Cambodian children in foster care, safe from immediate adoption, while efforts are made to learn who they are and where they are from. The first thing learned was that twenty-one of the children had one living parent. The U.S. Immigration Service was forced by congressional pressure to send a letter to the foster parents advising them that the children's identity was being investigated and that adoption would be delayed.)

A class-action suit has been brought in California by the Center for Constitutional Rights, asking that the adoption of *all* these children be held up, that they remain in foster care with their records open and their short lives unsealed while Vietnam reorders itself and time without war brings families forward to reclaim and renew their lives. At this writing, the case is in court. Witnesses are describing the confusion and exchange of children's names, not from unkindness, just from carelessness and pressure where rigor was particularly required. One woman, who had received a six-year-old Vietnamese girl for adoption, testified that the child was not an orphan and that she wanted to return to Vietnam. In addition, there should have been immediate photographing of each baby and child, in its own clothes, with its special characteristics—birthmarks and war wounds—described and recorded. In late June, a federal judge in San Francisco ordered the Immigration and Naturalization Service to determine within three months whether or not the 22,000 children are orphans.

I must say that I don't believe that women could have invented the insane idea of transporting these children. I have not met one woman who isn't passionate on the subject—against or in favor—which is quite different from the cynicism and manic energy required for its invention and enaction. Many women truly believed that the American care and ownership of these babies would be the only way their lives would be saved. But most women were wild at the thought of the pain to those other mothers, the grief of the lost children. They felt it was a blow to *all* women, and to their natural political rights. It was a shock to see the world still functioning madly, the world in which the father, the husband, the man-owned state can make legal inventions and take the mother's child.

The Vietnamese have protested again and again, calmly at first, in the way that they have of trying to explain to innocent or ignorant people their methods of caring for children, their view of family life, the extended family, the natural responsibility of community. Then in anger, Dan Ba Thi, Provisional Revolutionary Government ambassador to the peace talks, said: "This is an outrageous attack on our sovereignty; the 1954 Geneva Convention forbids this kind of kidnapping. We demand the return of our Vietnamese children."

And on May 19, 1975, Pham Van Ba, PRG ambassador in Paris, wired the U.S. District Court in California: "We demand that U.S. government return to South Vietnam children illegally removed by Americans. We will assist placement of these children in their families or foster homes."

These children are, after all, the "young shoots" of Vietnam. Surely all the parents and grandparents, the "aunties" who have suffered and fought for thirty years in horror and continuous loss of dear family, under French oppression and the napalm and bombs of the United States, who have seen the murder of their living earth—surely they will demand to be reunited in years of peace with the hopeful children. They must believe passionately that those small survivors are not to be deprived of the fruits of so many years of revolutionary and patriotic struggle.

A Ms. *reader's response:*
I am appalled by the misinformation and lopsided reporting in "Other People's Children" by Grace Paley (September 1975).

I worked on the staff of the agency with the longest and largest ongoing adoption program in South Vietnam, and observed first-hand the orphanages and halfway houses of Saigon. As the mother of four Vietnamese children, I feel that Grace Paley has failed to perceive the essence and philosophy of intercountry adoptions . . .

The vast majority of Vietnamese orphans who have been adopted are illegitimate and totally abandoned—with no relatives waiting to retrieve them at war's end. The death rate for abandoned infants and young children was often as high as 80 percent. Of those who stayed in the orphanages and survived, many were badly undernourished and neglected.

Starvation and emotional deprivation tend to foster weak bodies and dull minds. Were these children to be the hope of the future of Vietnam—its political and social leaders, its professors?

Paley quickly dismisses the racially mixed and handicapped children. Somehow her "iron-hearted god of irony" points out that these children would be better off left in an orphanage. Would she leave in an orphanage an abandoned, undernourished, Vietnamese/ black infant who had nerve damage in his arms and his hands from lead poisoning, as well as severe permanent damage to the retinas of his eyes? If he survived, perhaps he could look forward to being a blind street boy in Saigon. He is my son.

Would she leave an abandoned, six-pound, three-month-old Montagnard girl who had severe diarrhea, dehydration, badly infected ears, scabies, pneumonia, and cytomegalo (a virus which often causes debilitating birth defects or mental retardation)? She, who had been marked by death, is my daughter.

Would she leave an abandoned, sick Vietnamese/Cambodian asthmatic boy? He is my son.

Would she leave a nine-year-old boy whose entire family was killed by American bombs? Perhaps he could have stayed a bit longer and been drafted into the military. Then he could have fought in the war (which one of us ever knew when the war would end?) and, if not killed, he could have added more scars to the ones that already cover his body. He is my son.

These four children are unique and very special human beings— as are all children. Their stories, however, are not. The children could have come from Timbuktu. Does the name of the country matter when the child is starving, dying, or lonely? She or he is a member of the human family.

Finally, Paley states that she does not believe "women could have invented the insane idea of transporting these children," and that most women "felt it was a blow to *all* women, and to their natural political rights." The fact is that the decision to care for the orphans, nurse them, feed them, bury them, love them, process adoption papers for eight years, and, in the end, send them on the airlift, was made, on the whole, by women.

Most of these women were not attempting to save the children from Communism, offer them Christianity, salve their guilt about the war, steal babies from their mothers' arms, or deprive a country of its future generations. Their reverence for a single human life crossed national, cultural, racial, social, religious, political, and economic boundaries. These women gave the children a chance at life— the promise of a mother and father instead of no one; the warmth of a bed instead of hard wooden slats; the satisfaction of a full stomach instead of a swollen empty belly; the advantage of essential medical care instead of the threat of death from the measles, chicken pox, starvation; the security of knowing one is loved and wanted instead of rejected and lonely, and on and on.

Many of these women risked and lost their lives in order to give life. My children are in their debt.

Suzanne Dosh
Lakewood, Colorado

Grace Paley replies:
I do admire Suzanne Dosh's extraordinary generosity—the lifelong reality of it—not a gift of money alone but years of responsibility and affection.

However, I made three points—none of which are really discussed or argued by Ms. Dosh:

1. The Orphan Airlift was a cynical political game played by the government in the hope that drama and sentiment would persuade Americans to give military aid to Saigon and continue the war.

2. Many children in that airlift were not orphans, but no official procedure was followed—for example, photographing for the future of inquiry or for identification. There are, right now in *this* country, four or five Vietnamese women trying to get their children back.

3. There are other solutions to the problem of homeless children after war. Jewish children in the Netherlands after World War II were returned to their families, and more recently, 27,000 Nigerian children (many orphans) remained Nigerian.

(1975)

I have been harsh on the bomber pilots, and so might anyone who had traveled a couple of hundred miles across their insolent work: the hospitals, schools, villages, streams they made their own by destroying. I am not Vietnamese; I do not have to let go of these images in order to live in this world.

But I am, and was in '69, sadder than I seemed to be in my reports, about the pilots' long, long incarceration, their uncomfortable or tortured entrance into the world of human suffering.

I still believe the "orphan" airlifts were an outrageous political ploy. But I did not consider the fact of Vietnamese racism in the case of mixed-race children. There may be another word for it relating to family village centeredness, but there is no good word.

I still admire Ms. Dosh, who responded to my article in Ms., *though we might find even wider differences today. Certainly life in the middle-class homes of our defeated United States has been easier than life in unrepaired, impoverished, victorious Vietnam. Decades of American embargo have seen to that. Still, at a poetry reading organized by the Joiner Center at the University of Massachusetts, Boston, I heard American vets and Vietnamese vets read stories and poems. Among them, a wonderful American poet, a young Vietnamese American, Christian Langworthy. I told him how fine his work was, then felt obliged to truthfully tell him how angry I'd been when he and others first came to the United States, as children, part of one of America's war games; how glad I was he was here with another language tune in his head to give our English the jolts it has learned over the centuries to use so well.*

Some Notes on Teaching: Probably Spoken

A woman invented fire and called it
                    the wheel
Was is because the sun is round
             I saw the round sun bleeding to sky
And fire rolls across the field
            from forest to treetop
It leaps like a bike with a wild boy riding it

Oh   she said
                 see the orange wheel of heat
light   that turned me from the
            window of my mother's home
to home in the evening

Here are about fifteen things I might say in the course of a term. To freshmen or seniors. To two people or a class of twenty. Every year the order is a little different, because the students' work is different and I am in another part of my life. I do not elaborate on plans or reasons, because I need to stay as ignorant in the art of teaching as I want them to remain in the art of literature. The assignments I give are usually assignments I've given myself, problems that have defeated me, investigations I'm still pursuing.

1. Literature has something to do with language. There's probably a natural grammar at the tip of your tongue. You may not believe it, but if you say what's on your mind in the language that comes to you from your parents and your street and friends, you'll probably say something beautiful. Still, if you weren't a tough, recalcitrant kid, that language may have been destroyed by the tongues of schoolteachers who were ashamed of interesting homes, inflection, and language and left them all for correct usage.

2. A first assignment: to be repeated whenever necessary, by me or the class. Write a story, a first-person narrative in the voice of someone with whom you're in conflict. Someone who disturbs you, worries you, someone you don't understand. Use a situation you don't understand.

3. No personal journals, please, for about a year. Why? Boring to me. When you find only yourself interesting, you're boring. When I find only myself interesting, I'm a conceited bore. When I'm interested in you, I'm interesting.

4. This year, I want to *tell* stories. I ask my father, now that he's old and not so busy, to tell me stories, so I can learn how. I try to remember my grandmother's stories, the faces of her dead children. A first assignment for *this* year: Tell a story in class, something that your grandmother told you about a life that preceded yours. That will remind us of our home language. Another story: At Christmas time or Passover supper, extract a story from the oldest persons told them by the oldest person they remember. That will remind us of history. Also—because of time shortage and advanced age, neither your father nor your grandmother will bother to tell unimportant stories.

5. It's possible to write about anything in the world, but the slightest story ought to contain the facts of money and blood in

order to be interesting to adults. That is, everybody continues on this earth by courtesy of certain economic arrangements; people are rich or poor, make a living or don't have to, are useful to systems or superfluous. And blood—the way people live as families or outside families or in the creation of family, sisters, sons, fathers, the bloody ties. Trivial work ignores these two FACTS and is never comic or tragic.

May you do trivial work?

WELL

6. You don't even *have* to be a writer. Read the poem "With Argus" by Paul Goodman. It'll save you a lot of time. It ends:

*The shipwright looked at me
with mild eyes.
"What's the matter friend?
You need a New Ship
from the ground up, with art,
a lot of work,
and using the experience you
have—"
"I'm tired!" I told him in
exasperation,
"I can't afford it!"
        "No one asks you, either,"
he patiently replied, "to venture
forth.
Whither? why? maybe just forget it."
And he turned on his heel and left
me—here.*

7. Luckily for art, life is difficult, hard to understand, useless, and mysterious. Luckily for artists, they don't require art to do a good day's work. But critics and teachers do. A book, a story, should be smarter than its author. It is the critic or the teacher in

you or me who cleverly outwits the characters with the power of prior knowledge of meetings and ends.

Stay open and ignorant.

(For me, the problem: how to keep a class of smart kids—who are on top of Medieval German and Phenomenology—dumb? Probably too late and impossible.)

Something to read: Cocteau's journals.

8. Sometimes I begin the year by saying: this is a definition of fiction. Stesichorus was blinded for mentioning that Helen had gone off to Troy with Paris. He wrote the following poem and his sight was restored:

> *Helen, that story is not true*
> *You never sailed in the benched ships*
> *You never went to the city of Troy.*

9. Two good books to read:

> *A Life Full of Holes*, Charhadi
> *I Work Like a Gardener*, Joan Miró

10. What is the difference between a short story and a novel? The amount of space and time any decade can allow a subject and a group of characters. All this clear only in retrospect.

Therefore: Be risky.

11. A student says, Why do you keep saying a work of art? You're right. It's a bad habit. I mean to say a work of truth.

12. What does it mean To Tell the Truth?

It means—for me—to remove all lies. *A Life Full of Holes* was said truthfully at once from the beginning.* Therefore, we know it can be done. But I am, like most of you, a middle-class person of articulate origins. Like you I was considered verbal and talented,

* Really?

and then improved upon by interested persons. These are some of the lies that have to be removed:

    a. The lie of injustice to characters.

    b. The lie of writing to an editor's taste, or a teacher's.

    c. The lie of writing to your best friend's taste.

    d. The lie of the approximate word.

    e. The lie of unnecessary adjectives.

    f. The lie of the brilliant sentences you love the most.

13. Don't go through life without reading the autobiographies of Emma Goldman

      Prince Kropotkin

      Malcolm X

14. Two peculiar and successful assignments. Invent a person— that is, name the characteristics and we will write about him or her. Last year it was a forty-year-old divorced policeman with two children.

An assignment called the List Assignment. Because inside the natural form of day beginning and ending, supper with the family, an evening at the draft board, there are the facts of noise, conflict, echo. In other years, the most imaginative, inventive work has happened in these factual accounts.

For me too.

15. The stories of Isaac Babel and the conversation with him reported by Konstantin Paustovsky in *Years of Hope*. Also, Paustovsky's *The Story of a Life*, a collection of stories incorrectly called autobiography.

Read the poem "The Circus Animals' Desertion" by William Butler Yeats.

Students are missing from these notes. They do most of the talking in class. They read their own work aloud in their own voices and discuss and disagree with one another. I do interrupt, interject any one of the preceding remarks or one of a dozen others, simply bossing my way into the discussion from time to time, because, after all, it's my shop. To enlarge on these, I would need to keep a journal of conversations and events. This would be against my literary principles and pedagogical habits—all of which are subject to change.

Therefore: I can only describe the fifteen points I've made by telling you that they are really notes for beginners, or for people like myself who must begin again and again in order to get anywhere at all.

(1970)

Imagining the Present

I was trying to remember exactly how we started Teachers & Writers Collaborative. It was in 1965 or 1966 I think. I felt kind of shy with all those people: Anne Sexton, Muriel Rukeyser, Denise Levertov, Mitch Goodman, Tinka Topping, and Paul Lauter, and Florence Howe, who later created, with others, the Feminist Press. There were a lot of things happening around that time. We had learned about money becoming available from "up there," you know, from that bad old state that people are always talking about these days, and that the money was for the children of our city, for literature and literacy. And as it turned out, the ideas that were discussed in our early meetings were being talked about all over the country, so that wherever you go now, you'll find poets in the schools, and you'll find different organizations bringing them to elementary schools, high schools, and community centers. The results were far-reaching.

Not long ago I gave a talk at the Associated Writing Programs. The AWP is not as much about children as about extremely grown-ups, specifically people teaching writing in the colleges. It has become a profession, with a whole bunch of degrees that one has to have. But even that—the idea that writing could be taught! How extraordinary! The idea of teaching writing seems very peculiar to some people. Anytime I speak in public, someone will get up and say, "You can't teach writing." What they mean is that you can teach grammar and spelling, but you can't teach writing. They're under the impression that you can teach math—the same people!—whereas writing is language, something you've been doing all your life, since you were a little tiny kid, right? So the idea of teaching writing: what does it mean, finally?

For some people it meant that as a teacher you had to make great writers: either a student becomes a great writer or what's the point in teaching writing? Whereas the person who believes that you can teach math never thinks about whether or not the idea is to make a great mathematician. Nor does the history teacher believe that it is essential, in order to be an honorable teacher of history, to produce a great or famous historian. In a way, they are right about what they're doing: they want to produce women and men who love history, or math, or chemistry, and would understand what they (the teachers) are doing, and love and maybe understand the world a little bit better. Our idea was that children—by writing, by putting down words, by reading, by beginning to love literature, by the inventiveness or listening to one another—could begin to understand the world better and begin to make a better world for themselves. That always seemed to me such a natural idea that I've never understood why it took so much aggressiveness and so much time to get it started.

At one of our early meetings, we were walking along the beach, and Muriel, Anne, and Denise were reading poems to each other in the evening, which made it very beautiful and memorable for us. And then we found out that we had to write a grant! We had to figure out how to write a proposal to ask for the money. We sat there and wrote it, but one of our big arguments was about how to write it. Someone had already informed us that there was a whole grant-writing language. It was new at that time, but it was "inter-esting." But we argued among ourselves, saying, "We're trying to get money for this Teachers & Writers program, and we're writers, so let's just *write* it!" Finally, as we came to the end of it, there were a couple of people, more experienced in this kind of writing, who looked at it and said, "You can't do it this way. You have to use a certain kind of form for it." But we felt extremely brave, saying, "No, we're not going to end that way, we're going to end this with a noble statement as writers."

Now I want to say just a few things about the imagination. I've looked at a lot of other speeches about writing and the imagina-tion, and I'm all for it. I'm not against the imagination, so I don't want you to think that. But I read somewhere that Isaac Babel said that his main problem was that he had no imagination. And I thought about that a lot, because if you read him, you know that what he's trying to say—except for a few pieces, such as "The Sin of Jesus"—is very close to his life, the terrifying life that he led in the Cossack Red Army during, I guess, 1920, '21, '22. And so I tried to figure out exactly what he meant. I guess what he really didn't un-derstand was the amount of imagination it had taken for him to understand what had happened, what was real. There were people in his unit who, if they had tried to tell him what was going on in this particular hut or pogrom-suffering village, couldn't have. Yet he was able to use what he *did* know about life and poverty and war to stretch toward what he *didn't* know about the Cossack Red Army. So I think about that as the *fact* of the imagination.

That leads me to think of the headline that Jordan David held up when he introduced me: MCNAMARA ADMITS HE MADE A MISTAKE.* Well, McNamara finally developed an imagination is all I can say. Of course what he *may* have imagined is what was

---

* It turns out that—according to his tapes—Lyndon Baines Johnson in 1964 also thought the war might not be a good or workable idea.

going to happen to him in the next world if he didn't admit it. Something like George Wallace the other day at Selma, who also said he had been wrong. But the idea of McNamara's living through that time, allowing some of us to spend either our youth or the prime of our lives fighting in or against that war, and trying to help our neighbors imagine what was happening in Vietnam, while he and a few others were up there thinking, You know, it's possible we're not right, it's possible we shouldn't have gone in there, maybe we made a mistake, and then not speaking another word about it for the next thirty years!

At that time, hints came to us that there was dissension in the administrations, and that the children of a lot of those people, being young and healthy, had some idea that this was a terrible business that their parents were involved in. I mean, it's bad enough being the child of any parent: you suspect how wrong your parents are from the beginning. You *think* they're wrong, but you don't *know* they're wrong. But these young people *knew* their parents were wrong, and had to live with that. What I'm trying to say is: where is the imagination in that? What do we need our imaginations for?

First of all, we need our imaginations to understand what is happening to other people around us, to try to understand the lives of others. I know there's a certain political view that you musn't write about anyone except yourself, your own exact people. Of course it's very hard for anyone to know who their exact people are, anyway. But that's limiting. The idea of writing from the head or from the view or the experience of other people, of another people, of another life, or even of just the people across the street or next door, is probably one of the most important acts of the imagination that you can try and that can be useful to the world.

Certainly one of the things that haven't been sufficiently imagined yet, apart from the death of 60,000 Americans, is the terrible suffering that the Vietnamese people have been subjected to all these years. From the very beginning of the war, and then after the war, when everyone—the left with joy, the right with bitter rage—ran around saying that the poor little Vietnamese had beaten the Americans. Well, they never did. We—the United States, that is—beat them. And we continued to embargo them and keep them in terrible poverty, with unexploded bombs going off under their children for all these years. So, not to be able to imagine the suffering that we imposed directly on them, and for our 1996 congresspeople not to be able to imagine the suffering that they're going to impose on the poor people of this country—it's hard for me to believe that they can't imagine it. Unfortunately, I think they do. They simply don't care. Another subject.

So I'm talking about the imagination in another way. We're living in a very lucky time, in some respects, in this country. As far as literature is concerned, we're really fortunate, and I think that Teachers & Writers and poets-in-the-schools programs and the other organizations that have been involved in basic literacy work have had something to do with it. We're living in a time when the different peoples in this country are being heard from, for the first time. I'm happy to have lived into this period when we hear the voices of Native Americans—twenty or twenty-five years ago you didn't even know they were writing, apart from token publication. That was the general condition of American literature at that time. The voices of African-American men and women, the voices of women of all colors, Asian women, Asian men, all these people— *this is our country*—and we're living at a time when we can hear the voices of all these people. So whenever I hear complaints about what's going on in literature in this country—those people without imagination talk that way—I want to remind them: when before now did this happen? Then they will say with that denigrating tone, "multiculturalism." Or "diversity." Or "political correctness." They use those words to try to shut all of us up. This is what the imagination means to me: to know that this multiplicity of voices is a wonderful fact and that we're lucky, especially the young people, to be living here at this time. My imagination tells me that if we let

this present political climate defeat us, my children and my grandchildren will be in terrible trouble.

I will probably think of other things to say to you when I'm asleep,
but it won't bother me so much because I'll know you're all asleep
too! But I would like to thank all of you. I think you've overrated
me somewhat, but if there's ever a time in your life when you like
to be overrated, it's when you're old. I thank you for doing it, and I
thank all the young people and children who are here tonight, who
have been writing poems and plays. They honor us with their presence. The child, you know, is the reason for life. Thank you, all.

(1996)

The Value of Not
Understanding Everything

The difference between writers and critics is that in order to function in their trade, writers must live in the world, and critics, to survive in the world, must live in literature.

That's why writers in their own work need to have nothing to do with criticism, no matter on what level.

In fact, since seminars and discussions move forward a lot more cheerily if a couple of bald statements are made, I'll make one: you can lunge off into an interesting and true career as a writer even if you've read nothing but the Holy Bible and the New York *Daily News*, but that is an absolute minimum (read them slowly).

Literary criticism always ought to be of great interest to the historian, the moralist, the philosopher, which is sometimes me. Also to the reader—me again—the critic comes as a journalist. If it happens to be the right decade, he may even bring great news.

As a reader, I liked reading Wright Morris's *The Territory Ahead*. But if I—the writer—should pay too much attention to him, I would have to think an awful lot about the Mississippi River. I'd have to get my mind off New York. I always think of New York.

I often think of Chicago, San Francisco. Once in a while Atlanta. But I never think about the Mississippi, except to notice that its big, muddy foot is in New Orleans, from whence all New York singing comes. Documentaries aside, my notions of music came by plane.

As far as the artist is concerned, all the critic can ever do is make him or break him. He can slip him into new schools, water-log him in old ones. He can discover him, ignore him, rediscover him . . .

Apart from having to leave the country in despair and live in exile forever—or as in milder situations, never having lunch up-town again—nothing too terrible can happen to the writer's work. Because what the writer is interested in is life, life as he is *nearly* living it, something which takes place here or abroad, in Nebraska or New York or Capri. Some people have to live first and write later, like Proust. More writers are like Yeats, who was always be-ing tempted from his craft of verse, but not seriously enough to cut down on production.

Now, one of the reasons writers are so much more interested in life than others who just go on living all the time is that what the writer doesn't understand the first thing about is just what he acts like such a specialist about—and that is life. And the reason he writes is to explain it all to himself, and the less he understands to begin with, the more he probably writes. And he takes his ununder-standing, whatever it is—the face of wealth, the collapse of his father's pride, the misuses of love, hopeless poverty—he simply never gets over it. He's like an idealist who marries nearly the same woman over and over. He tries to write with different names and faces, us-ing different professions and labors, other forms to travel the short-est distance to the way things really are.

In other words, the poor writer—presumably in an intellectual profession—really oughtn't to know what he's talking about.

When people in school take their first writing classes, it is some-times suggested to them that they write about their own experience.

Put down what you see. Put down what you know. Perhaps describe a visit you have just had with a friend.

Well, I would suggest something different. I would say, don't
knock yourself out. You know perfectly well what happened when
your friend Helen visited last Friday. This is great practice for a
journalist and proper practice for a journalist. As for an inventing
writer, I would say something like this:

Now, what are some of the things you don't understand at all?
You've probably taken all these psych courses, and you know pretty
well what is happening between your mother and yourself, your
father and your brother. Someone in your family has surely been
analyzed, so you've had several earfuls as well as a lot of nasty remarks at dinner. Okay—don't write about that, because now you
understand it all. That's what certain lessons in psychology and analytical writing effect—you have the impression that you know and
understand because you own the rules of human behavior, and that
is really as bad as knowing and understanding.

You might try your father and mother for a starter. You've seen
them so closely that they ought to be absolutely mysterious. What's
kept them together these thirty years? Or why is your father's second wife no better than his first?

If, before you sit down with paper and pencil to deal with them,
it all comes suddenly clear and you find yourself mumbling, Of
course, he's a sadist and she's a masochist, and you think you have
the answer—*drop the subject*.

If, in casting about for suitable areas of ignorance, you fail
because you understand yourself (and too well), your school friends,
as well as the global balance of terror, and you can also see your last
Saturday-night date blistery in the hot light of truth—but you still
love books and the idea of writing—you might make a first-class
critic.

What I'm saying is that in areas in which you are very smart
you might try writing history or criticism, and then you can know
and tell how all the mystery of America flows out from under Huck

Finn's raft; where you are kind of dumb, write a story or a novel, depending on the depth and breadth of your dumbness. Some people can do both. Edmund Wilson, for instance—but he's so much more smart than dumb that he has written very little fiction.

When you have invented all the facts to make a story and get somehow to the truth of the mystery and you can't dig up another question—change the subject.

Let me give you a very personal example: I have published a small book of short stories. They are on several themes, at least half of them Jewish. One of the reasons for that is that I was an outsider in our particular neighborhood—at least I thought I was—I took long rides on Saturday, the Sabbath. My family spoke Russian, but the street spoke Yiddish. There were families of experience I was cut off from. You know, it seemed to me that an entire world was whispering in the other room. In order to get to the core of it all, I used all those sibilant clues. I made fiction.

As often happens when you write something else, a couple of magazines asked to hear from me. They wanted a certain kind of story—which I'd already done—

But the truth of the matter is, I have probably shot my Jewish bolt, and I had better recognize that fact and remember it. It's taken me a long time, but I have finally begun to understand that part of my life. I am inside it. I could write an article, I imagine, on life in the thirties and forties in Jewish New York, but the tension and the mystery and the question are gone. Except to deceive my readers and myself, in honor I could never make fiction of that life again. The writer is not some kind of phony historian who runs around answering everyone's questions with made-up characters tying up loose ends. She is nothing but a questioner.

Luckily for my craft—for my love of writing—I have come up against a number of other inexplicable social arrangements. There are things about men and women and their relations to each other, also the way in which they relate to the almost immediate destruction of the world, that I can't figure out. And nothing in critical or historical literature will abate my ignorance a tittle or a jot. I will have to do it all by myself, marshal the evidence. In the end, probably all I'll have to show is more mystery—a certain juggled translation from life, that foreign tongue, into fiction, the jargon of man.

(mid-1960s)

Feelings in the Presence
of the Sight and Sound of the
Bread and Puppet Theater

ADMIRATION

Oh! Ah! The gorgeousness   the solemn size   the humorous disparities

HAPPINESS

Sheer happiness   just plain happiness

RESTFULNESS

In some of the long slow pieces often of holy intention—rest— the spirit—also the body rests inside the event the work-with room and permission for absence. The gathering of knowledge at the "five senses' entry to the soul"—so with rest comes thought— time—room for thinking *during* the work not only after it.

ARTISTIC INSPIRATION

Why not speak the truth directly? Just speak out! Speak to! Why not?

POLITICAL INSPIRATION

Why not speak the truth directly? Just speak out! Speak up! Speak to! Why not?

CORROBORATION
Yes! That's just what's happening.

ENVY
Because the work is so useful the courage of its usefulness in a long period when usefulness was mocked   Envy as an artist for the beauty and usefulness of the huge puppet figures like legends out of history   the gray women of suffering the ridiculous evil Uncle Fatso   the lovely oxen turning round and round in the dance of silent beasts   the white deer on the hill under the red ball of the sun   the high birds bravely carried that have flown before and after us on our demonstrations and have waited fluttering in the wind outside the jails of New York Vermont Washington.

To have been useful As an Artist to the important movements of our times   to have spoken out as artists for the poor, the oppressed and humiliated in Europe Africa and at home *and been heard.*

AND FINALLY LOVE AND GRATITUDE
for Peter Schuman and Elka Schuman and that solid core of puppeteers—also for those who came, worked with Peter for a couple of years, and then went off to Maine California France Italy Germany Ninth Street New York Brooklyn   Gratitude for their gifts to us of labor and beauty from the earliest unknown days on Delancey Street when we were sometimes fewer than they—to these wonderful summer circus days in Vermont where we, their comrades and friends, meet one another in the thousands   AND GRATITUDE also for the opportunity generously given to be one of them an ox   a deer   a stilt walker   a horse   a maintenance man   a washerwoman.

And thanks Peter for the tens of thousands of Loaves of Bread and the music

(1981)

Traveling

My mother and sister were traveling south. The year was 1927. They had begun their journey in New York. They were going to visit my brother, who was studying in the South Medical College of Virginia. Their bus was an express and had stopped only in Philadelphia, Wilmington, and now Washington. Here, the darker people who had gotten on in Philadelphia or New York rose from their seats, put their bags and boxes together, and moved to the back of the bus. People who boarded in Washington knew where to seat themselves. My mother had heard that something like this would happen. My sister had heard of it too. They had not lived in it. This reorganization of passengers by color happened in silence. My mother and sister remained in their seats, which were about three-quarters of the way back.

When everyone was settled, the bus driver began to collect tickets. My sister saw him coming. She pinched my mother: Ma! Look! Of course, my mother saw him too. What frightened my sister was the quietness. The white people in front, the black people in back—silent.

The driver sighed, said, You can't sit here, ma'am. It's for them, waving over his shoulder at the Negroes, among whom they were now sitting. Move, please.

My mother said, No.

He said, You don't understand, ma'am. It's against the law. You have to move to the front.

My mother said, No.

When I first tried to write this scene, I imagined my mother saying, That's all right, mister, we're comfortable. I can't change my seat every minute. I read this invention to my sister. She said it was nothing like that. My mother did not try to be friendly or pretend innocence. While my sister trembled in the silence, my mother said, for the third time, quietly, No.

Somehow finally, they were in Richmond. There was my brother in school among so many American boys. After hugs and my mother's anxious looks at her young son, my sister said, Vic, you know what Mama did?

My brother remembers thinking, What? Oh! She wouldn't move? He had a classmate, a Jewish boy like himself, but from Virginia, who had had a public confrontation with a Negro man. He had punched that man hard, knocked him down. My brother couldn't believe it. He was stunned. He couldn't imagine a Jewish boy wanting to knock anyone down. He had never wanted to. But he thought, looking back, that he had been set down to work and study in a nearly foreign place and had to get used to it. Then he told me about the Second World War, when the disgrace of black soldiers being forced to sit behind white German POWs shook him. Shamed him.

About fifteen years later, in 1943, in early summer, I rode the bus for about three days from New York to Miami Beach, where my husband in sweaty fatigues, along with hundreds of other boys, was trudging up and down the streets and beaches to prepare themselves for war.

By late afternoon of the second long day, we were well into the

South, beyond Richmond, maybe South Carolina or Georgia. My excitement about travel in the wide world was damaged a little by a sudden fear that I might not recognize Jess or he, me. We hadn't seen each other for two months. I took a photograph out of my pocket; yes, I would know him.

I had been sleeping waking reading writing dozing waking. So many hours, the movement of the passengers was something like a tide that sometimes ebbed and now seemed to be noisily rising. I opened my eyes to the sound of new people brushing past my aisle seat. And looked up to see a colored woman holding a large sleeping baby, who, with the heaviness of sleep, his arms so tight around her neck, seemed to be pulling her head down. I looked around and noticed that I was in the last white row. The press of travelers had made it impossible for her to move farther back. She seemed so tired and I had been sitting and sitting for a day and a half at least. Not thinking, or maybe refusing to think, I offered her my seat.

She looked to the right and left as well as she could. Softly she said, Oh no. I became fully awake. A white man was standing right beside her, but on the other side of the invisible absolute racial border. Of course, she couldn't accept my seat. Her sleeping child hung mercilessly from her neck. She shifted a little to balance the burden. She whispered to herself, Oh, I just don't know. So I said, Well, at least give me the baby. First, she turned, barely looked at the man beside her. He made no move. So, to my surprise, but obviously out of sheer exhaustion, she disengaged the child from her body and placed him on my lap. He was deep in child-sleep. He stirred, but not enough to bother himself or me. I liked holding him, aligning him along my twenty-year-old young woman's shape. I thought ahead to that holding, that breathing together that would happen in my life if this war would ever end.

I was so comfortable under his nice weight. I closed my eyes for a couple of minutes, but suddenly opened them to look up into the face of a white man talking. In a loud voice he addressed me: Lady, I wouldn't of touched that thing with a meat hook.

I thought, Oh, this world will end in ice. I could do nothing but look straight into his eyes. I did not look away from him. Then I held that boy a little tighter, kissed his curly head, pressed him even closer so that he began to squirm. So sleepy, he reshaped himself inside my arms. His mother tried to narrow herself away from that dangerous border, too frightened at first to move at all. After a couple of minutes, she leaned forward a little, placed her hand on the baby's head, and held it there until the next stop. I couldn't look up into her mother face.

I write this remembrance more than fifty years later. I look back at that mother and child. How young she is. Her hand on his head is quite small, though she tries by spreading her fingers wide to hide him from the white man. But the child I'm holding, his little face as he turns toward me, is the brown face of my own grandson, my daughter's boy, the open mouth of the sleeper, the full lips, the thick little body of a child who runs wildly from one end of the yard to the other, leaps from dangerous heights with certain experienced caution, muscling his body, his mind, for coming realities.

Of course, when my mother and sister returned from Richmond, the family at home wanted to know: how was Vic doing in school along all those gentiles? Was the long bus ride hard, was the anti-Semitism really bad or just normal? What happened on the bus? I was probably present at that supper, the attentive listener and total forgetter of information that immediately started to form me.

Then last year, my sister, casting the net of old age (through which recent experience easily slips), brought up that old story. First I was angry. How come you never told me about your bus ride with Mama? I mean, really, so many years ago.

I don't know, she said, anyway you were only about four years old, and besides, maybe I did.

I asked my brother why we'd never talked about that day. He said he thought now that it had had a great effect on him; he had

tried unraveling its meaning for years—then life family work happened. So I imagined him, a youngster really, a kid from the Bronx
in Virginia in 1927; why, he was a stranger there himself.

In the next couple of weeks, we continued to talk about our
mother, the way she was principled, adamant, and at the same time
so shy. What else could we remember . . . Well, I said, I have a
story about those buses too. Then I told it to them: How it happened on just such a journey, when I was still quite young, that I
first knew my grandson, first held him close, but could protect him
for only about twenty minutes fifty years ago.

(1997)

FROM *Long Walks and Intimate Talks*

Midrash on Happiness

What she meant by happiness, she said, was the following: she meant having (or having had) (or continuing to have) everything. By everything, she meant, first, the children, then a dear person to live with, preferably a man, but not necessarily (by live with, she meant for a long time but not necessarily). Along with and not in preferential order, she required three or four best women friends to whom she could tell every personal fact and then discuss on the widest deepest and most hopeless level, the economy, the constant, unbeatable, cruel war economy, the slavery of the American worker to the idea of that economy, the complicity of male people in the whole structure, the dumbness of men (including her preferred man) on this subject. By dumbness, she meant everything dumbness has always meant: silence and stupidity. By silence she meant refusal to speak; by stupidity she meant refusal to hear. For happiness she required women to walk with. To walk in the city arm in arm with a woman friend (as her mother had with aunts and cousins so many years ago) was just plain essential. Oh! those long walks and intimate talks, better than standing alone on the most admirable mountain or in the handsomest forest or hay-blown field (all of which were certainly splendid occupations for the wind-starved soul). More important even (though maybe less sweet because of age) than the old walks with boys she'd walked with as a girl, that nice bunch of worried left-wing boys who flew (always slightly handicapped by that idealistic wing) into a dream of paid-up mortgages with a small room for opinion and solitude in the corner of home. Oh do you remember those fellows, Ruthy?

Remember? Well, I'm married to one.

But she had, Faith continued, democratically tried walking in the beloved city with a man, but the effort had failed since from about that age—twenty-seven or eight—he had felt an obligation, if a young woman passed, to turn abstractedly away, in the middle of the most personal conversation or even to say confidentially, wasn't she something?—or clasping his plaid shirt, at the heart's level, oh my god! The purpose of this: perhaps to work a nice quiet appreciation into thunderous heartbeat as he had been taught on pain of sexual death. For happiness, she also required work to do in this world and bread on the table. By work to do she included the important work of raising children righteously up. By righteously she meant that along with being useful and speaking truth to the community, they must do no harm. By harm she meant not only personal injury to the friend the lover the coworker the parent (the city the nation) but also the stranger; she meant particularly the stranger in all her or his difference, who, because we were strangers in Egypt, deserves special goodness for life or at least until the end of strangeness. By bread on the table, she meant no metaphor but truly bread as her father had ended every single meal with a hunk of bread. By hunk, she was describing one of the attributes of good bread.

Suddenly she felt she had left out a couple of things: love. Oh yes, she said, for she was talking, talking all this time, to patient Ruth and they were walking for some reason in a neighborhood where she didn't know the children, the pizza places or the vegetable markets. It was early evening and she could see lovers walking along Riverside Park with their arms around one another, turning away from the sun which now sets among the new apartment houses of New Jersey, to kiss. Oh I forgot, she said, now that I notice, Ruthy I think I would die without love. By love she probably meant she would die without being *in* love. By *in* love she meant the acuteness of the heart at the sudden sight of a particular person or the way over a couple of years of interested friendship one is suddenly stunned by the lungs' longing for more and more breath in the presence of that friend, or nearly drowned to the knees by the salty spring that seems to beat for years on our vaginal shores. Not to omit all sorts of imaginings which assure great spiritual energy for months and when luck follows truth, years.

Oh sure, love. I think so too, sometimes, said Ruth, willing to hear Faith out since she had been watching the kissers too, but I'm really not so sure. Nowadays it seems like pride, I mean overweening pride, when you look at the children and think we don't have time to do much (by time Ruth meant both her personal time and the planet's time). When I read the papers and hear all this boom boom bellicosity, the guys out-daring each other, I see we have to change it all—the world—without killing it absolutely—without killing it, that'll be the trick the kids'll have to figure out. Until that begins, I don't understand happiness—what you mean by it.

Then Faith was ashamed to have wanted so much and so little all at the same time—to be so easily and personally satisfied in this terrible place, when everywhere vast public suffering rose in reeling waves from the round earth's nation-states—hung in the satellite-watched air and settled in no time at all into TV sets and newsrooms. It was all there. Look up and the news of halfway round the planet is falling on us all. So for all these conscientious and technical reasons, Faith was ashamed. It was clear that happiness could not be worthwhile, with so much conversation and so little revolutionary change. Of course, Faith said, I know all that. I do, but sometimes walking with a friend I forget the world.

PART III

Rs

POEMS

Fidelity

After supper I returned to
my reading book   I had
reached page one hundred
and forty   two hundred and twenty
more to go I had been thinking that
evening as we spoke
early at dinner with a couple of young
people   of the dense improbable
life of that book in which I had become so comfortable
the characters were now my troubled companions
I knew them   understood I could
reenter these lives without loss
so firm my habitation   I scanned the shelves
some books so dear to me   I had missed them
leaned forward to take the work into
my hands   I took a couple of deep breaths
thought about the acceleration of days
yes   I could reenter them but . . .
No   how could I desert that other whole life
those others in their city basements
Abandonment   How could I have allowed myself
even thought of a half hour's distraction
when life had pages   or decades to go
so much about to happen to people
I already know and nearly loved

For Danny

My son enters the classroom
There are thirty-two children waiting for him
He dreams that he will teach them to read
His head is full of the letters that words are looking for

Because of his nature
his fingers are flowers
Here is a rose   he says   look   it grew right
into the letter R

They like that idea very much   they lean forward
He says   now spell garden
They write it correctly in their notebooks   maybe
        because the word rose is in it

My son is happy
Now spell sky
For this simple word the children
turn their eyes down and away   doesn't he know
the city has been quarreling with the sky all of their lives

Well, he says   spell home   he's a little frightened
        to ask this of them   What?
They laugh   they can't hear him say
What's so funny?   they jump
up out of their seats laughing

My son says hopefully   it's three o'clock
but they don't want to leave   where will they go?
they want to stay right in the classroom   they probably
want to spell garden again   they want
to examine his hand

My Mother: 33 Years Later

I

There are places
   garden
   music room
   stove
   dining room

Death bed   her eyes are open   she doesn't speak
   My sister and I hold up a picture of Frannie the first grandchild
   Mama do you know who this is?
   Fools! Who do you think you're talking to?
   Oh!   she cried and turned away

My room   she says
   I've heard that expression
   I know how you talk
   don't think I'm so dumb
   hot pants! that's what you say, you girls!

Bobby and I are walking, arm and arm, across the camp field
Our mothers are behind us. We're nine years old.
We're wearing swimming trunks.
                                        She says
   look   see the line of soft soft
   hair along their spines
   like down   our little birds

One of the mothers
the mother out of whose body
I easily appeared

Once I remembered her

2

This is what I planned:
To get to the end of our life quickly

And begin again

Everyone is intact   talking
Mother and Father   Mira   Babashka
all of us eating our boiled egg
but the poplar tree on Hoe Avenue
has just been cut down and the Norway maple
is planted in Mahopac

Then
my mother gives me
a vase full of zinnias
"as straight as little Russian soldiers"

Yes
mama
as straight as the second grade
in the P.S. 50 schoolyard
at absolute attention
under its woolen hats
of pink   orange   lavender   yellow

Suddenly There's Poughkeepsie

what a hard time
the Hudson River has had
trying to get to the sea

it seemed easy enough to
rise out of the Tear of
the Cloud and tumble
and run in little skips
and jumps   draining
        a swamp here and
    there   acquiring
streams and other smaller
rivers with similar
longings for the wide
imagined water

suddenly
there's Poughkeepsie
except for its spelling
an ordinary town but
the great heaving
ocean sixty miles away is
determined to reach
that town every day
and twice a day   in fact
drowning the Hudson River
in salt and mud
it is the moon's tidal
power over all the waters
of this earth at war with
gravity   the Hudson
perseveres   moving down

down   dignified
slower   look it has
become our Lordly Husdon
hardly flowing
                 and we are
now in a poem by the poet
Paul Goodman   be quiet heart
home home
            then the sea

In the Bus

Somewhere between Greenfield and Holyoke
snow became rain
and a child passed through me
as a person moved through mist
as the moon moves through
a dense cloud at night
as though I were cloud or mist
a child passed through me

On the highway that lies
across miles of stubble
and tobacco barns our bus speeding
speeding disordered the slanty rain
and a girl with no name   naked
wearing the last nakedness of
childhood   breathed in me
                        once   no
                        two breaths
a sigh   she whispered   Hey you
begin again
                    Again?
again   again   you'll see
it's easy   begin again   long ago

A Poem About Storytelling

The artist comes next
she tells the story of the stories

The first person may be the child who
says   Listen!   Guess what happened!
The important listener is the mother
The mother says   What?

The first person can be the neighbor
She says   Today my son told me   Goodbye
I said   Really?   Who are you?   You
didn't even say hello yet   The listener
is probably her friend   She remembers
Well wasn't he always like that   as a small boy
I mean   The neighbor says   That's not
true   You're absolutely wrong   He was like a
motorcycle   a little horse   every now
and then at rest   a flower

The first person is often the lover who
says   I never knew anyone like you
The listener is the beloved   She whispers
Who?   Me?

The first person is the giver of testimony
He rises and tells   I lived in that village
My father shouted   He returned from the fields
I was too small   My father cried out
Why don't you grow up and help me   My mother said
Help him   you're eight years old   it's time
The listeners say   Oh! It was just
like that   I remember

The giver of testimony rises and tells
I lived in the hut   behind the barn
The padrone   the master   the manager came
to me   I can take you whenever I want
he said   Now you're old enough   The right
age is twelve he said   The giver of testimony
rises   She looks into her village   She
looks into the next village   Where
are the listeners

The artist comes next   She waits for
the listeners too   What if they're all dead or
deafened by grief or in prison   Then
there's no way out of it   She will listen
It's her work   She will be the listener
in the story of the stories

News

although we would prefer to talk
and talk it into psychological theory the prevalence of small genocides
or the recent disease floating
toward us from another continent we
must not   while she speaks her eyes
frighten us   she is only one person
she tells us her terrible news   we
want to leave the room we may not
we must listen   in this wrong world this
is what   we must do   we must bear it

Connections: Vermont   Vietnam (I)

Hot summer day
on the River Road
swimmers of the Ompompanoosuc
dust in my eyes
       oh
       it is the hot wind from Laos
       the girl in Nhe An covers her face with a straw hat
       as we pass   she breathes   through cloth
       she stands between two piles of stone

       the dust of National Highway 1 blinds

me
summertime
I drive through Vermont
my fist on the horn, barefoot
    like Ching

Connections: Vermont   Vietnam (II)

The general came to the President
We are the laughingstock of the world
What world? he said
                    the world
                    the world

Vermont
    the green world
    the green mountain

Across the valley
someone is clearing a field
he is making a tan rectangle
he has cut a tan rectangle on Lyme Hill
the dark wood
the deposed farm
                        the mist is sipped up by the sun
                        the mist is eaten by the sun

What world?   he said

What mountain?   said the twenty ships of the Seventh Fleet
rolling on the warm waves   lobbing shells all the summer day
into green distance

        on Trung Son mountain Phan Su told a joke:
        The mountain is torn, the trees are broken
        how easy it is to gather wood
        to repair my house in the village which is broken by bombs

His shirt is plum-colored, is brown like dark plums

the sails on the sampans that fish in the sea of the Seventh Fleet
        are plum-colored

the holes in the mountain are red
the earth of that province is red   red
                       world

In San Salvador (1)

Come   look   they said
here are the photograph albums
these are our children

We are called The Mothers of the Disappeared
we are also the mothers of those who were seen once more
and then photographed   sometimes part of them
could not be found

A breast   an eye   an arm is missing
sometimes a whole stomach
that is why we are called   The Mothers
of the Disappeared   although we have these large
heavy photograph albums full of beautiful
torn faces

That Country

This is about the women of that country
Sometimes they spoke in slogans
They said
    We patch the roads as we patch our sweetheart's trousers
    The heart will stop but not the transport
They said
    We have ensured production even near bomb craters
    Children let your voices sing higher than the explosions
                                        of the bombs
They said
    We have important tasks to teach the children
    that the people are the collective masters
    to bear hardship
    to instill love in the family
    to guide the good health of the children (they must
    wear clothing according to climate)
They said
    Once men beat their wives
    now they may not
    Once a poor family sold its daughter to a rich old man
    now the young may love one another
They said
    Once we planted our rice any old way
    now we plant the young shoots in straight rows
    so the imperialist pilot can see how steady our
    hands are

In the evening we walked along the shores of the Lake
                                of the Restored Sword

I said   is it true?   we are sisters?
They said   Yes, we are of one family

On the Ramblas
A Tree   A Girl

Anyone would love to paint from memory
the bark of a plane tree in Barcelona
little geographies of burgundy turn to olive
before your very eyes or peel to that yellow
that pale cream of all the apartment rooms
in the Bronx

or write one proper grieving song for the girl
beautiful but burned in face and arm
smoke smeared into lifelong recognition
screaming in Catalan at the man who stands
before her   who supplicates   whose hands
brought together in supplication
beg   for what
        pimp   lover   father?

I say father because I'm old
and know how we beg the young to live
no matter what

People in My Family

In my family
people who were eighty-two were very different
from people who were ninety-two

The eighty-two-year-old people grew up
    it was 1914
    this is what they knew
    War   World War   War

That's why when they speak to the child
they say
    poor little one . . .

The ninety-two-year-old people remember
    it was the year 1905
    they went to prison
    they went into exile
    they said   ah   soon

When they speak to the grandchild
they say
    yes   there will be revolution
    then there will be revolution   then
    once more   then the earth itself
    will turn and turn and cry out   oh I
    have been made sick

        then you   my little bud
            must flower and save it

My Father at 85

My father said
        how will they get out of it
        they're sorry they got in

My father says
        how will they get out
        Nixon   Johnson   the whole bunch
        they don't know how

Goddamn it he says
        I'd give anything to see it
        they went in over their heads

He says
        greed   greed   time
        nothing is happening fast enough

Sisters

My friends are dying
well we're old   it's natural
one day we passed the experience of "older"
which began in late middle age
and came suddenly upon "old"   then
all the little killing bugs and
baby tumors that had struggled
for years against the body's
brave immunities found their
level playing fields and
victory

but this is not what I meant to
tell you   I wanted to say that
my friends were dying but have now
become absent   the word dead is correct
but inappropriate

I have not taken their names out of
conversation   gossip   political argument
my telephone book or card index in
whatever alphabetical or contextual
organizer   I can stop any evening of
the lonesome week at Claiborne   Bercovici
Vernarelli   Deming and rest a moment
on their seriousness as artists   workers
their excitement as political actors in the
streets of our cities or in their workplaces
the vigiling   fasting   praying in or out
of jail   their lightheartedness which floated
above the year's despair

their courageous sometimes hilarious
disobediences before the state's official
servants   their fidelity to the idea that
it is possible with only a little extra anguish
to live in this world   at an absolute minimum
loving brainy sexual energetic redeemed

On Occasion

I forget the names of my friends
and the names of the flowers in
my garden   my friends remind me
Grace   it's us   the flowers just
stand there stunned by the sun

A long time ago my mother said
darling   there are also wildflowers
but look   these I planted

my flowers are   pink and rose and
orange   they're sturdy   they make
new petals every day to fill in
their fat round faces

suddenly before thought I
called out ZINNIA   zinnia
zinnia   along came a sunny
            summer breeze   they swayed
            lightly bowed   I said   Mother

Anti-Love Poem

Sometimes you don't want to love the person you love
you turn your face away from that face
whose eyes lips might make you give up anger
forget insult   steal sadness of not wanting
to love   turn away then turn away   at breakfast
in the evening   don't lift your eyes from the paper
to see that face in all its seriousness   a
sweetness of concentration   he holds his book
in his hand   the hard-knuckled winter wood-
scarred fingers   turn away   that's all you can
do   old as you are to save yourself   from love

My Sister and My Grandson

I have been talking to my sister   she
may not know she's been dust and ashes
for the last two years   I talk to her
nearly every day

I've been telling her about our new baby
who is serious   comical   busy   dark   my
sister   out of all the rubble and grit
that is now her   my sister mutters   what
about our old baby   he was smart   loving
so beautiful

yes yes I said   listen   just last week
he stopped at my hallway door   he saw
your small Turkish rug   he stared at it
he fell to his knees his arms wide   crying
Jeannie   oh my own auntie Jeannie

remembered   ah   her hard whisper came to me
thank you Grace   now speak to him tell him
he's still my deepest love

Fathers

Fathers are
more fathering
these days   they have
accomplished this by
being more mothering

what luck for them that
women's lib happened   then
the dream of new fathering
began to shine in the eyes
of free women and was
irresistible

on the New York subways
and the mass transits
of other cities   one may
see fatherings of many colors
with their round babies on
their laps   this may also
happen in the countryside

these scenes were brand new
exciting for an old woman who
had watched the old fathers
gathering once again in
familiar army camps and comfortable war rooms to consider
the necessary eradication of
the new fathering fathers
(who are their sons) as well
as the women and children who
will surely be in the way

Luck

She looks at me   you're
lucky   you always were a
lucky person   what she means
is her life is hard   the man's
far off   the boy's mad

I make a joke   take it easy
there's time for me to be totally wrecked   I grab her grief
jam it into the grief pack between
my shoulders   when my head
turns right or left   I know it

She laughs   mentions God   throws
her life up up into the sky
in fearful sleep   I see it   a
darkness widening among my
lucky stars

The Hard-Hearted Rich

Oh how hard the hard-hearted rich are
when they meet a working person in their places
of work   a cab or a restaurant kitchen
and the hard heart   beats and eases   the mouth
into saying well they do get minimum wage
probably and when they meet   an
ordinary bum or maybe a homeless person
on their street or broad boulevard
standing on the pavement common to
all the good shops   holding a paper cup or cap
asking for change   oh say the hard-hearted rich
they will use it for drugs or drink and be found
at midnight in drunken sleep in the doorway
of one of the best shops of all
Then the hard-hearted rich and
there are many many in our city
just as there are many many women and
men working in hard-driven poverty
or not working at all   oh the hard-hearted rich
move into the glorious evening of drinking and talking
and eating and drinking   again   into sleep
in their queen-sized beds as though they
were queens with kings beside each other
and it's night and the moon's bright
light falls through the huge windows
then they decide to try
love   as a kind   of heart softener
they are tired and think to try   love

Responsibility

It is the responsibility of society to let the poet be a poet
It is the responsibility of the poet to be a woman
It is the responsibility of the poet to stand on street corners
        giving out poems and beautifully written leaflets
        also leaflets they can hardly bear to look at
        because of the screaming rhetoric
It is the responsibility of the poet to be lazy   to hang out and
        prophesy
It is the responsibility of the poet not to pay war taxes
It is the responsibility of the poet to go in and out of ivory
        towers and two-room apartments on Avenue C
        and buckwheat fields and army camps
It is the responsibility of the male poet to be a woman
It is the responsibility of the female poet to be a woman
It is the poet's responsibility to speak truth to power as the
        Quakers say
It is the poet's responsibility to learn the truth from the
        powerless
It is the responsibility of the poet to say many times: there is no
        freedom without justice and this means economic
        justice and love justice
It is the responsibility of the poet to sing this in all the original
        and traditional tunes of singing and telling poems
It is the responsibility of the poet to listen to gossip and pass it
        on in the way storytellers decant the story of life
There is no freedom without fear and bravery   there is no
        freedom unless
        earth and air and water continue and children
        also continue
It is the responsibility of the poet to be a woman   to keep an eye on
        this world and cry out like Cassandra, but be
        listened to this time

For My Daughter

I wanted to bring her a chalice
or maybe a cup of love
or cool water   I wanted to sit
beside her as she rested
after the long day   I wanted to adjure
commend   admonish   saying don't
do that   of course   wonderful   try
I wanted to help her grow old   I wanted
to say last words   the words famous
for final enlightenment   I wanted
to say them now   in case I am in
calm sleep when the last sleep strikes
or aged into disorder   I wanted to
bring her a cup of cool water

I wanted to explain   tiredness is
expected   it is even appropriate
at the end of the day

Letter

I am writing to the
Chinese Association for the Study
of Jewish Literature

They have asked for the addresses
of a couple of other Jews
Ozick and Kazin to be specific

Of course there are hundreds
probably thousands now alive
writing in Spanish and Portuguese

Russian   even German   the great languages
of nations into whose histories
we were admitted and began almost

immediately to talk   exclaim   praise
make metaphor   despair   raise children
ask questions of the authorities

in their own tongue!   succeed   multiply
and finally be driven out

They say a thousand Jews fled Bombay
in the 12th century   traveled to
Kaifeng City to live in the center

of China   to live   to live   ah   into
the generations they disappeared
in the terrible Yahweh-defying act
of assimilation

Fear

I am afraid of nature
because of nature   I am mortal

my children and my grandchildren
are also mortal

I lived in the city for forty years
in this way I escaped fear

Families

The sheep families are out in the meadow
Caddy and her two big lambs   Gruff and Veronica
Veronica raises her curly head   then bends to the grass
Usefully she shits green grass and wool is her work

Gruff is going away   he will become something else
Father of generations?   What?   more likely meat   that
is a male in war or pasture   his work is meat

Saint-John's-wort!
it must be summertime
buttercup   gone
hawkweed   gone

black eyed Susan
         before you
know it   Queen Anne's lace

goldenrod   and that
will be that

Goldenrod

What would happen
if there were a terrific shortage of goldenrod
in the world
and I put my foot outside this house
to walk in my garden and show city visitors
my two lovely rosebushes
and three remarkable goldenrod plants
that were doing well this year

I would say: Look!
how on each of several sprigs
there are two three dozen tiny stems
and on each stem three four tiny golden
flowers   petals stamen pistil and the pollen
which bees love
                    but insufficiently
otherwise
            can you imagine the fields
on rainy days in August   brass
streaking the lodged hay heads
dull brass in the rain
and under the hot sun
the golden flowers
    floating   gold dust in August fields
for miles and miles

Then

Vera stopped at the flower called fireweed
three fireweed in that old field   year after year
I watch from the kitchen window   I wonder

when the earth is a repository of seed   a seed bank   a
bed where seed rest comfortably   some say for years
waiting for the nudge from weather and light   year after

year   there are three fireweed   no more no less   then
Vera disappeared into the woods and our dog Bear
followed her   I said to myself   WORK! and walked

east toward the far sunny haze of Smarts Mountain   down
into the swale   which had gathered vervain boneset and
meadowsweet   where were the beginnings of those late

asters that should have started their leaves toward
blue and lavender September   still we are the gardeners
of this world and often talk about giving wildness

its chance   it's I who cut the field too late   too
early   right on time   and therefore out of the earth which
is a darkness of timed seed and waiting root the sunlight

chose vervain   jewelweed   boneset   just beyond
our woodchuck-argued garden a great nation of ants
has lived for fifteen years in a high sandy anthill

which I honor with looking and looking and never disrupt
(nor have I learned their lesson of stubborn industry)
they ask nothing except to be not bothered and I personally

agree   though it is my nation that has refined sugar
in bowls of sugar   far from their sandy home   I've often
found them   drunk and bathing

Is There a Difference
Between Men and Women

Oh the slave trade
    the arms trade
death on the high seas
    massacre in the villages

        trade in the markets
            melons mustard greens
        cloth shining   dipped in
            onion dye beet grass
        trade in the markets   fish
            oil   yams   coconuts   leaves
        of water spinach   leaves
            of pure water   cucumbers
        pickled   walking back
            and forth along the stalls
        cloth bleached to ivory
            argument from stall to stall
        disgusted and delighted
            in the market

oh the worldwide arms trade
    the trade in women's bodies
the slave trade
    slaughter

        oranges coming in from
            the country in one
        basket on the long
            pole   coconuts in
        the other   on the
            shoulders of women

walking   knees slightly bent
   scuffing   stumbling
along the road   bringing
   rice into the city
hoisting the bundles of dry
   mangrove for repair
of the household   trade
   in the markets on
the women's backs and shoulders
   yams   sometimes peanuts

oh the slave trade
   the trade in the bodies of women
the worldwide unending arms trade
   everywhere man-made slaughter

Definition

My dissent is cheer
a thankless disposition
first as the morning star
    my ambition: good luck

and why not   a flight
over the wide dilemna
and then good night to
    sad forever

Education

To have lived long enough
and not too far from the dying
of a couple of ancient trees
the high leaf and flowering
above broken arms   to have known
one great tree full and sturdy
then in my own years
the arbitrary swords of sunscald
lightning   scar   scab   rot

in the woods behind our house
uprooted storm-thrown hemlock
(hurricane of 'thirty-eight) a humped
and heaving graveyard   do you see that

it's good in one ordinary life
to have witnessed the hard labor
of a long death   the way one
high branch can still advance alone   pale green
and greener   into the sun's
nutritious light

One Day

One day
one of us
will be lost
to the other

this has been
talked about but
lightly   turning
away   shyness   this
business of con-
fronting the
preference for
survival

      my mother said   the
      children are grown   we
      are both so sick   let us
      die together   my father
      replied   no no   you
      will be well   he lied

of course I
want you in the world
whether I'm in it or
not   your spirit
I probably mean
there is always
something to say   in
the end   speaking
without breath   one
of us will be lost
to the other

This Hill

this hill
crossed with broken pines and maples
lumpy with the burial mounds
of uprooted hemlocks (hurricane
of 'thirty-eight)   out of their rotting hearts
generations rise trying once more
to become the forest

just beyond them
tall enough to be called trees
in their youth like aspen   a bouquet
of young beech is gathered

they still wear last summer's leaves
the lightest brown almost translucent
how their stubbornness decorates
the winter woods

on this narrow path
ice holds the black undecaying
oak leaves in its crackling grip
oh   it's become too hard to walk
        a sunny patch   I'm suddenly
in water up to my ankles   April

AFTERWORD
by Nora Paley

Who Grace Paley was and that she was my mother are naturally inseparable for me. That is the luck I carry, now that it is "afterward."

As her child I absorbed the global way my mother took in the day. She experienced time as a bathtub calibrated by stories however they were sensed. As a young kid I recognized her open water intelligence but there was always a shark swimming through it. I witnessed how hard she worked to get it right on the page as well as how much of her work was out in that day, not at her kitchen table typewriter. I learned from her that precision requires a warm eye, not a cold one. This involved a lot of city walking. In the second half of her life, it involved country walking in Vermont.

I can give you a daughter's snapshot of my mother's life in the 1950s early 1960s. In my memory, my brother, mother, and I were walking the cracked pavement and cobblestone streets of our neighborhood every day, on the way to the park (Washington Square), the grocery store where we had seemingly endless credit (Jefferson Market), or the beautiful dark old library (Jackson Square branch).

We walked through our streets always to public spaces, always meeting friends, my child self tugging on her long full 1950s cotton skirt to keep going, stop talking! The women we ran into were mothers who were artists, anti-atomic-bomb-testing activists, often also in the PTA, mothers working to keep the buses out of Washington Square Park, many single parents (or all of these). They are varied, radiant, smart, grown women in my memory. The men we ran into seemed clever, fanciful, sometimes lovable, but brittle, as a species. I noticed as a little girl how these expansive women narrowed down to "handle" the men in family life as well as at political meetings. They accepted this task and seemed to love them anyway.

I had a difficult depressed funny father of my own who required quite a bit of "handling." Eventually, late in my teens, my mother left him and remarried a very different difficult, complicated, though not depressed husband. Both men supported her writing totally. This was a time when women's lives were not considered interesting enough to be the subject of stories.

The segmentalization of life, now talked about in terms of balancing, was something my mother was incapable of, so luckily did not believe in it. In the '60s there were people who knew her as a political activist and did not know she was a writer, and vice versa. She was criticized for spending so much time in antiwar (American War in Vietnam) activities versus at her "desk."

In order to get courage she'd say to herself, before going onstage in front of large audiences for literary or political events, "The worst they can do is kill me!" Then she'd laugh.

Her way of living in a time of increasing compartmentalization and disintegration had confluence with the women's movement. She often said that when people say nothing happened in the 1970s, it is because so much was going on with women. The phrase "The Personal is political," which came out of the late '60s early '70s, described to me the culture of my family and community in the very pre-affluent Greenwich Village. I assumed it originated in Jewish scripture (we were atheists).

My mother's powerful optimism annoyed me as a grouchy teen-ager. Later, I understood it. In her last illness she wanted to keep that thin silver thread of her life going as long as she could—like she always did in her gardens after the frost with the slim green stem hiding under the frozen ended summer. Her dying was not like her, but she knew everyone else did it.

My mother's voice is strong in my ears, but I am the daughter. It is also strong on the page and that is lucky for all of us. I am grate-ful that the wonderful poet and painter Kevin Bowen was inspired to put this book together.

CHRONOLOGY

1906 Isaac Goodside and Manya Ridnyik immigrate to the Bronx, New York, from the Ukraine.

1906 Birth of Isaac and Manya's son, Victor.

1908 Birth of Isaac and Manya's daughter Jeanne.

1922 December 11, birth of Grace Paley, third child of Isaac and Manya.

1938 Grace Paley drops out of high school, attends classes at Hunter, City College, and Merchants and Bankers Business and Secretarial School.

1940 Enrolls in W. H. Auden's poetry class at The New School for Social Research. Encouraged by Auden to write in her own voice, she publishes poems in school paper.

1942 Marries filmmaker and photographer Jess Paley, lives with him near Army camps in the South and Midwest. Publishes poems in *Experience*.

1944 Moves into Greenwich Village. Manya Ridnik Goodside dies of breast cancer.

1949 Birth of daughter, Nora.

1951 Birth of son, Danny.

1956 First short story, "Goodbye and Good Luck," published in *Accent*. Joins other mothers in blocking buses passing through Washington Square.

1958 "The Contest" published in *Accent*.

1959 *The Little Disturbances of Man* published by Doubleday. Joins in organizing antinuclear protests and with protests against air-raid drills in schools.

1961 With John W. Darr, Mary Gandall, Sybl Clairborne, Karl Bissinger, Erika Weihs, Robert Nichols, Judith Malina, Theodore Willentz, David McReynolds, and other neighbors founds The Greenwich Village Peace Center. Protests against atomic testing, civil defense drills with PTA members from PS 41. With Eva Kollich and Sybl Clairborne begins five o'clock protests before draft board. Publishes "Faith in the Afternoon" in *Noble Savage*. At suggestion of Otto Nathan, executor of the estate of physicist Albert Einstein, organizes one of the first teach-ins on Vietnam, with performances around the city of music, stories, and history of Vietnam. Women Strike for Peace founded. Awarded Guggenheim Fellowship for Fiction Writing.

1963 Begins lifelong friendship with Peter and Elka Schuman and the Bread and Puppet Theater.

1965 Begins works as instructor in general studies at Columbia.

1966 Arrested in New York City on Armed Forces Day for civil disobedience, sentenced to six days in prison. Begins teaching creative writing at Sarah Lawrence College.

1967 With Artists and Writers Against the Vietnam War and Greenwich Village Peace Center helps organize Angry Arts Week. Over 250 artists and writers perform from trucks and in venues across the city of New York. With Karl Bissinger and Paul Goodman founds Support in Action, organizing the public burning of over 1,500 draft cards on the Sheep Meadow in Central Park on April 15. Joins Muriel Ruckeyser, June Jordan, Kenneth Koch, Herbert Kohl, Victor Hernandez Cruz, Anne Sexton, and others in founding Teachers and Writers Collaborative. Writes Teachers and Writers Collaborative "Manifesto." Separates from Jess Paley. Publishes "Distance" in *The Atlantic*. "Faith in a Tree" published in *New American Review*.

1968 Travels with writers and clergy to France and Sweden to meet with young men who have left the country in opposition to the draft. Publishes "Two Stories from Five Boroughs" in *Esquire*.

1969 Travels to North Vietnam with small delegation of peace activists to receive three U.S. prisoners of war. "Distances" is awarded O'Henry Award.

1970 Award from National Institute for Arts and Letters for short stories.

1971 Publishes "A Conversation with My Father" in *New American Review*. "Two Stories: I. 'Debts,' II. 'Wants'" published in *The Atlantic*.

1972 Marries writer, landscape architect, and urban planning activist Bob Nichols at Judson Church. "Enormous Changes at the Last Minute" published in *The Atlantic*.

1973 Death of Isaac Goodside. Attends World Peace Congress in Moscow as representative of War Resisters League.

1974 Travels with Bob Nichols and small group to China under the sponsorship of *The Guardian*. *Enormous Changes at the Last Minute* published by Doubleday. "The Long Distance Runner" published in *Esquire*.

1975 Travels to Paris as representative of War Resisters League to meet with Vietnamese delegation at peace negotiations.

1977 Attends First National Women's Year Conference in Houston.

1978 Arrested in antinuclear demonstration on White House lawn, receives six-month suspended sentence. Publishes "Somewhere Else" in *The New Yorker*.

1979 Cofounds Woman and Life on Earth. Drafts "Women and Life on Earth Unity Statement." Arrested for unfurling banner against nuclear energy on White House lawn. October, participates in Clamshell Alliance's "Take it to Wall St." action against nuclear power and weapons. Publishes "Friends" and "Love" in *The New Yorker*.

1980 Attends spring ecofeminist conference "Women and Life on Earth" at Amherst College. Works organizing November 17 Women's Pentagon Action in Washington, D.C. Arrested with 140 other women. Writes "Women's Pentagon Action Unity Statement."

1981 Second Women's Pentagon Action, Washington, D.C.

1982 Publishes "The Story Hearer" in *Mother Jones*. Special Issue of *Delta* dedicated to Grace Paley.

1983 July, Women's Encampment for a Future of Peace and Justice held outside Romulus Army Base, Seneca Falls, New York. Begins teaching at City College. Stories adapted by John Sayles filmed as *Enormous Changes at the Last Minute*.

1985 *Later the Same Day* published by Farrar, Straus and Giroux. *Leaning Forward*, a poetry collection, published by Granite Press. Travels to El Salvador and Nicaragua under sponsorship of MADRE, a group of North and Central American women opposed to U.S. policy in Central America.

1985 PEN/Faulkner Prize for *Later the Same Day*.

1986 Receives Edith Wharton Citation of Merit from New York State Writers Institute, becomes first State Author of New York. Arrested at sit-in at Seabrook Nuclear Power Plant in New Hampshire.

1987 Receives Senior Fellowship from the Literature Program of the National Endowment for the Arts for "major contribution to American Literature over a lifetime of lifetime of creative endeavor." Special dinner honoring her work held by The War Resisters League. Travels to Israel to International

Conference of Women Writers, cofounds the Jewish Women's Committee to End the Occupation of the West Bank and Gaza.

1988   Retires from Sarah Lawrence.

1989   *365 Reasons Not to Have Another War*, a calendar for The War Resisters League, published.

1991   *Long Walks and Intimate Talks*, a collection of essays and poems with artwork by Vera Williams, published by Feminist Press.

1992   *New and Collected Poems* published by Tisbury House. Receives Rea Award for the Short Story.

1994   *The Collected Stories* published by Farrar, Straus and Giroux, receives National Book Award. Receives Pen/Malamud Award for Excellence in Short Fiction. Begins teaching at William Joiner Center Summer Writers' Workshop.

1996   Travels to Vietnam with delegation from William Joiner Center to meet with Vietnamese writers and publishers.

1998   *Just As I Thought*, essays, published by Farrar, Straus and Giroux.

2000   *Begin Again: Collected Poems* published by Farrar, Straus and Giroux.

2003   Named Vermont State Poet Laureate. Receives Robert Creeley Award for Poetry.

2006   Receives Rabbi Marshall T. Meyer Risk Taker Award from Jews for Racial and Economic Justice.

2007   Grace Paley passes away at home in Thetford, Vermont, from breast cancer. *Here and Somewhere Else*, with Bob Nichols, published by Feminist Press.

2008   *Fidelity* published by Farrar, Straus and Giroux. *Massachusetts Review* publishes special issue on Grace Paley.

A SHORT LIST FOR
SUGGESTED FURTHER READING

Book-Length Studies

Conversations with Grace Paley. Ed. Gerhard Bach and Blaine Hall. Jackson: University Press of Mississippi, 1997.

Grace Paley: A Study of the Short Fiction. Neal Isaacs. Boston: G. K. Hall/Twayne, 1990.

Grace Paley: Illuminating the Dark Lives. Jacqueline Taylor. Austin: University of Texas Press, 1990.

Grace Paley's Life Stories: A Literary Biography. Judith Arcana. Champaign: University of Illinois Press, 1994.

Special Journal Issues and Monographs Dedicated to Grace Paley's Work

Delta: Revue du Centre d'Étude et de Recherches sur les Écrivains du Sud aux États-Unis. Special Issue on Grace Paley. Ed. Kathleen Hulley. No. 14, May 1982.

Contemporary Women's Writing: Grace Paley Writing the World. Ed. Mariannne Hirsch. Special Issue. Vol. 3, no. 2. Oxford University Press, 2009.

Massachusetts Review: Grace Paley. Ed. Dara Wier, Chris Bachelder, Noy Holland and Lisa Olstein. Special Issue. Vol. 49, no. 4, Winter, 2008.

Literary Criticism

No Man's Land: The Place of Women Writers in 20th Century Fiction. Ed. Sandra M. Gilbert and Susan Gubar. New Haven: Yale University Press, 1988.

Women Writers Talking. Ed. Janet Todd. New York: Holmes and Meier, 1983.

The American Short Story 1945–1980: A Critical History. Gordon Weaver. Boston: Twayne, 1983.

The Writer in the World. Ed. Reginald Gibbons. Boston: Atlantic Monthly Press, 1986.

History and Memoir

American Gandhi: A. J. Muste and the History of Radicalism in the Twentieth Century. Leilah Danielson. Philadelphia: University of Pennsylvania Press, 2014.

Climbing Fences, Sybil Clairborne. New York: War Resisters League, 1987.

David Dellinger: The Life and Times of a Non-Violent Revolutionary. Andrew Hunt. New York: NYU Press, 2006.

Prisons That Could Not Hold. Barbara Deming. Athens: University of Georgia Press, 1995.

The Vietnam Wars 1945–1990. Marilyn Young. New York: Harper Collins, 1991.

Women on War: An International Anthology from Antiquity to the Present. Daniela Gioseffi. New York: Feminist Press, 2003.

Interviews

"Every Action Was Essential: An Interview with Grace Paley, Phyllis Ekhaus and Judith Mahoney Pasternak." *The Nonviolent Activist,* March–April 2002.

"Grace Paley, The Art of Fiction No. 131," *Paris Review,* no. 124, Fall, 1992.

"Grace Paley Writing Against War," Marianne Hirsch. *PMLA,* vol. 124, no. 5, October 2009.

"Inches of Progress," in *A God in the House: Poets Talk About Faith.* Ed. Ilya Kaminsky and Katherine Towler. North Adams: Tupelo Press, 2009.

Film

Grace: A Documentary. Sonya Friedman. New York: Four Corners Productions, 2010.

Grace Paley: Collected Shorts. Lilly Rivlin. www.gracepaleythefilm.com, 2009.

Resources

GracePaleylegacy.blogspot.com.

Teachers and Writers Collaborative: www.twc.org

War Resisters League: www.warrestisters.org

Waves of Change: www.deepdishwavesofchange.org

Books by Ama Ata Ato, Edwidge Danticat, Carolyn Forché, Jamaica Kincaid, Maxine Hong Kingston, Tony Kushner, Ursula LeGuin, Toni Morrison, Tillie Olson

A NOTE ABOUT THE AUTHOR

Grace Paley, born in the Bronx in 1922, was a renowned writer and activist. Her *Collected Stories* was a finalist for both the Pulitzer Prize and the National Book Award. Her other collections include *Enormous Changes at the Last Minute* and *Just As I Thought*. She died in Vermont on August 22, 2007.